Social Space and Governance in Urban China

Social Space and Governance in Urban China

Social Space and Governance in Urban China

The Danwei *System from Origins to Reform*

DAVID BRAY

Stanford University Press

Stanford, California

2005

Stanford University Press
Stanford, California
www.sup.org

Library of Congress Cataloging-in-Publication Data

Bray, David, 1965–
    Social space and governance in urban China : the danwei system from ori-
gins to reform / David Bray.
        p. cm.
    Includes bibliographical references and index.
    ISBN 978-0-8047-5038-7
    1. Social structure—China.   2. Urban planning—China.   3. Gover-
nance, urban—China.   4. Danwei.   I. Title.
HM716.B73 2005
301'.0951—dc22   2004013445

Printed and bound by CPI Group (UK) Ltd, Croydon, CR0 4YY

Original Printing 2005

Last figure below indicates year of this printing:

14   13   12   11   10   09   08   07   06   05

Designed and typeset at Stanford University Press in 10.5 / 12 Bembo.

For Louise

Contents

Figures and Table

Figures

Table

Acknowledgments

This study is based on my doctoral dissertation and I would like to thank a number of organizations for providing financial assistance toward the research. The University of Melbourne funded my doctoral candidacy through an Australian Postgraduate Research Award and supported two research visits to China under their visiting scholar programs with Beijing University and the Chinese University of Politics and Law. I am grateful to the Australian Vice Chancellors Association for providing a substantial grant toward my research in China through their Australian Awards for Research in Asia scheme. Many thanks also to the Department of Political Science at the University of Melbourne for travel grants and other support through my years of doctoral study. Staff and scholars at Beijing University and the Chinese University of Politics and Law offered valuable assistance during my various field trips to China, and the Contemporary China Center at the Australian National University were kind enough to fund several weeks of research at the center. Finally, I must thank the Faculty of Oriental Studies at Cambridge University for funding my most recent visit to China to gather additional research materials, for a publishing grant, and for providing the time and space to complete the revisions.

The personal debts accrued during the research and writing of this book have been many. I would particularly like to express my thanks to the following friends and colleagues: my doctoral supervisor, Michael Dutton, for his years of support, encouragement, and friendship, without whose inspiration I would never have pursued postgraduate study; my unofficial "doctoral committee," Elaine Jeffreys, Kaz Ross, and David Stokes, for the hours they spent reading my work, for their criticisms, suggestions, insights, and comradeship; Graham Marsh and Beno Engles at the Department of Social Science, RMIT, for giving me my first teaching job; Bruce Jacobs and Gloria Davies at the Department of Asian Languages and Studies, Monash University, for employing me and providing crucial support over the latter stages of the doctorate; and David McMullen, Professor of Chinese Studies at Cambridge University, for his support over the last four years. I would also like to thank Chris Buckley, Peter Micic, Xu Zhangrun, Xu Ping, Liu Guang'an, Zhang Jie, Wang Fenyu, Liang Kun, Jon Unger, Gu Zhiming, Serena Lillywhite, Pan Yi, Zhu Yong, Chang Xinxin, Zhang Wei, Lou Jianbo, Roel Sterckx, Stephen Fagg, Clive of Economics, the "good bunch o' lads" at Wolfson, all my students, and many others who have generously assisted, encouraged, and kept me sane over the years.

I am very grateful to Muriel Bell at Stanford for her interest in my work and to Carmen Borbón-Wu, Tony Hicks, and Mary Ray Worley for their assistance through the publishing process. Stanford's two anonymous reviewers did a wonderful job in identifying errors, offering sound advice on amendments, and generally sharing their wisdom. I am very appreciative of their contribution to the final product. Naturally I take full responsibility for the views expressed and for any errors or omissions within the text.

I owe a special debt of gratitude to "Madame Mao" for her tireless devotion to the task of keeping my knees warm over many long winters of research and writing in Melbourne, and to "Harriet the Spy" for similar devotions in Cambridge. Heartfelt thanks to my parents, Kevin and Gwenyth Bray, and my sister, Jennifer Crone, for their unconditional support over the years. Most of all, I thank my partner, Louise Freckelton, whose love, support, encouragement, faith, wisdom, and bush-sense have made all the difference.

ACFTU	All China Federation of Trade Unions
CCP	Chinese Communist Party
FFYP	First Five-Year Plan
GMD	Guomindang (Nationalist Party)
MCA	Ministry of Civil Affairs
NPC	National People's Congress
PLA	People's Liberation Army
PRC	People's Republic of China
RC	Residents' committee
RMRB	*Renmin ribao* (People's Daily)
RSFSR	Russian Soviet Federated Socialist Republic
SOE	State-owned enterprise

Social Space and Governance in Urban China

Social Space and Governance in Urban China

CHAPTER 1

Introduction

A whole history remains to be written of *spaces*—which would at the same time be the history of *powers* (both these terms in the plural)—from the great strategies of geo-politics to the little tactics of the habitat, institutional architecture from the classroom to the design of hospitals, passing by economic and political installations. . . . Anchorage in a space is an economico-political form which needs to be studied in detail.

Michel Foucault, 1977[1]

This book is an attempt to write a history of a particular kind of space in urban China—the space of the socialist work unit, or *danwei*. The point of doing this is not simply to provide descriptions of physical spatial forms and their transformation over time, but rather, as Foucault suggests, to explore the relationships between space and power. In focusing on the *danwei*, the basic unit of urban life under socialism, I particularly want to investigate how the political and economic strategies of government in China have impinged upon the everyday lives of the urban population through the ways in which they create and structure particular forms of spatial order. The underlying premise of this book is that detailed study of spatial formations can provide new insights into the nature of political and social relationships in China. The *danwei*, as I hope to demonstrate, provides especially rich terrain upon which to develop this kind of analysis.

The approach I adopt here is based heavily on methodologies developed in the work of Michel Foucault. First, in tracing the history of the *danwei* I utilize what Foucault referred to as the "genealogical" method. This approach differs from conventional historical method in that it does not seek to reconstruct the past or provide a seamless narrative of development; rather the aim is to explore how particular institutions of the present took shape through the layering of often disparate, unrelated, and discontinuous practices.[2] Since the *danwei* emerged through the juxtaposition of a wide range of disciplinary, governmental, biotechnical, and spatial practices over a considerable period of time, it seems to me that the genealogical method offers a particularly appropriate framework for analysis. Second, I adopt Foucault's conception of power as a complexity of interrelationships between knowledge, institutional disciplinary practice, and biotechnical strategies at the micro level of everyday life. Saturated as it has been with social, political, and economic significance, the *danwei* provides fertile ground for applying and developing this micro-physical model of power. Third, I employ Foucault's technique for analyzing the rationalities of government, or what he terms "governmentality." In this body of work Foucault challenges many conventional assumptions in posing a whole series of questions on the nature of government: what is the object of government? what problems are deemed appropriate for government intervention? how is intervention made thinkable? how can populations be mobilized to govern themselves? and so on. The rationalities that underpin modern forms of governmental activity and the practices through which they operationalize their objectives have varied over time and location. In the case of China, I argue in this book that the *danwei* has been central to a distinctive form of socialist governmentality. Initially the *danwei* was an answer to a range of organizational and practical problems faced by the CCP-led government in the 1940s and 1950s and became one means through which a form of socialist governance could be deployed among the urban population. Later the *danwei* itself became part of the problem, influencing the parameters and possibilities for governmental intervention. Through detailed study of the *danwei*, fundamental questions on the nature of governance in China can be further illuminated and refined.

The research strategy underpinning this work is avowedly interdisciplinary. I have attempted to develop an analytical perspective based on the use of primary and secondary materials covering a long historical period from a range of disciplinary fields including architecture, urban planning, anthropology, sociology, cultural studies, and political science. Since I am neither an anthropologist nor a sociologist I did not attempt to undertake systematic fieldwork, case studies, or surveys. Instead I sought to build upon the many fine existing empirical studies of urban China and to integrate my own research findings with the existing archive of knowledge within a new interpretive framework. But before providing more detail on my approach to the topic, it is perhaps appropriate to introduce more fully the subject of my study.

What Is a Danwei*?*

"Foreign academics usually translate this term [*danwei*] as *unit*; however, the word *unit* comes nowhere near to expressing the rich substance contained by the Chinese concept of *danwei*. The *danwei* phenomenon is the most typical and most comprehensive expression of the many unique features that have been formed over many years as a result of China's economic and political practices."[3] The problem of terminology is always magnified in translation—especially in translating from a character-based language into a phonetic-based language. The Chinese term *danwei* can mean "unit," as in "unit of measurement." It can also mean something quite different and far more complex: namely, a specific form of social organization that came to dominate socialist China's cities. Like Zhu Guanglei (quoted above), I feel that *unit* is entirely inadequate as a representation for the "rich substance" implied by this second meaning of *danwei*. Rather than adopt an English approximation, then, I think it is preferable to simply use the romanized form of the term, *danwei* (as it is represented in the *pinyin* system of romanization for modern standard Chinese). This goes some way, at least, toward capturing a sense of the uniqueness of the institution and its grounding in Chinese socialist practices.

Perhaps the best strategy is to begin with a fairly simple definition: *danwei* is a generic term denoting the Chinese socialist workplace and the specific range of practices that it embodies. In the introduction to his pioneering study of the *danwei*, Lu Feng highlights the way in which the term *danwei* marks a common "system" shared by all urban Chinese workplaces: "In China everyone calls the social organization in which they are employed—whether it be a factory, shop, school, hospital, research institute, cultural troupe, or party organ—by the generic term *danwei*. This phenomenon clearly shows that, over and above their individual characteristics, . . . all types of social organization in China have a common characteristic: the characteristic of being a *danwei*."[4] Clearly, then, there can be many kinds of *danwei*, as He Xinghan explains: "There are big units [*danwei*[5]] and there are small ones, there are enterprises and businesses, there are publicly owned units as well as collectively owned utilities, there are even Party, government and military units. Even Buddhist temples can be divided into rank order in this way, with prefectural level and county level units and so on."[6]

Despite the wide variety in the type and size of *danwei*, they all share a common range of functions. As Li Hanlin points out, the *danwei* offers far more to its members than simply a regular salary: "In China the *danwei* not only provides members of society with economic reward for their work; in addition, through the provision of housing, free medical care, child care centers, kindergartens, dining halls, bathing houses, service companies, and collective enterprises to employ the children of staff, the *danwei* provides its members with a complete social guarantee and welfare services."[7]

A full complement of material benefits—the so-called iron rice bowl (*tiefanwan*)—is, however, only one aspect of *danwei* functions, for, as He Xinghan acknowledges, "It is also in charge of ideological remolding, political study, policing and security matters, marriages and divorce, entry into the Party, awarding merit and carrying out disciplinary action."[8] The *danwei*, then, takes on a wide range of political, judicial, civil, and social functions. Because of this, the *danwei* has become the principal source of identity for urban residents:

> It bestows upon its members rights, social identity, and political status to act within and without the *danwei*. For example, to go to another *danwei* on business, to buy an airline ticket, or to stay in a hotel . . . a Chinese citizen requires a letter of introduction from his or her *danwei*. Members of any *danwei* respond to an outsider according to the status of the outsider as set out in the letter of introduction provided by his or her *danwei*.[9]

The question of status is critical to the *danwei* member, for it bears heavily upon the important issue of *mianzi*, or "face." Yi Zhongtian illustrates this point in the following passage:

> The work unit is one's rice bowl but it is also one's "face." So if a person doesn't have a work unit then they will have no face. Not only does the lack of a work unit exclude the possibility of a person having face, but even worse, without a work unit they are often pigeon-holed as being "suspicious characters" or "dangerous persons." One can even go so far as to say that, without a work unit, such people come to be regarded as "unemployed idlers."[10]

If the *danwei* provides identity and face to its members within broader society, it also supplies them with a social identity, a community, and a sense of belonging:

> "We are of the same work unit" at once captures the warmth and feeling between sisters and brothers, but also potentially signifies the enmity between those in the grip of an on-going struggle. Because the traditional conception of self is so dim, it is only within a life built around human inter-relationships that Chinese people feel comfortable. . . . So, even though the work unit isn't perfect, it is preferable to being lonely and roaming around in society without one.[11]

Feelings of community and belonging are further bolstered by the design of the archetypal *danwei*—a walled compound that has become the basic spatial unit of the Chinese city. This point is well illustrated by American reporter Fox Butterfield in his description of a Chinese informant's *danwei* compound:

She lived in an apartment in a vast compound of five-story gray-brick buildings managed by her ministry. All her neighbors were also employed by the ministry. To go in or out of the one entrance, she had to walk past an army guard in uniform, and if she brought any visitors into the compound, they had to register in the sentry box. The woman's nine-year-old son went to school in another building inside the compound; she shopped for groceries in the compound store; when the family was sick there was a clinic in the compound.[12]

In summary, it would be no great exaggeration to contend that the *danwei* is the foundation of urban China. It is the source of employment and material support for the majority of urban residents; it organizes, regulates, polices, trains, educates, and protects them; it provides them with identity and face; and, within distinct spatial units, it forms integrated communities through which urban residents derive their sense of place and social belonging. The importance of the *danwei* is further highlighted by the fact that any person who does not have a *danwei* is considered to be "suspicious" or even "dangerous."

Readers who are familiar with contemporary China will no doubt protest that I should refer to the *danwei* in the past rather than the present tense. I readily admit that some of the features outlined above are no longer common or universal, that many urban residents now survive comfortably outside of the *danwei* and that for many others the role and importance of the *danwei* has diminished significantly in recent years.[13] In my defense, however, I can offer two points for consideration. First, the bulk of this book focuses on examining the origins of the archetypal, pre-reform socialist *danwei*.[14] In this respect, the description outlined above provides a useful and relevant introduction to the subject as archetype. Second, for the moment at least, I would like to forestall premature claims as to the demise of the *danwei*. As I will argue in Chapter 7, it seems to me that certain aspects of the *danwei* system remain influential to the present. One of the major themes throughout this study is that forms and practices from the past are constantly redeployed and reinvented in the present. For this reason I believe it is unwise for us to write the *danwei* out of China just yet.

Studying the Danwei

In the last decade the *danwei* has emerged from relative obscurity to become a major area of concern within Chinese studies. This occurrence has undoubtedly been due to a conjunction of events: first, the greater access since the mid-1980s afforded Western scholars to undertake case studies of grassroots Chinese workplaces; and second, the reemergence of sociology within the Chinese academy.[15] In China the latter development has meshed with the particular concerns of the reform period, namely the desire to transform economic and institutional modes of operation, resulting in much academic investigation being focused upon the basic-level economic and social structures that have underpinned what is now termed the "traditional" socialist system.[16]

The growing literature on the *danwei* is characterized by a number of key fault lines which divide scholarly opinion. The first area of contention concerns the question of origins: is the *danwei* a purely socialist institution, or was its formation primarily influenced by traditions from China's presocialist past? Scholars have also developed quite divergent views on the nature of the *danwei*; it has been characterized variously as a remnant of feudal paternalism, a tool of social control, a welfare community, and a system for cultivating political and managerial elites. Finally, debate has raged over the fate of the *danwei*; some commentators have readily forecast its demise at the hands of economic and structural reform, while others argue that although diminished, its influence remains significant.

In relation to the origins of the *danwei* there have been a wide range of views. Andrew Walder, perhaps the best known and most often quoted authority in this subfield, specifically rejects the need for a cultural perspective in understanding the *danwei*.[17] According to his analysis, the methods of industrial personnel management developed under socialism in China had more in common with practices in the Soviet Union and other socialist states than with traditional practices of China's past.[18] With the exception of Barry Naughton, who provocatively claims that "the danwei system emerged during the mid-1960s,"[19] most other scholars venture across the 1949 divide in looking for its origins. Some, including Lu Feng, Xiaobo Lü, and Brantly Womack, focus on what they see as the *danwei*'s "revolutionary" origins in the "communist supply system" and other practices developed by the Chinese Communist Party (CCP) during the Yan'an period.[20] Others, like Elizabeth Perry and Wen-hsin Yeh, have looked to labor and management practices in urban Republican China to find the precedents for the *danwei*.[21]

In one of the more recent additions to the subfield, based on case studies of several Chinese factories that operated both before and after 1949, Mark Frazier concludes that the *danwei* system "can be understood as a matrix of labor management institutions overlaid at different periods between the 1930s and the late 1950s."[22] In many respects, Frazier's work can be seen as providing a synthesis of previous scholarly efforts. Rather than looking for a definitive point of origin in a particular policy or period, he suggests that the *danwei* emerged through the layering of a whole range of practices over time. In this way, we can view the *danwei* as a composite institution that bears the marks of Republican, CCP, and Soviet influence. While this model appears to provide satisfactory explanations in relation to practices like labor management, wage systems, and welfare distribution, it leaves other aspects of the *danwei* system unanswered. How, for example, can we explain the spatial arrangements of the archetypal *danwei* compound—the high enclosing walls and the symbolic axial layout of the key buildings? To my mind such questions necessitate a deeper look into the question of origins.

A few scholars have hinted at much earlier origins for the *danwei*. While Lu Feng traces the organizational foundations of the contemporary *danwei* to the Yan'an period,[23] he also argues that it was founded upon a much deeper historical connection to the clan system of feudal times: "In form, the *danwei* and the traditional style clan have a lot in common: they both exert a patriarchal-type authority over their members; the responsibility of individuals to the group is more emphasized than are individual rights, while the group must take total responsibility for the care of its members."[24] Having made the comparison, however, Lu provides no evidence to support a historical link between the two. Indeed, this part of his argument seems to be founded upon a fairly simplistic binary opposition between tradition and modernity. Under this model, the fact that the *danwei* exhibits signs of "patriarchy" and "collectivity" is taken as sufficient evidence of feudal influence.

Cultural historian Yang Dongping provides a more convincing argument that the *danwei* has earlier historical links. In his comparative study of Beijing and Shanghai, Yang identifies "walls" as the key sign that there is a connection between the modern *danwei* and cultural practices in premodern China.[25] In particular, he argues that the persistent use of the walled compound spatial form from ancient times to the present provides clear physical evidence to support this link. Unfortunately, Yang provides little actual evidence to bolster his observation, but he has flagged a line of inquiry that seems to me very worthy of further exploration. My study, then, will begin with a reexamination of China's traditional spatial practices and formations in order to more fully explore the genealogy of the *danwei* as a sociospatial artifact.

To posit a connection between the modern *danwei* and practices from the premodern past, however, is not to suggest that the *danwei* is itself a "feudal remnant." On the contrary, I argue that the *danwei* is certainly an entirely modern institutional formation. The point is that what is "modern" invariably bears many traces and influences from all those practices that preceded it. The *danwei* has been influenced by spatial practices from China's past, but also by practices from the more recent Republican period, from the CCP's own revolutionary history, and from the Soviet Union. There is no one point of origin or primary source of influence, but rather a complex process of layering disparate practices on top of each other. It is impossible for a conventional historical approach to bring this complexity to the fore—the genealogical method, however, is well suited to precisely this kind of problem.

Toward a Genealogy of the Danwei

Foucault's genealogical method is instructive in that it makes no a priori assumptions about the nature of "the state" or the relevance of conceiving of social organization in terms of a binary state/society relationship. On the contrary, by taking seriously the complexity of mundane daily practices, it aims to challenge the view that deeper "truths" lie at the root of surface appearances. In this respect such a project could be thought of not as a conventional narrative history, but rather as a "history of the present."[26]

Four broad areas of concern are central to Foucault's genealogical studies. First, Foucault insists on the interconnectedness of power and knowledge: "There is no power relation without the correlative constitution of a field of knowledge, nor any knowledge that does not presuppose and constitute at the same time power relations."[27] Foucault's genealogical study of the prison system illustrates this relationship clearly by showing the close connection between fields of knowledge such as criminology and regimes of disciplinary power that emerged within the institutional practices of the modern prison.[28] In the following chapters I will argue that the power/knowledge nexus is, likewise, critical to understanding the emergence and operation of the Chinese *danwei*. Through analysis of a number of different fields—for example, economic planning, labor management, and architecture—I will demonstrate the ways in which the production and practices of knowledge were intimately tied to the modes of power relationships that operated within the *danwei*.

Second, Foucault's genealogical studies emphasize the importance of technologies of the body to modern power relations. "Bio-power," as Foucault terms it, "brought life and its mechanisms into the realm of explicit calculations and made knowledge/power an agent of transformation of human life."[29] This occurred particularly through institutional settings such as workshops, barracks, prisons, and hospitals, where bodies were subjected within disciplinary regimes aimed at maximizing the usefulness and uniformity of individuals.[30] As I will show, bio-power played an important role in the *danwei* through a range of disciplinary spatial practices aimed specifically at transforming individual bodies into productive proletarian subjects. Unlike in the Western institutions studied by Foucault, however, body-centered technologies within the *danwei* tended to promote collectivized rather than individualized subjects.

Third, the genealogical method emphasizes the importance of uncovering the operational principles, or rationalities, of government. Governmentality, as Foucault refers to it, is closely related to bio-power since it is concerned with "the welfare of the population, the improvement of its condition, the increase of its wealth, longevity, health, etc."[31] However, where bio-power refers to the various micro-level disciplinary practices which bear directly upon individual bodies, governmentality invokes the numerous sciences of population—policing, economic management, accounting, statistics, insurance, welfare, education, sanitation, urban planning—concerned not with individual bodies but rather with the management of the many bodies that constitute a population.[32] Based on the premise that planned intervention can improve society, the practice of government everywhere is underpinned by an element of utopianism. Under socialism, where the end objectives are more clearly articulated, the scope of governmental intervention tends to be much wider than under capitalism. From their beginnings during the Yan'an period, the practices developed by CCP-led governments emerged to create a distinctive form of socialist governmentality. In the chapters that follow, I explore the emergence of these practices, the logic that informed them, and the key role played by the *danwei* as the basic unit within this system of urban governance.

Finally, Foucault insists upon the necessity of incorporating the problem of space into his broader modes of genealogical analysis.[33] The linkages that connect space to the broader genealogical project and, specifically, to the issues of power/knowledge and bio-power are most fully developed by Foucault in *Discipline and Punish*, with his analysis of Bentham's "Panopticon."[34] According to Foucault, the Panopticon is much more than merely a device for maintaining surveillance within a prison; rather it should be viewed as a symbol of a new kind of relationship between power and space. In the Panopticon, careful spatial planning has been deployed in order to produce an individuating disciplinary effect.[35] Foucault's analysis demonstrates the importance of spatial techniques to the operation of modern forms of power, alerting us to the realization that the spatial dimension can no longer be ignored in the study of modern institutions.

Spatial considerations are obviously fundamental to this study. As I will show, the archetypal *danwei* is a highly determined, regularized, and ordered spatial formation. Through application of the genealogical method, I describe the ways in which the spatiality of the *danwei* emerged and became linked to the particular strategies of power, knowledge, discipline, government, and subject formation within urban China. Spatial arrangements are significant, then, not simply for aesthetic or descriptive purposes, but more importantly because space itself is a productive medium implicitly bound up with and constitutive of the various biotechnical practices that define the *danwei*.

Despite the groundbreaking work of Foucault and a few other scholars, spatial analysis has remained at the margins of scholarly work in the social sciences and humanities.[36] In Chinese studies, the neglect of the spatial question is perhaps even more marked. Histories of Chinese architecture and urban planning have seldom strayed beyond conventional aesthetic concerns and standard periodizations, while only a very small handful of studies from other disciplines have attempted to incorporate spatial analysis into commentaries on economic, social, and political themes. The exceptions include Paul Wheatley's study of the spatial heritage of the imperial city;[37] Francis Hsu's study of traditional family life in southwestern China, which contains a detailed examination of spatial forms within the traditional home;[38] and Francesca Bray's exploration of gendered space and the role of women's work in late imperial society.[39] Until quite recently the archive of scholarly work on post-1949 China was even more devoid of studies relating to space. Lisa Rofel's case study of factory space,[40] Michael Dutton's work on the prison and on "streetlife,"[41] and Li Zhang's analysis of "migrant" space in Beijing's Zhejiang Village[42] are all good examples of ways in which this long-term neglect is beginning to be redressed.[43] Nevertheless, there are still many gaps in our understanding of space in contemporary China. This study of the *danwei* aims to help fill some of the remaining gaps.

Theorizing Urban Space

After a long period of neglect, *space* has recently become somewhat of a buzzword within certain branches of contemporary scholarship. However, many of the studies that purport to examine space or even that contain the word *space* in the title in fact provide negligible genuine analysis of spatial formations or practices.[44] In this light, it is worth exploring in more detail the problematic of space and the implications of "spatial analysis." I have already referred to Foucault's work on the Panopticon as a reference point for developing a methodology for spatial analysis, but there are other perspectives on this question that need consideration.

The relevance of spatial formations and the analysis of space to the study of human society—in particular, the study of urban society—has been the subject of some debate over the last four decades. The debate has crossed a number of fields: urban sociology, geography, architecture, planning, cultural studies, and the interdisciplinary field of critical theory.[45] Yet even among those scholars who have championed its importance, there has been much controversy on the basic question of what is meant by the term *space*. For example, should space be considered a geopolitical concept, a geographical concept, an economic commodity, a product of architectural design, or a realm of governmental planning? Commentators, of course, have reached different conclusions depending upon their disciplinary background and methodological outlook. However, much of the credit for the recent surge in interest on the question of space can be attributed to developments in the discipline of geography.

The conventional view of geography as an applied science based on descriptive and quantitative analysis of the physical and human environment was challenged in the late 1960s with the appearance of Marxist geographers who sought to link questions of space to their critique of capitalism.[46] David Harvey, for example, sought to build a spatial dimension onto Marxist theories of capitalist economic cycles, while Doreen Massey proposed that class relations could be properly understood only within a spatial context.[47] These approaches, however, tended to subordinate the question of space to the Marxist valorization of social relations or, to be more precise, class inequality. By privileging the socioeconomic domain as the fundamental element in modern human society, they relegated spatial considerations to the role of mere geographical variable.

Henri Lefebvre demands a much broader and more central role for spatial analysis.[48] He rejects what has hitherto been acknowledged as the orthodox Marxist position on space: namely, that spatial form is simply a superstructural reflection of underlying economic relations. In contrast, Lefebvre asserts that space is one of the central elements driving the production, reproduction, and constant transformation of capitalism.[49] Moreover, he sees multiple forms and possibilities implicit within the spatial problematic and attempts to develop a multilayered theoretical analytic to account for this complexity. Thus Lefebvre considers not only geographical and geopolitical space but also the architectural and institutional spaces of everyday life. As well as addressing the built spaces of capitalism, he attempts to account for the imaginative and theoretical processes involved in the thinking and planning of spaces. For Lefebvre, space is integral to capitalism not simply because it mirrors or bolsters class inequalities as expressed in regional unevenness, but because the multiple aspects of capitalist space structure the practices and possibilities inherent within all aspects of everyday life. It is Lefebvre who insists that the political conception of space be extended to include not just the macro geographical spaces of convention—the nation, region, city, town, village, and so on; but also the micro spaces of daily life—the home, school, workplace, street, and so on. It is this innovation in spatial thinking that influenced Foucault and others to introduce a spatial dimension into their genealogies of everyday institutions. And it is the methodology that has developed out of this trend that is the starting point for my analysis of the Chinese *danwei*.

Having established his broad conception of space, Lefebvre theorizes that the actual production of space is driven by a dialectical struggle between what he terms "social space" and "abstract space." Social space describes the complex array of spatial practices that emerged layer upon layer over centuries of "natural" social interaction.[50] With the rise of capitalism, however, social space became subject to all sorts of interventions demanded by capital's pursuit of productive economic relations. Lefebvre considers these interventions to be "abstract" in the sense that they were predicated upon developing a series of technical, theoretical, and intellectual processes that allowed space to be conceived of as an object amenable to manipulation, planning, and reconstitution in ways favorable to the more efficient and productive operation of capitalism. Abstract space, then, is the space of the administrator, the technocrat, the urban planner, and the architect. But above all, abstract space is the space of the capitalist state: "Each new form of state, each new form of political power, introduces its own particular way of partitioning space, its own particular administrative classification of discourses about space and about things and people in space. Each such form commands space, as it were, to serve its purposes."[51]

Although Lefebvre's work is insightful in many respects, it is overly skewed toward a state-centered analysis. His contention that all attempts to plan and program the production of space necessarily serve the interests of the capitalist state is, to my mind, both too generalized and too simplistic. It is too generalized because it subsumes all types and strategies of planned intervention under a single generalized category;[52] and it is too simplistic because it ignores the complex interests involved in the development and implementation of spatial interventions. The true level of complexity becomes apparent if we abandon the assumptions inherent within the Marxist position and instead apply the principles of the genealogical method. Utilizing this approach, I suggest that the planning of space should be viewed as a governmental practice which has emerged, on the one hand, out of particular rationalities of governmental action and, on the other hand, within particular contexts of social relationships. It is not something that has been simply imposed from above, but rather a set of practices that has developed through long processes of experimentation, theoretical debate, and practical experience. To analyze a particular regime of spatial practice, it is necessary to consider the logic and rationality that informs it, the particular spatial forms that it attempts to realize, as well as the historical and social context into which these interventions are made. Only through attending to all these interrelated aspects can a full understanding of such spatial practices be reached. Lefebvre's method is simply unable to account for this degree of complexity in the production of space.

It is no doubt true that there is a close relationship between the rise of capitalism and the emergence of spatial planning as a strategy of government. However, to view this new spatial practice as entirely monolithic and seamlessly dominant is to misconstrue and overestimate its role. For although it is premised on the belief that strategic interventions into spatial formations can transform social reality for the better, attempts to implement governmental plans are rarely straightforward. To begin with, the logic that informs planned spatial intervention is an unstable and ever-changing field of applied knowledge, subject at any given time to numerous contesting positions. Moreover, accepted views on what constitutes appropriate intervention can change rapidly within a short space of time.[53] Second, planning is routinely constrained by competing economic and political interests which often mean that projects are only partially realized, or realized in quite a different form from that intended by the planners. Third, even when fully realized the effect of the spatial intervention is unpredictable; it may be used or appropriated by communities in ways quite different from those that were intended. Finally, spatial formations have a physical presence that may remain for many years. Over its life span, any given space may be reappropriated, redeployed, or reinterpreted in many different contexts. In short, the planning and implementation of spatial interventions involves the complex interweaving of several factors: unstable and contestable fields of knowledge, competing priorities among governmental agencies, the unpredictable response of subjects to new spatial forms, and the unimagined outcomes of historical transformation. These are among the factors I will take into account as I reconstruct a genealogy of the *danwei* over the subsequent chapters.

I should emphasize here that for the most part throughout this study I treat the *danwei* as an archetype. Clearly there has been wide variation in the size and spatial layout of individual *danwei*. My point, however, as many other scholars have averred, is that there is an overall unity in the history, function, purpose, and design of *danweis* such that it makes sense to treat them all as variations on a general archetypal theme. Moreover, it is through analysis of the archetype that we can most fully understand the genealogical heritage, the spatial significance, and the governmental rationale of the *danwei*. Many individual *danwei*, in various ways and for various reasons, fall short of the archetype, but this fact does not negate the relevance of the overall study. It merely indicates that within some *danwei* the archetypal system was not fully realized or developed.

I commence the genealogical project, in Chapter 2, with an exploration of the ways in which sociospatial practices from premodern China have influenced the contemporary *danwei*. I focus on the ubiquity of walls and walled compounds throughout Chinese history and examine how these spatial forms were linked to specific regimes of discipline and governance. I suggest that the principal role of the walled compound was to define realms of social governance and that internally these spaces were organized to promote the production of collective-oriented subjectivities. While the defining logic of this presocialist spatial order was Confucian, the spatial forms that emerged proved readily adaptable to other forms of collective society.

In Chapter 3, I pursue the genealogy of the *danwei* in two key modern locales: the industrializing cities of Republican China and the revolutionary base areas under CCP control. I show that, despite significant differences in rationale, in both locations the organization of work and regulation of communities was influenced by traditional practices emphasizing the collective over the individual. Moreover, in my analysis of CCP organizational practice, I point to the rise of a distinctly pastoral mode of socialist governmentality that was centered on the *danwei* system and implemented by a corps of highly dedicated cadres.

The analysis in Chapter 4 is premised on my contention that some aspects of *danwei* spatial practice are influenced by a modern European tradition of revolutionary architecture and planning. Utilizing Foucault's concept of governmentality, I discuss the way in which the discipline of urban planning emerged in Europe as a technique for policing and transforming social relations through intervention in spatial formations. I then show how revolutionary architects and utopian socialist planners appropriated some of the strategies of urban planning in order to facilitate radical transformations of society. The Russian Revolution provided great impetus to this movement, and a sympathetic political environment under which radical spatial planning could actually be realized in practice. Subsequent developments in Soviet architecture and urban planning became very influential in China after 1949.

Discussion in Chapter 5 centers on the emergence of the *danwei* as the key unit of social and political organization in post-1949 China. I outline the way in which key CCP governmental practices, particularly those related to the provision of a social guarantee (*baoxialai*) and the political mobilization of the urban population (*zuzhiqilai*), contributed to the formation and solidification of the *danwei* system. I show how some of the practices that were to become emblematic of the *danwei* were actually adopted as contingent and temporary solutions to unforeseen circumstances. Moreover, I also consider how the rejection of the Soviet model affected the *danwei* and signaled the reaffirmation of pastoral forms of leadership amongst grassroots cadres.

The significance of the *danwei* as a spatial unit is the focus of Chapter 6. First, I explore the development of urban planning after 1949, especially around the question of how to deal with traditional city formations like that of Beijing. Second, I seek to explain how central government planning and investment strategies resulted in the *danwei* becoming a virtually independent spatial realm within relatively weak city jurisdictions. Then, through a detailed reading of architectural and design practice and the emergence of standardization, I argue that *danwei* space was arranged in order to directly promote socialist collectivity and proletarian consciousness among its members. In this respect, the *danwei* became a spatial machine for the production of good socialists.

Chapter 7 looks at some of the effects of economic reform and restructuring on the *danwei* over the last two decades. The emergence of "scientific" labor management, a nonstate sector of the economy, and new spatial forms brought about through the large-scale reconstruction of the urban environment have all contributed to displacing the socialist *danwei* as the focus of urban life. However, as I demonstrate, in other respects the *danwei* still plays a critical and influential role in the lives of urban residents and has even adapted to take advantage of opportunities brought by the market. Moreover, some of the new institutions that have begun to take over the role of the *danwei*—the *xiaoqu* and the *shequ*—have clearly adopted some of its characteristics. The trends explored in this chapter illustrate the complexity of the social, spatial, economic, and political transformations that China is currently undergoing. My analysis highlights the weaknesses inherent within the simplistic "market transition" models of change favored by many commentators.

Chapter 8 concludes the study with a reconsideration of the key methodological issues that underpin this book and a summary of the main arguments. In particular, I emphasize the points of divergence with previous studies. I argue that my interdisciplinary analysis of the *danwei* system provides ample evidence to justify a deep skepticism as to the existence of the so-called party/state in China. The *danwei* is and was an institutional formation made of many disparate and even contradictory practices. The only way to understand its significance is to examine each of its various practices in its specificity and in combination, rather than impute some overall coherence, coordination, and control to a mythical party/state.

CHAPTER 2

Walls and Compounds

Toward a Genealogy of *Danwei* Spatial Practice

> In the past the basic unit of the city was the courtyard house (*siheyuan*), which corresponded to the family; now the basic unit of the city is the compound (*dayuan*), which corresponds to the *danwei* or "department" (*bumen*). While these two basic organizational units in fact represent two different types of social structure, the enclosed compound (*yuanluo*) form and the implications of wall culture have continued in an unbroken historical line.[1]

Even today most Chinese cities retain some architectural "skeletons" of the past[2]—walled temples, palaces, and courtyard homes—which not only give us a glimpse into the glories of bygone days, but also permit us to compare these premodern spatial forms with those of the socialist period. Such a comparison would seem to support Yang Dongping's claim as to the historical continuity in the utilization of walled compounds to define social space. For, like the cities of the past, the modern Chinese city is dominated by walls—the walls that were constructed from the early 1950s to enclose the *danwei* of the socialist state. In urban China it seems that the role of the walled compound as a technology of spatial demarcation transcends any simple historical divide between "traditional" and "modern" China.[3]

In this chapter I begin tracing the genealogy of the *danwei* through a study of certain traditional, or premodern, spatial practices in China. My principal contention is that the modern *danwei* has been influenced by a long-standing Chinese tradition in which carefully ordered walled spaces are used to demarcate and to regulate distinct social units. I commence with a discussion of the literature on the role of walls in Chinese history before moving on to analyze the internal organization of traditional walled spaces and the close connections between spatial and social order.

Walls and Culture in China

Fifty years ago Osvald Sirén observed the ubiquity of walls within urban China. "Walls, walls and yet again walls, form the framework of every Chinese city. They surround it, they divide it into lots and compounds, they mark more than any other structures the basic features of the Chinese communities."[4] But only in recent years has the Chinese wall been elevated to the status of cultural trope. From the Great Wall of China to ancient city walls to the walls enclosing the modern *danwei*—they are all interpreted now as variations on a uniform cultural theme. For a new breed of cultural historians, walls seem to point to deeper truths about the nature of Chinese culture.

In his wide-ranging historical and cultural study of China, W. J. F. Jenner, for example, dedicates an entire chapter to the subject of walls.[5] The opening statement sets the scene for the chapter: "This is a chapter about enclosures, walls and boxes. Walls on the ground and walls in the mind. Enclosures within which all can be controlled and safely structured."[6] Jenner's discussion ranges from the walls of ancient cities to the walls of the contemporary *danwei*, from physical walls to so-called invisible walls such as the limits on internal migration and obstructions to transferring workplace. However, beyond the broad metaphor of "enclosure" as suggested by the opening statement, Jenner fails to establish any more concrete connection between these various kinds of "walls." For example, precisely in what respects walls that enclose traditional courtyard homes are similar to (or different from) the more recent walls that enclose *danwei* is not established, nor are we given any insight into how these physical walls may be connected to the so-called walls in the mind. Nevertheless, in juxtaposing the physical enclosure of walls with various institutional practices, Jenner clearly intends to draw a parallel between the ideas of "enclosure" and "social control." Indeed, he devotes far more attention to various social, political, and cultural practices—the "walls in the mind"—than to actual physical walls. This reinforces the view that Jenner reads walls as a metaphor for social control. The physical walls ubiquitous to China thus are viewed principally as symbols of a much deeper truth about the nature of Chinese culture. According to Jenner's analysis, the significance of the wall transcends historical change and stands for enclosure, limitation, and social control. Since the wall signifies this deeper reality of Chinese culture, there is apparently no need to explore the specific manifestations, forms, or daily practices associated with actual physical walls.

The significance of the wall as a metaphor for understanding Chinese culture is similarly emphasized by Geremie Barmé and John Minford.[7] The first chapter in their edited collection is also entitled "Walls" and is introduced as follows: "It takes the image of the Great Wall as a starting point, and from there story writer, poet, social psychologist, and dramatist branch out, to confront various 'dead ends', culs-de-sac, and traps—cultural, economic, political, and psychological."[8] As with Jenner, Barmé and Minford read the wall in purely negative terms—it closes off, limits, and entraps those caught within its embrace. Indeed, through its very act of enclosure the wall is taken to be an architectural exemplification of a culture that has become hopelessly inward-looking and moribund and a society which lives in the past and rejects the possibilities of change. Such a reading posits the wall as a universal signifier for many aspects of Chinese political, social, and cultural life, ranging from foreign policy to family relationships.[9] Thus the various types of wall that exist in China, from the Great Wall to the traditional walled family compound and the modern wall enclosing the *danwei* are all seen as repetitions of a universal Chinese cultural trait.

In a similar vein, the writers of the controversial television documentary series *He Shang (River Elegy)*, broadcast throughout China in 1988, adopted the Great Wall as one of the defining symbols of Chinese culture.[10] Controversy surrounded the series owing to its brutally unfavorable treatment of Chinese culture in comparison to Western culture. It characterized China as mired in a closed-off, earth-bound, backward-looking, and conservative peasant culture, in contrast to the West, which was seen as outward-looking, forward-thinking, innovative, and exploratory.[11]

One key episode in the series compared China and the West in the fifteenth century. The writers pointed out that whereas in the West the fifteenth century saw the beginnings of the conquest of the seas and rapid expansion of economic, military, and political power over the globe, in China the same period was dominated by a massive project to rebuild and renovate the Great Wall. Thus, while Europe was busy expanding its borders and developing trade, China was apparently building a wall to close itself off from the rest of the world. The authors of the series attribute China's failure to look outward or to respond constructively to the rise of the West as the result of a particularly conservative cultural outlook. The central components of this culture are represented symbolically by the Yellow River, the dragon, and the Great Wall. While the Yellow River was taken to symbolize a culture tied to the earth, the seasons, and the cycles of flood and famine and the dragon to exemplify a culture ruled through despotism and superstition, the Great Wall was interpreted as representing the imperial force which bound the whole culture together: "Thus, whoever built the Great Wall would effectively own the land, mountains, rivers and people inside the Great Wall. To the ruler, the Great Wall became the wall surrounding the courtyard of his house."[12] For the authors of *River Elegy*, the Great Wall appears as a tragic embodiment of the fate that befell China. To them it represents both the rejection of Western culture and a general cultural malaise or inertia exemplified by an inward rather than outward gaze.[13] In describing the Great Wall as the wall around the emperor's courtyard, they draw an analogy between the Great Wall and the courtyard walls that surrounded the homes of each family. If the emperor's "courtyard" was walled in, then so were the courtyards of his subjects. The Great Wall, according to this analysis, represents all the walls in China. It symbolizes not only the isolation of China from the outside world, but also the confinement of an entire society within the binds of a narrowly conservative and restrictive culture.

The authors of *River Elegy* draw similar conclusions to those made by Jenner and Barmé and Minford. They each bestow symbolic status on the Chinese wall, reading it as an expression of a transhistorical unity binding Chinese culture together. For these commentators, the wall is important not for its mundane, day-to-day functions, but rather because it supposedly represents a deep truth about the nature of Chinese culture. This form of analysis, however, is highly problematic.

The problem with attributing universal cultural significance to the Chinese wall in general is that it necessarily erases all the multiple meanings inherent within the many different forms of walls. In making their generalizations about "the wall," these critics at once empty a multiform architectural technology of its own specific historical development and wide variety of functional uses. As Michel Foucault has shown with his discussions on the Panopticon, architectural forms are open to a range of possible appropriations.[14] The variety of uses to which the walled compound form has been put throughout Chinese history attests to this flexibility. Therefore, by homologizing the various forms of walls—courtyard walls, city walls, border walls—into one symbolic unity, the ability to differentiate between the various realms of social space, which these different walls demarcate, is lost. The operation of the empire within the Great Wall is of an order very different from the operation of a family within its courtyard walls. It is true that there are common points of reference that impart an element of cultural unity to the different types of walls, particularly in respect to a unifying Confucian cosmology which underpins and influences the ordering of society within enclosed spaces. Nevertheless, the generalizations that associate all Chinese walls with ideas of limitation, enclosure, inwardness, and so on are too reductionist.

The central problem with this body of work is that it focuses too much on the walls themselves while failing to address what lies within them. Yang Dongping alludes to this problem in pointing out that "the function of walls is to define, segregate, and defend the space of power."[15] Thus it is not the walls, nor the fact that they enclose per se, which is crucial; rather it is the *space* which they create and the spatial arrangements and practices that operate there which are of primary significance. Chinese walls, then, should be

considered not in the predominantly negative sense of enclosure and con-
tainment, as they are in the works examined above, but rather as positive
technologies productive of particular relations of spatial practice. Moreover,
each form of the walled compound must be examined in its own right as a
distinct ensemble of spatial and institutional practices, rather than as a
straightforward example of a universal cultural trope. A more rigorously specific mode of analysis is necessary to arrive at a more nuanced understanding of the significance of walls within Chinese cultural and social practice.

Toward a Genealogy of Walls

In the remainder of this chapter, I focus upon the mundane walls of everyday life and, more particularly, the social spaces that are created inside those
walls. I develop an analysis of the archetypal spatial forms of the past and the
social practices which corresponded to them. In doing so, I show the close
relationship between the production of lived space and the norms of social
organization and behavior within traditional Chinese society. Through this
analysis it will become clear that in many respects the traditional courtyard
home, ubiquitous through Chinese history, can in some ways be thought of
as a "machine" for the production of Confucian subjects. In later chapters I
build upon this analysis to suggest that the modern *danwei* redeploys these
spatial tactics to produce quite a different kind of subject.

No one can be sure precisely when, or to what purpose, the first walls in
China were built. However, in his study of the Great Wall, Arthur Waldron
hypothesizes that the first walls were probably built to separate households.
At a later stage the use of walls was extended to enclose whole villages and
towns.[16] It is the latter rather than the former form of ancient walls that have
survived the longest and hence provide the earliest evidence of Chinese wall
building. One of the earliest examples of a city wall is the seven-kilometer
wall surrounding the Shang dynasty town of Erligang in Henan (modern-
day Zhengzhou). Built around 1500 BC, it is about twenty-two meters thick
at the base and has sections that still stand nine meters in height.[17] Evidence
for the building of walls around individual houses is not quite as old, yet still
stretches back to around the eleventh century BC, as in the case of the
Zhouyuan site in Shaanxi Province.[18] The precise origin and embryonic history of the wall in China is unlikely to be resolved for certain; however, what
these archaeological sites do reveal is that at least as early as three thousand
years ago the Chinese had already begun to use walls in two specific forms:
to surround towns and cities and also to enclose individual dwellings.

The purpose of city and household walls is generally assumed to be defensive. However, some anthropologists and cultural historians argue that a
more critical function of these kinds of walls is to mark out sacred social

space. Mircea Eliade, for example, argues that within traditional cultures, like those of ancient Rome, India, Iran, and China, urban and household spaces were arranged to imitate or mirror the religious universe.[19] In his analysis of the Kabyle house in Algeria, Pierre Bourdieu demonstrates how the traditional household was organized spatially to symbolize the sacred nature and order of family life.[20] Reflecting on this conception of household space, Francesca Bray characterizes the house (in general) as "a mechanism that converts ritual, political and cosmological relationships into spatial terms experienced daily and assimilated as natural."[21]

Scholars who have studied the cities and houses of ancient China appear to concur with this view. In his work on Han China, Michael Loewe, for example, points out that the Han capital city was designed to "symbolize the ideal regularity of the imperial order and the view of society as a series of interrelated groups, each placed in its own rightful position in the universe."[22] Likewise, one of the leading experts on Chinese residential architecture, Ronald Knapp, believes that the design and arrangement of the traditional house "evokes connections with many other aspects of Chinese culture, imitating in multiple 'little traditions' the cosmological predilections of 'the great tradition.'"[23] In reproducing the sacred order of the cosmos, the spatial forms of the traditional city and the traditional house imbue the everyday physical environment with religious and philosophical significance. This sacred spatial order is further bolstered, according to Eliade, through the practice of ritual. Spatial arrangements, then, provide a cosmological grid that underpins and orders the ritual practices of day-to-day social and religious interaction.

Cosmologically ordered space makes no internal distinction between the sacred and the secular or profane. Or, to put it another way, the profane is simply excluded from this spatial ordering. Thus, all space inside the walls created through the imposition of a cosmologically defined order is by definition sacred. Conversely, that which lies outside of the walls—unordered space—is necessarily profane. The wall marks the point of demarcation between the two. Yet the wall is much more than just the dividing line between the sacred and profane; indeed to see it simply in these terms would imply a return to the position criticized above, which sees the wall as a universal signifier of cultural unity and reads the house, the temple, the palace, and the city as simple repetitions of the same cultural order.[24]

To avoid this pitfall, it is important to note that space created within the walls is also a world of social relationships in which difference and differentiation are central features. It is in this respect that the specificity of various architectural forms takes on a crucial importance, for each different form demarcates a different domain of social relationship. In this context, as F. W. Mote observes, the most important role of the city wall "was to mark the presence of the government."[25] The city walls thereby demarcated the realm of the state and spatially structured the relationships between state officials and the general populace. Similarly, the walls around the compound house, as Francesca Bray points out, "marked the boundaries of a patriarchal domain."[26] While each of these spatial realms may be linked through a common cosmological origin, as realms within which the highly ordered rituals and practices of Confucianism held sway, in daily practice they represent distinct social domains, each characterized by a set of differentiated social relationships.

The Walled City: Cosmology, Government, and Social Order

Walled cities in China, as I have noted above, can be traced back as far as the fifteenth century BC. However, the earliest surviving written records that set down principles for the design of cities are those found in the *Kaogongji* section of the *Zhou Li*, or *Rites of Zhou*, a text that probably dates from around the time of the Han dynasty emperor Han Wudi (141–87 BC).[27] It prescribes that the imperial capital should be set out as "a square with sides of nine *li*, each side having three gateways. Within the capital there were nine meridional and nine latitudinal avenues, each of the former being nine chariot tracks in width."[28] This layout created a regular grid pattern that formed the basic skeleton of the city (Figure 2.1). The emperor's palace was sited at the heart of the grid, facing south and approached by a long ceremonial avenue from the central gate in the southern wall. Other important government buildings and places of ritual and worship were also placed along this central axis, gathered in symbolic order around the heart of the state. Confucius likened the emperor to the polestar—the body around which all the heavens revolve[29]—hence the central position of the palace symbolized the role of the emperor as the central pivot of the empire.[30] The designs of all the great historical capitals, from the Chang'an of the Western Han through to Ming and Qing Beijing, were based upon the precepts laid down in the *Kaogongji*.[31] Beijing, the last imperial capital, still preserves much of its original central axis culminating in the Forbidden City, despite having lost its city wall and undergone enormous development. Many other administrative cities and towns were also built according to these principles of design, though on a much smaller scale.[32]

While the central axis of the traditional city represented the power of the emperor and the state in China, this was only one aspect of the grid system set down in the *Kaogongji*. As urban theorist Zhu Wenyi rightly points out, most commentaries have placed too much emphasis upon the center of the grid, while neglecting the everyday social spaces that constituted the rest of the city.[33] Apart from the central axis and areas set aside for markets, storage,

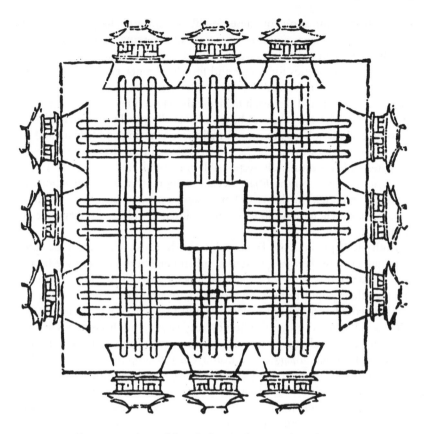

FIGURE 2.1. Representation of the ideal capital city as described in the *Kao-gongji*.
Source: Reproduced in Liu Dunzhen, *A History of Classical Chinese Architecture* (Beijing: Chinese Architecture Industry Press, 1980), 23.

or other official uses, the majority of the city grid was given over to residential usage. The spatial form of these residential neighborhoods and the way in which they were policed offer significant insight into the social order of the traditional city.

The residential areas within the city walls were divided into blocks defined by the interlocking grid of avenues. In turn, each block—known variously as *li*, *lüli*, or, later, *fang*[34]—was enclosed by its own walls. In this way the walled city was itself made up of numerous walled residential compounds, antecedents to the walled *danwei* compounds of modern China.

The earliest justification for these neighborhood walls has been found in the writings of Guanzi, a philosopher from the Warring States period (475–221 BC). He believed that a system of enclosed residential areas would reduce the opportunities for crime and for illicit contact between men and women.[35] In order to facilitate the policing of social and moral order, Guanzi also stipulated that each *li* have only one central avenue with a gate at either end. The gates were to be guarded at all times by an official known as *lüyousi*, whose job was to monitor all those entering and leaving and report to the head of the *li*, the *liwei*. This latter official also held the key to the gates and was ultimately responsible for overall management.[36] Under this style of regulation the *li-fang* became integral to the everyday policing of social order within the city. This system operated until the Northern Song dynasty, when the walls were pulled down in order to facilitate greater commercial activity.[37]

Both He Yeju and Yang Kuan point out the close relationship between the emergence of the *li-fang* system of urban neighborhoods and the household registration systems, or *baojia*, developed by the early Chinese states to organize their populations.[38] The *Zhou Li*, for example, stipulated that five families would form a unit called a *bi* and that five *bi* form a larger unit called a *lü*.[39] Thus, during the Zhou dynasty, twenty-five households formed the basic residential unit of the city. In later periods the number of households constituting a *li-fang* varied from twenty-five up to as many as eighty, but whatever the number, internally the *li-fang* was always ordered according to a strict hierarchical code of responsibility. There was a twofold purpose in organizing the population in this way. First, this system facilitated the collection of taxes and the enforcement of corvée labor and army service.[40] Second, it was intended to foster the maintenance of social order and safety. Thus, the *bi* was charged with the role of mutual protection, while the *lü* was designated as the basic unit of community administration.[41]

The close relationship between the *li-fang* and the *baojia* systems is worthy of note, for it illustrates the ways in which spatial forms were linked both to the organization of community and to the policing of social order within China's traditional urban environment. To understand this nexus, it is necessary to take seriously Michael Dutton's point that the *baojia* system did not, as many commentators contend, operate purely as a repressive institution of state coercion, but also embodied a range of positive community functions related to education, welfare, self-defense, and other forms of mutual self-help.[42] Although the *baojia* system provided the authorities with a "window" into every household, it also invested the grassroots level of the population with an organizational structure designed to promote its viability and harmony. The *li-fang* system clearly reinforced the delineations of community units under *baojia*, as well as providing an added dimension of security.

Through spatial reinforcement, it further bolstered the practices of collective responsibility and mutual obligation that were cornerstones of the Confucian moral code. In traditional urban China, the walls of the *li-fang* created the ordered space in which the regimes of the *baojia* could be fully realized.

As previously mentioned, the walled *li-fang* system disappeared during the Northern Song dynasty.[43] Despite this development, and perhaps even because of it, the *baojia* system was actually strengthened during this period through reforms instituted by Wang Anshi (1021–86).[44] *Baojia* remained central to dynastic strategies of government through to the Qing dynasty and was even redeployed by the Guomindang government during the Republican period.[45] Although the walls had gone, the memories of *li-fang* lived on in urban place names,[46] and *baojia* continued to be tied closely to local community and the policing of the urban population.[47] The disappearance of the *li-fang* walls may have presaged a shift in urban function during the Song dynasty from a purely symbolic and administrative role to a more commercially oriented role, but this development by no means implied a shift away from the core values of the Confucian moral code, nor its basis in the institution of the family. Thus, while the *li-fang* walls quickly vanished, the walls of the courtyard-style traditional home remained firmly in place. Although more intimate, the enclosed space of the family compound nonetheless played a critical role in organizing and policing social order within the Chinese city.

The Courtyard House: Cosmology, Family, and the Confucian Moral Code

According to Confucian texts, the ideal society is one ordered through virtue and correct behavior, rather than governed through adherence to laws and punishments.[48] "The Master said, 'Guide them by edicts, keep them in line with punishments, and the common people will stay out of trouble but will have no sense of shame. Guide them by virtue, keep them in line with the rites [*li*], and they will, besides having a sense of shame, reform themselves.'"[49]

The rulers of society ought to be steeped in virtue, and their method of leadership was through promoting *li*—the rites or rules of propriety. Virtue was considered to be innate to the educated, well-bred "gentleman," or *junzi*, and implied a deep understanding of ritual and ethical codes. The rules of *li*, variously translated as ceremony, ritual, rites, propriety, rules of propriety, good custom, decorum, and good form,[50] were the means through which the less enlightened majority of the population were to be taught how to behave.

As the passage quoted above demonstrates, the codes of *li* were not conceived of as legal precepts, but rather were taken to be values and practices intrinsic to the virtuous conduct of social relationships. The social nature of *li* is crucial, as Tu Wei-ming points out, since in Confucian society "man authenticates his being not by detaching himself from the world of human relations but by making sincere attempts to harmonize his relationships with others."[51] Confucian relationships, however, were based not on notions of equality, but rather upon a hierarchy of social roles. To "harmonize relationships with others," then, required strict adherence to the rules of behavior set down for each different social role. The central relationships within Confucian society were referred to as "the five duties of universal obligation." The five duties were "those between sovereign and minister, between father and son, between husband and wife, between elder brother and younger, and those belonging to the intercourse of friends."[52] The grid of social order was founded upon the ritualized differentiation between social positions as embodied through these five intrinsic relationships.[53]

Since three of the "five duties of universal obligation" concern family relationships (those between father and son, husband and wife, and elder brother and younger brother), it is clear that the family household was critical to Confucian ideals of social order. The practice of *li*, therefore, was not something restricted to state affairs or to the polite society of palace life; it was a code that sought to regulate behavior at all levels of society. The importance afforded the conduct of family life by Confucianism is evident in the pronouncement, attributed to Confucius, that "the duty of children to their parents is the foundation whence all other virtues spring."[54] This indicates that the correct regulation of family relationships was the basis of Confucian society.

A great deal of scholarship has been produced on the importance of family relationships to Confucian society. Conversely, as Francesca Bray points out, surprisingly little scholarship has been produced on the role of the traditional house in the reproduction of family relationships.[55] In her insightful study on gender and technology in late imperial China, Bray illustrates the ways in which traditional household space encoded relationships between man and woman, husband and wife, parents and children, and so on. Adopting a technological allusion, Bray suggests that "one can picture the Chinese house as a kind of loom, weaving individual lives into a typically Chinese social pattern."[56] The spatial order of the traditional home, then, is not simply an idealized reproduction of cosmological space but is more importantly a machine for the reproduction of Confucian family order. This "machine" appeared in its archetypal form from a very early period.

I noted above that there is archaeological evidence of walled housing complexes dating back to the eleventh century BC. The Zhouyuan structures from the early Western Zhou period, as well as being enclosed by walls, were arranged in the courtyard-style pattern that was later to become ubiquitous.[57] It seems that this kind of courtyard form had become the architectural ideal very early, but for many centuries it was utilized only for the most important ceremonial and royal buildings. Meanwhile, at least until the Warring States period (481–221 BC), the majority of the population lived in semisubterranean thatched huts.[58] There are references to walled courtyard-style residences in some of the pre-Han classical texts. The *Analects*, for example, contain some oblique reference to household spatial arrangements (see discussion below), and Mencius compares those who seek office through improper means to boys who *climb over walls* to meet girls from other families without the prior approval of their parents.[59] However, it is the Han dynasty that furnishes the earliest detailed evidence of residential architecture, in the miniature clay models of houses that have been unearthed from burial chambers.[60] These clay models of courtyard-style walled compounds reveal that the basic principles of classical Chinese residential architecture were already well established by the Han dynasty.

The fact that these basic principles of residential architecture remained essentially unchanged from ancient times right through to the Qing dynasty is confirmed by an examination of any basic architectural history of dynastic China.[61] A review of this literature confirms Knapp's comment that "unlike the cities and countryside of the West which may be read as museums of changing architectural styles, the cultural landscapes of China are remarkably ahistorical."[62] Similarly, while regional differences in architectural style do occur, the architectural records tend to suggest that these differences are relatively minor variations of the same general spatial principles. Where differences do occur, they are largely due to climatic factors. For instance, while the house in northern China has a large central courtyard to make the most of winter sun, the traditional home in southern China, where the climate is much warmer, has a very small courtyard, known as "the well of heaven" (*tianjing*), which ensures the summer sun is largely kept out.[63] Despite the variation in courtyard size, however, internal spatial arrangements within northern and southern homes are remarkably similar.[64]

In his study of Chinese architectural and urban planning history, Andrew Boyd suggests that the basic principles of design were remarkably straightforward. "They appeared early in the tradition and were applied very widely, whether to the plan of a little homestead, the layout of a temple, a palace or a city ensemble." These basic principles were "(a) *walled enclosure*; (b) *axiality*; (c) *north-south orientation*; and (d) *the courtyard*."[65] The remarkable persistence of the walled courtyard-style residence across historical and regional divides parallels the long dominance of Confucianism as the primary source of ethical order within Chinese society. This correlation is by no means coincidental; rather it serves to underscore the intimate linkage between spatial forms and the production of social order.

At the most basic level the enclosed family compound created a distinct realm of familial authority, distinguishing the family from other families as well as from other levels of social organization.[66] The enclosed space also represented family unity and solidarity, symbolized by the one central stove or hearth that fed all family members.[67] If an extended family divided up its property, each new family branch would set up a separate stove, symbolizing the division.[68] Yet, although the reinforcement of family authority and unity were significant effects of the walled residential form, in my view the most singular feature of traditional family space was the manner in which it demarcated difference within the Confucian family. In short, the traditional home reproduced in spatial form the hierarchical family relationships that were defined through the precepts of *li*. This becomes evident through a careful reading of a passage from the Confucian *Analects*.

Chen Kang asked Boyu, saying, "Have you heard any lessons [from your father] different [from what we have all] heard?"

Boyu replied, "No. He was standing alone once, when I passed below the hall with hasty steps, and said to me, 'Have you learned the Odes?' On my replying 'Not yet,' [he added,] 'If you do not learn the Odes, you will not be fit to converse with.' I retired and studied the Odes.

"Another day, he was in the same way standing alone, when I passed by below the hall with hasty steps, and said to me, 'Have you learned the rules of Propriety?' On my replying 'Not yet,' [he added,] 'If you do not learn the rules of Propriety, your character cannot be established.' I then retired and learned the rules of Propriety.

"I have learned only these two things from him."

Chen Kang retired, and, quite delighted, said, "I asked one thing, and I have got three things. I have heard about the Odes. I have heard about the rules of Propriety. I have also heard that the superior man maintains a distant [reserve] towards his son."[69]

Boyu was the eldest son of Confucius, so the passage quoted above recounts events which are supposed to have occurred within the Master's own household. According to traditional Chinese rules of etiquette, to "walk with hasty steps" was a sign of respect toward one's superiors, in this case indicating the respect of the son toward his father. The "hall" (*ting*), below which the son passed, was the central and most prominent room of the classical Chinese compound house; it faced onto and dominated the internal courtyard.[70]

After hearing Boyu relate the two encounters with his father (Confucius), Chen Kang was astute in observing that much more than just direction for study was at issue. Apart from the father exhorting his son to study *The*

Odes and *The Rules of Propriety*, the very manner of the encounters reveals significant features of the Confucian father/son relationship. The father, standing alone outside the central hall, looks over and dominates the courtyard below. As all rooms lead onto this courtyard, the father's gaze may instantly take in everything happening within his family domain. The son, moving from one room to another, must cross the courtyard and come within the gaze of the father. The son crosses "with hasty steps," reverential within the sight of his father, and hoping not to impinge too overtly on his father's space. Conversation is initiated by the father and takes the form of interrogation and direction—no pleasantries are exchanged. The son answers respectfully, obeying at once the father's instructions.

As Chen Kang remarks, it is clear from the interaction that the Confucian father keeps a distance between himself and his son.[71] Yet this distance appears not only in the severe and detached way the father deals with the son, but also in the physical distance maintained between the two. The father standing outside the hall in a position elevated above the courtyard and the son scurrying across below in the courtyard illustrate as eloquently as the exchange of words the distance between the two and their relative status. The regulation of difference between father and son is thus expressed, in a manner transparent to all, by the spatial distance that separates them and the positioning of each within that space. The architectural arrangement of the house conspires with ritualized behavior to establish distance and difference between social roles within the family (Figure 2.2).

This link between spatial form and social relationship is further underscored through a detailed examination of the distribution of rooms within the household.[72] In a typical traditional house consisting of a single enclosed courtyard, the principles of spatial distribution were relatively simple. The most important part of the house was the building sited along the northern side of the courtyard facing south. It was known as the *zhengfang* (also referred to sometimes as the *gaotang*, or *zutang*) and was always occupied by the most senior male, the patriarch of the family, and his wife (or wives).[73] As with other wings of the courtyard, this building generally consisted of three rooms: a central room with an externally opening door (to the south), known as the *ting*, or *tangwu*; and two side rooms, one opening off each side of the *ting*, known as *jian*. The *ting* was central to the household not only because of its dominating position but also because it was the site through which families were linked to their ancestors.[74] Ancestor tablets, images of elders, and sometimes genealogical scrolls were displayed there while offerings of food and other valuables were regularly left out to placate the ancestral spirits.[75] As well as being used for ceremonial and ritual purpose, the *ting* was used for greeting important guests and for family or clan meetings. In short, the *ting* was the center of family power, its symbolism expressing the

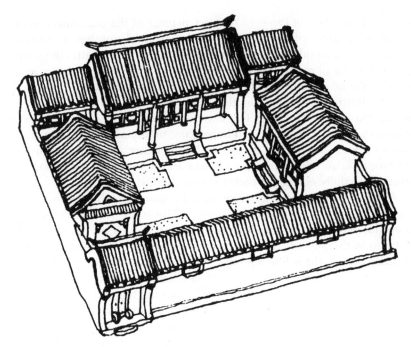

FIGURE 2.2. Bird's-eye view (*above*) and floor plan (*opposite*) of a single court-yard *siheyuan*.
Source: Generic type derived from numerous sources.

continuity from past to present and the ancestral authority invested in the living occupier of its space. Its spatial domination of the courtyard bolstered its centrality to family ritual and the empowerment of patriarchal authority.

The rooms that opened off the *ting*, the *jian*, were generally used as bedrooms for the patriarch and his wife (or wives). Here again spatial arrangement played an important function. For of the three rooms that constituted the *zhengfang*, only the central one, the *ting*, had an external door. Thus, as the seat of the patriarch, the *ting* commanded domination not only over the whole courtyard but also over the rooms he occupied with his wife (or wives). To enter or exit the *zhengfang* necessitated passing through the *ting* and under the gaze of the patriarch. The terminology used in describing these rooms reflected this hierarchical spatial order. Because it communed with the outside, the *ting* was referred to as *ming*, or bright, while the *jian*, which communed only internally with the *ting*, were termed *an*, or dark.[76] These terms relate directly to the Chinese metaphysical concepts of *yin* and *yang*—*yin* being the dark, female principle; *yang* the bright, male principle.

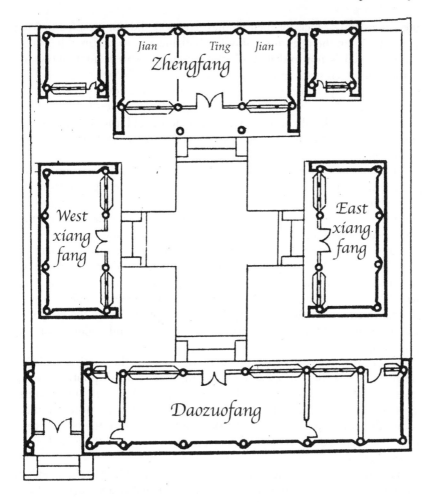

The rooms occupied primarily by the women were, both literally and symbolically, internal and dark, while those primarily occupied by the men were external and bright. In this way the relationship between *ting* and *jian* is imbued with cosmological as well as social significance. Where the former speaks to metaphysical understanding of gendered difference, the latter realizes the hierarchical domination of husband over wife in concrete spatial form. Just as the patriarch spatially dominates the whole courtyard, so the husband dominates his quarters within the *zhengfang*.

The spatial differentiation between women and men explicit in the design of the home is confirmed by many of the rules of conduct set down in the *Liji*, or the *Book of Propriety*. For example, "Males and females did not use the same stand or rack for their clothes. The wife did not presume to hang up anything on the pegs or stand of her husband; nor to put anything in his boxes or satchels; nor to share his bathing house."[77] This example shows the manner in which spatial practices were reinforced by the strict regime of social and bodily practices set out in the ancient codes. For relationships between husbands and wives, as for the relationship between father and son discussed above, the physical arrangement of household space conspired with the formulas of ritual to mark in a most visible fashion the differentiation of social roles.

Flanking the courtyard to the east and west, lower in height and smaller in scale than the *zhengfang*, were the *xiangfang*. These were generally of the same three-room form as the *zhengfang*, with a central *ting* opening to the outside and a *jian* on each side opening internally into the *ting*. These wings were occupied by those male members of the family, and their wives and children, who ranked next below the patriarch in the family hierarchy: either the sons of the family patriarch or his younger brothers. Normally the second-ranking male took the east *xiangfang* and the third the west *xiangfang*.[78] Within each *xiangfang* the same spatial arrangements applied as with the *zhengfang*, such that within each subdomain of the family the hierarchical dominance of the husband over the wife (wives) and children was expressed spatially.

The fourth side of the courtyard house, sited to the south and facing north, known as the *daozuofang*, occupied the least favorable position, having no access to direct sunlight and often being separated from the main courtyard by an internal wall. The purpose of such a wall was to show that these rooms did not properly form part of the family structure as they would generally be occupied by servants (if the family had any), house the kitchen, or be used for storage.[79]

The size of courtyard homes varied, of course, according to the wealth of the family; nevertheless the basic principles of spatial arrangement and distribution remained the same. No doubt smaller homes were far more common than larger ones, and many descriptions and illustrations of these various forms can be found in the standard architectural surveys.[80] Based upon these studies and my own observations in modern rural villages where homes are still built on this model, the smallest residences consist of a single wing divided into three spaces like the *zhengfang* described above: a central room (*tang*) opening to the outside, usually facing south, which often combined the roles of kitchen and ancestor shrine, and two internal rooms opening off it, one usually occupied by the parents, the other by the children (Figure 2.3).[81] Slightly wealthier families may have an additional wing at right angles to the first to form an L-shaped house, or two such side wings making the house U-shaped. But regardless of whether it contains one, two,

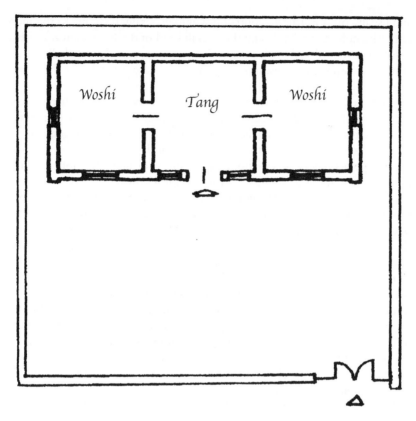

FIGURE 2.3. Floor plan of single-wing courtyard residence. The central hall (*tang*) is flanked on both sides by bedrooms (*woshi*).
Source: Generic type based on author's observations in rural Shandong.

or three wings, these smaller-scale houses invariably reproduce the enclosed courtyard form. This is achieved by simply building a wall around the sides not enclosed by buildings. Thus even the poorest families could maintain a secure, enclosed space to reinforce and reproduce Confucian family relationships.

At the other extreme of wealth, homes were naturally much larger but still conformed to the basic design principles. Wealthy families occupied homes generally made up of many courtyards of the type described above, linked together along an axis, each opening into the next one. In these residential complexes it was possible to house numerous branches of one large extended family, each branch occupying its own courtyard. The innermost, and usually most northerly, courtyard would generally be home to the most senior branch of the family and the overall head of the lineage group. Other courtyards were distributed, as with the various rooms discussed above, according to family hierarchy, allocating the most senior branches to the courtyards at the northern end of the axis, and the more junior branches to the southern end. In this manner, distribution of space differentiated both among social roles within each smaller family unit as well as between different branches of the extended family. Indeed, the household arrangements for a large extended family virtually mirrored the hierarchy set down in the family's genealogical tables—both home and genealogy positioned family members according to a transparent hierarchical order.

Whether we consider the homes of the poor or the wealthy, the distribution of rooms shows the link between spatial organization and social relationships within the traditional household. Moreover, with each member of the household fixed spatially in this manner, according to their position within the family hierarchy, the traditional compound house operated as a machine for the reproduction of Confucian *li*. In this way, the space of the compound household not only reproduced cosmological order but also positioned social actors spatially within this cosmological order so as to bolster the hierarchical family relationships demanded by Confucian principles. Spatio-cosmological order thus conspired with social practice to reinforce a collective family-centered mode of subjectivity; bodies were positioned spatially, not as individuals, but rather as specific role-players within the highly differentiated family organization.

Situated around a central courtyard, the occupant of each space within the home was easily visible to all others, and particularly to the family patriarch, who occupied the most central position. In consequence, the allocation of space to individual family members did not result in the creation of private realms. On the contrary, it placed each family member visibly within the hierarchical order of the social group. In this way each individual was tied to his or her designated role within the family, and the individual's behavior was policed through the transparency of the open courtyard formation and the ritual practices prescribed to daily life.

Conclusion

Throughout China's history, walls have been widely utilized to demarcate social spaces. For this reason, many historians have interpreted the wall as a symbol of Chinese culture. To them, the wall represents enclosure, conservatism, introspection, and even totalitarianism. In contrast, I have argued that what is most significant about the wall is not the act of enclosure or exclusion per se, but rather the spaces created by the wall and the forms of spatial and social practice which are inscribed within these spaces. In taking this position, I have built upon the work, discussed in Chapter 1, of theorists like Henri Lefebvre and Foucault in order to show that important insights into social practice and subjectivity can be gained through analysis of the spatial environments of everyday life.

The walled city and the walled household compound were the two most significant spatial realms in traditional China. The former was the realm of imperial government, while the latter was the realm of the Confucian family. The walled city embodied a complex array of cosmologically determined symbolic spaces designed to reinforce the might of the emperor and his government, but also, in its simple grid design it provided a template for the ordering of everyday social life. This grid was the foundation for the *li-fang* system of walled neighborhoods that inscribed communities within a clear spatial realm. The spatial arrangements of the city then, mirrored and bolstered the local community group that the Confucian state relied upon for the maintenance of social order. This was reflected in the close correspondence between the *li-fang* system of neighborhood space and the *baojia* system of mutual-aid and policing.

The traditional Chinese compound house was the realm of the Confucian family and was designed to reproduce the differentiated social relationships demanded by Confucian moral philosophy. Space was arranged in highly symbolic form within the house so that the allocation of spaces to family members provided transparent representation of social position within the family. Moreover, the ritual practices of *li* through which social behavior was regulated and bodily discipline enforced further bolstered the spatial order of the family.

In both the walled city and the walled family compound, spatial practice operated to produce and regulate particular kinds of subjects. Within the walled city, the object of regulation was the local community group. The *li-fang* and *baojia* systems functioned to demarcate, legitimize, and bolster the effectiveness of the community in its designated roles of localized self-help and self-policing. Within the walled compound, it was the family unit that was the object of regulation. Allocation of space and the practices of *li* together operated to reproduce the ideally ordered family of Confucian legend. The subject of city governance, then, was the community group, while the subject of the household compound was the family.

But what has all this to do with the *danwei* of socialist China? In the beginning of this chapter I suggested a link between the *danwei*, the traditional city, and the compound house on the basis of a common reliance upon the enclosing wall. While this connection may have seemed tenuous at first, the close relationship between spatial form, social regulation, and the production of subjects, which has been revealed in this chapter, sheds new light on the genealogy of the *danwei* as both the basic social unit and basic spatial unit of the socialist city. In making this genealogical link, however, I do not mean to imply that the *danwei* is a remnant of the traditional past, as some have suggested. On the contrary, as will become clear in subsequent chapters, my view is that the *danwei* has a complex and many-layered genealogy. The complexity and the way in which a range of quite disparate practices came together and were invested with new meanings, implications, and effects makes the *danwei* such an interesting and important object of study.

It must also be remembered, as Foucault has pointed out in his discussion of the Panopticon, that spatial forms are quite flexible and open to a range of reappropriations.[82] If the socialist *danwei* adopted the walled compound form, it was not because the *danwei* was an inherently Confucian institution, but rather because this spatial form had a certain mimetic resonance as a technology that could be productively utilized for the ordering of collective forms of social relationship. The *danwei* is clearly a modern institution, but one that has reemployed a familiar spatial repertoire to the service of a new social purpose. Where the traditional courtyard house defined the realm of the Confucian family, the *danwei* compound established the territory of the socialist collective. But many other factors and influences were also to contribute to the formation of the *danwei*, as the following chapters attest.

CHAPTER 3

Modernity and Social Organization Before 1949
The Emergence of the Proto-*Danwei*

With victory over the Nationalist forces in 1948–49, the CCP was finally able to return to the cities after twenty-two years of rural-based struggle. As victors of the civil war, they were now in a position to establish a new
government and begin the huge task of transforming China into a modern
socialist state. One of the outcomes of the Chinese transition to socialism
was the emergence of the *danwei* as the key basic unit of urban life. But this
didn't happen overnight—the establishment of the *danwei* was never pro-
claimed, and there is no particular date or event or even specific policy to
which we can solely attribute its origin. Its emergence was the result of a
complex layering of various disparate practices, institutions, and policies over
a long period. In this chapter, I trace genealogical strands of the *danwei* from
two distinct pre-1949 social settings. I examine the institutional structures of
workplace organization in the cities of Republican China—guilds, gangs,
and corporations—and consider the ways in which traditional forms of family-centered subjectivity were transformed and adapted to the demands of a
modernizing and industrializing urban environment. Second, I focus on the
Yan'an period in order to chart the emergence of the CCP's approach to
modern social and workplace organization. I show how the CCP developed
a distinctive rationale of governance which led directly to the formation of
the proto-*danwei*.

More than just chronological proximity justifies bringing the Republican
and the Communist worlds together in this context. Although they pursued
quite different policies, protagonists in Yan'an and the Republican cities
were both looking for modern institutional forms of organization that were
suited to contemporary Chinese realities. Beyond sharing a common modernizing theme, however, there were more direct links between the two
worlds. Many prominent leaders within the CCP had spent their earliest

revolutionary years working within the nascent labor movements of the Republican cities. Although forced to flee after 1927, their experiences of urban industrial organization from that period, as Elizabeth Perry has shown, had a long-term effect on CCP policy and influenced the implementation of urban strategies after 1949.[1] However, it is also important to recognize that the CCP's return to the cities did not simply lead to a resumption of 1920s-era policy—much had changed in the meantime. Rather, the new government adapted the mobilization practices developed during the Yan'an period to its understanding of urban society. From the genealogical perspective, however, perhaps the most striking connection between the Republican and Communist worlds was how both developed modern institutional practices that fostered collective rather than individual forms of subjectivity. It was primarily because of this common feature that the transition from a nascent capitalist system to a socialist system in urban China was far less socially disruptive than it might otherwise have been.

Subjectivity and the Danwei

The question of subjectivity is one that has been largely neglected in previous studies of the *danwei*. This omission can no doubt be attributed to a fairly widespread assumption that there is only one kind of human subject—namely, the individual self-conscious subject that has dominated Western philosophical thought since the Enlightenment. Despite its apparent dominance, this assumption has been subject to critical challenge on a number of fronts. First, it has been questioned with respect to its accuracy in accounting for social phenomena within Western society itself. Marx and Durkheim, for example, each developed influential analytical frameworks which denied the primacy of individual subjectivity in favor of overriding mechanisms at the level of society itself: respectively, the mode of production and organic solidarity. The constitutive importance of social structure over individual agency was further emphasized—or overemphasized as many critics now suggest—by structuralists like Levi-Strauss and Althusser. More recently Foucault and a range of other post-structuralist scholars have problematized the assumed autonomy of the individualized subject in different ways.[2] They have shown how various social and institutional practices and regimes of knowledge production have constituted individualized forms of subject in the West. Individual autonomy, therefore, should be seen as neither a natural nor a universal human attribute, but rather as the result of a complex ensemble of practices, knowledges, and power relationships associated with the emergence of Western liberalism over the last two centuries. In particular, the notion of individual autonomy is crucial to this form of subjectivity because it encourages practices of self-regulation (through self-awareness and self-knowledge) that are essential to the operation of liberal modes of government.[3]

Assumptions about the autonomous nature of the individual human subject have also been critiqued as Eurocentric. Anthropologist Marcel Mauss, for example, demonstrates that the privileged position afforded the notion of the individualized self-conscious subject is specific to postenlightenment Western culture. In contrast, many non-Western societies conceive of subjectivity predominantly in ways in which individual identity is tied to group identity through various relationships of kinship, ritual, and economic exchange.[4] Despite the obvious implications of this anthropological work and the developments in post-structuralist theory, categories deriving from the Western experience of modernity have continued to operate as epistemological givens within the mainstream of Chinese studies; alternative notions of subjectivity are seldom acknowledged.

In recent years, however, a small archive of new, theoretically nuanced scholarship has appeared to challenge the mainstream position and to assert the specificity of Chinese subjectivities. Angela Zito and Tani Barlow, for example, point to the great diversity and multiplicity of subject positions in China as demonstrated by the various contributions to their timely edited collection *Body, Subject, and Power in China*.[5] While I certainly acknowledge the significance of diversity, for the purposes of this study, which focuses on a particular institutional formation, I take my lead from the argument, elaborated by both Michael Dutton and Ann Anagnost, that governmental practices in China have tended to promote collective rather than individual forms of subjectivity.[6] It is this specific nexus between institutional formation and collective subjectivity that I examine in this chapter.

To emphasize the collective orientation of institutions does not, of course, imply a necessarily egalitarian form of collectivism; after all, the traditional Confucian family was a highly differentiated form of collective social unit in which the various roles carried vastly unequal degrees of status and power. The socialist *danwei* is also underpinned by differentiation between various roles—workers, cadres, party activists, and so on—but like the traditional family, its overall orientation reproduces collective rather than individual subjects. The purpose of this chapter is to trace the points of transition from the premodern to modern social institutions to see how new collective subjects could be produced as the foundation for organizational practice both in the Republican cities and in Yan'an and the implications of this for the subsequent emergence of the *danwei*.

Refiguring Traditional Subjectivities: Guilds, Gangs, and Corporations in the Cities of Republican China

A number of urban historians have pointed to the important role played by traditional forms of organization—artisan guilds, native-place associations, gangs, and sworn brotherhoods—in mediating labor relations during the emergence and development of industry in Chinese cities.[7] In a study of the Shanghai labor movement, Perry argues that artisan guilds and the skilled artisan constituents they represented were particularly influential in establishing the agenda for workplace-based welfare provision that was to become such a significant part of the future *danwei* system. Links between the guilds and influential members of the CCP were important to future developments, but of more interest from the genealogical perspective is the question of how the guilds as institutions adapted to the rise of modern industry.

As Perry relates, the artisan guilds of early-twentieth-century Shanghai were based upon a very old form of association known as the "native-place" association.[8] For centuries, native-place associations had operated in China's towns and cities to provide support and welfare for people with common places of origin.[9] Their function, in part, was to replicate in the cities the traditional family and community networks that surrounded rural residents. In organizational form they were modeled upon the traditional Confucian family. The guild had a set hierarchical order with the guild head occupying a position and status analogous to the family head, or *jiazhang*, of the traditional family system.[10] Likewise, ordinary members of the guild would address each other as "elder brother" and "younger brother" according to their particular age and rank. Within the cities, authorities viewed the guilds as equivalent to extended families or clans and bestowed upon them the same status in law. Thus, like family heads, guild leaders were expected to ensure that their members respected and adhered to the prevailing moral and legal codes. In the event of anyone transgressing these codes, it was the guild leader, rather than the offender, who was held primarily accountable to local authorities.[11]

To join a guild, an applicant had to be a native of the region the guild represented and obtain a formal introduction from an existing member. The sponsor was also required to vouch for the moral character of the applicant and could be held responsible if the new member broke any rules of the guild. Other qualifications varied from guild to guild. Some were very strict on membership; for example, to join the Wuxi boilermakers' guild, an applicant had to be the son of a Wuxi boilermaker.[12] Guild members paid an annual fee and were expected to participate in guild ritual and social activities as well as uphold the guild's interests and status within the business community.

The advantage of guild membership was that it provided newcomers with all that was necessary to establish life in an otherwise unfamiliar and alienating urban setting. In urban China, guilds had traditionally held monopolies over certain crafts, which meant they could guarantee their members a relatively constant source of employment.[13] In addition to the provision of employment, the guild offered a ready-made social network for new members. The guild buildings operated as a community center for members and generally provided facilities like meeting halls, theaters, temples to worship guild deities and local gods, as well as space to accommodate new arrivals.[14] New members were inducted in ritual services where they were required to pledge loyalty to the guild leadership and master craftsmen as well as to kowtow before the guild's patron deity. Within each guild, strict hierarchical order was maintained, centering on the relationship between master and apprentice. This relationship was modeled upon the father/son relationship of the Confucian tradition and, hence, did not simply turn upon instruction in a set of technical skills but also implied the adherence to the same Confucian familial codes and practices that regulated the actions of father and son within the traditional family.[15]

Unlike in Europe, the advent of industrialization in late-nineteenth-century Chinese cities did not herald the demise of the traditional guild. Instead Chinese guilds succeeded in expanding their monopolies over the provision of skilled labor into the newly emerging industrial factories. This meant that when a new factory required skilled workers it would contract with the guild that represented that particular craft to provide the necessary workers. In this way the native-place artisan guilds, which represented an essentially traditional mode of social relationship, were interpolated into the operational practices of ostensibly modern industrial enterprises.[16] Consequently, the guild structure and the social relationships it implied were reproduced in factories that employed skilled workers.[17] Within these factories, workers who belonged to the same guild would live, socialize, and practice their common rituals together, virtually as a subbranch of the parent guild.[18] Moreover, it was through these guild structures that the skilled workers of Shanghai organized themselves to carry out collective action to advance and defend their working conditions against increasing attacks from employers.

The way in which artisan guilds adapted to the rise of modern industry in China demonstrates, as Perry and other historians have argued, the inadequacies inherent in applying conventional understandings of modernity to the Chinese context.[19] It challenges the neat binary opposition between modernity and tradition that informs much of the "grand theory" in Western social sciences. More specifically, the Shanghai example shows the inaccuracy of the contention that the rise of modernity must inevitably result in the destruction of traditional social and community structures.[20] In the case of China, the rise of modern industry did not lead to the isolation and atomization of the worker, as predicted by Marxist and Weberian modes of analysis; on the contrary, the industrialization process in urban China saw the adaptation of traditional collective-oriented social practices to the new circumstances.

While the scholars cited above have made a strong historical case against the conventional discourse of modernity, they have largely neglected the question of subjectivity. From the genealogical perspective, the most significant feature of the guild system is the manner in which it carried a traditional collective mode of subjectivity into the newly emerging industrial enterprises of urban China. The guild system not only provided social contact, sources of employment, a locus for industrial activism, and a welfare safety net for its members; it structured their very mode of daily practice. In short, the guild was not just an organization that an individual joined to enhance his opportunities within a new environment; it was the group through which his very identity as a human subject was created. Just as the traditional Confucian family conferred a collective mode of identity upon its members, so the urban guild, operating in many respects as a surrogate family, conferred upon its members a collective social identity within a modernizing urban setting.

The importance of this kind of group identity to the processes of industrialization in urban China is further underlined when we examine the history of unskilled migrant workers, who did not belong to artisan guilds and hence arrived in Shanghai with little or no access to support networks. Not surprisingly, unskilled workers had a much more difficult time establishing themselves within the urban environment. They did not have the native-place associations or artisan-based social networks of skilled workers. In addition, the working conditions they were forced to labor under were far harsher, and job security was generally poorer than that experienced by artisans and skilled workers. Yet, according to the studies of Perry and Hershatter, much of this unskilled labor sector was rapidly absorbed into the networks of urban society through the intercession of underworld gangs.[21] These gangs had initially centered their activities around the opium trade and other organized criminal activities but quickly seized the opportunity to take control of that part of the labor market that fell outside the scope of the guild system.[22] Consequently, new unskilled immigrants from the countryside found that their only access to urban employment was through affiliation with one of these criminal gangs.[23]

Gangs were prominent in the direct organization of businesses such as prostitution, begging, and night soil collection.[24] However, they also came to play a major role as labor contractors for other forms of business and industry that required a ready supply of workers. The waterfront, transport, and the cotton industry, in particular, came under the control of gang-affiliated labor contractors.[25] These contractors would travel to poor rural areas and recruit workers directly from the villages.[26] The relationship between the contractor and the contracted did not end when the latter began work in the city, as labor contractors derived an ongoing income through taking a percentage commission from the wages of every worker they had recruited.[27] Workers had no choice but to pay this commission, since the foremen in their workplace were invariably gang associates of the labor contractors and could make life unbearable for them if they did not acquiesce to this exploitative system.[28] Workers recruited under this system were also forced to join the gang as "disciples" of the foreman whom they worked under.[29]

Despite the obvious negative aspects of this system, it nevertheless provided new workers with a degree of protection as well as access to social networks in a harsh urban environment.[30] In this respect, the gang network to which they had been unknowingly tied played a positive role in the socialization of rural workers into the complexities of urban life. One direct way in which gang affiliation benefited these unskilled workers was in the gang's power to demand pay raises and organize widespread protest actions in support of such demands. Perry notes several occasions on which gang-led industrial action proved successful.[31] While such activity was by no means entirely altruistic, since a wage raise naturally meant an increase in commission for the gang-affiliated labor contractors, it nevertheless resulted in some improvement in the conditions of work for unskilled workers.[32]

Living and working in the shadow of the foreman and the labor contractor, the average unskilled worker was subject to a highly authoritarian social hierarchy. This was further accentuated by the formal structure of the gangs themselves. New workers were generally required to join the gang of their labor contractor, and in so doing enter into a ritualized master/disciple relationship with their mentor. In this respect, gangs, like artisan guilds, were structured as fictive kinship-style hierarchies. Indeed, according to Brian Martin, the Green Gang referred to itself as "the family."[33] Under this organizational structure, superior/inferior relationships were modeled upon the Confucian father/son relationship, and gang disciples were expected to behave as brothers to each other and as devoted and obedient followers of the gang leadership.[34] Like the Confucian family, the gang was an inherently collective-oriented organization; as such, gang disciples were defined not as individuals but rather through their position within the hierarchically structured group. In this sense, the gang played a similar role among unskilled workers to that played by the guild for the skilled workforce—namely, it functioned as a surrogate family, providing solidarity and identity for its members as well as material benefits and basic welfare.[35]

The preceding discussion demonstrates the extent to which collective forms of subjectivity based upon the traditional Confucian family were re-produced within the social networks of both skilled and unskilled work-ers in the industrializing cities of China. It could be argued that this was simply because much of the industrial workforce of the time consisted of first-generation arrivals from the countryside, where traditional forms of social organization were naturally strong, and that over time such forms of organization would weaken as the patterns of modern urban life and more individualized modes of subjectivity gained hold. This kind of assumption, however, does not hold up under scrutiny, as Wen-hsin Yeh's study of so-cial practices among Shanghai middle-class professionals during the 1920s and 1930s shows.[36] This group, the best-educated and most Westernized of Shanghai's social classes, could be assumed to be the most likely to break with the traditional collective-oriented ways of the past and embrace more individualistic, autonomous modes of subjectivity. Yet, as Yeh demonstrates, while they enjoyed a degree of affluence associated with the influx and popularization of certain Western-style commodities, many among the professional middle classes remained closely tied to their work-place under organizational formations that, notwithstanding the appear-ance of modernity, reproduced key aspects of the traditional collective form of subjectivity.

Based on an analysis of developments at the Bank of China in Shanghai from the late 1920s through to the Communist takeover in 1949, Yeh charts the rise of a new form of urban Chinese corporate culture that combined a distinctly Confucian social order with the operation of a modern corporate enterprise. This development was the result of reforms begun in 1928 under which the bank aligned its business practices to meet modern international financial standards at the same time as implementing a neo-Confucian model of employee relations. The latter feature was achieved through the development of a complex set of disciplinary practices to which employees were subject.

The focus of the new regime of employee relations was that the man-ager/clerk relationship should be modeled upon the father/son relationship of traditional Confucianism. As Yeh illustrates, this involved not only the constant deference of clerks to their superiors but also participation in ac-tivities aimed at moral self-improvement, such as attendance at lectures on ethics and moral conduct given by the management staff, as well as partici-pation in periodic ceremonies "analogous to the rituals traditionally ob-served by an apprentice in relation to his master."[37] To augment these pub-lic displays, bank clerks had to model their everyday behavior according to the strictures and regulations outlined in the "employee handbook" (*hangyuan shouce*) and were required to record personal reflections and self-evaluations in a diary. The diary formed an integral part of the disciplinary regime since it was regularly reviewed by the clerk's manager/mentor in order to assess attitudes and moral progress.[38] It is clear that the purpose of these institutional practices was to mold the behavior of employees according to the norms of a new form of communal corporate life based upon a reinterpretation of traditional Confucian values.

The new norms of behavior were reinforced when the bank constructed a residential compound for its employees in the late 1920s. Within this compound, managers, assistant managers, and ordinary clerks were provided accommodation appropriate to their status, thereby reinforcing the hierarchies of the bank's management structure. In addition, the compound contained gardens, sports facilities, classrooms, and a meeting hall and could thus cater to almost all the daily needs of its residents. The classrooms were used as a school for children of the compound during the day and for evening classes for employees after work, while the hall was used for large meetings and special celebrations in which all the residents of the compound came together. Participation in sports was advocated as a way of strengthening the solidarity of the group, as well as promoting an active, healthy, and modern lifestyle. By providing such facilities and activities, the bank ensured that there was little need for its employees or their families to venture outside into what was in that period a rather chaotic and dangerous urban environment. In short, the bank provided a complete community environment in the form of a comfortable middle-class sanctuary for its employees. Yet, as Yeh points out, while this middle-class world may have reproduced some of the trappings of a Westernized lifestyle, at its heart it remained a Neo-Confucian moral code and hierarchical order underpinned by a collective rather than individualistic orientation.[39]

According to Yeh, the Bank of China model was adopted by numerous other commercial institutions within Shanghai and contributed to the smooth transition to the *danwei* system in post-1949 Shanghai. This meant that "by the time the Communists moved into the city with their system of collective residential and work arrangements, a significant portion of Shanghai's middle-class urbanites had already been socialized by decades of comparable communal experience."[40] There certainly appear to be many parallels between the corporate communities described above and the post-1949 socialist *danwei*; however, Yeh does not venture an explanation as to precisely why this was the case. Was it simply coincidence, or could it instead be put down to some other underlying cause? The evidence in relation to other sectors of early industrial society, discussed above, would seem to point to the latter explanation. In Republican China, it seems apparent that urban modernization led to the adaptation of traditional Confucian models of social relationship to the new industrial order. Through this process collective modes of subjectivity were reproduced in all sectors of the modern workforce—skilled and unskilled workers, as well as the white-collar middle class. It was this feature of modernization in the Republican period that ensured that the socialist *danwei* found ready acceptance in the cities after 1949.

But to understand more fully why the *danwei* dovetailed so neatly into preexisting urban social formations, we need to explore the parallel developments in CCP organizational strategy during the years of rural-based revolutionary mobilization.

Yan'an and the Emergence of the Proto-Danwei

The proto-*danwei*, as a basic unit of grassroots socialist organization, first emerged in the early 1940s in the CCP-governed Shaan-Gan-Ning Border Region.[41] Its appearance was one outcome of a CCP strategy to promote economic production through grassroots mobilization. Yet it also reflected a more deep-seated Maoist commitment to grassroots politics, represented by the famous "mass line" policy. In operational terms, the *danwei* rapidly assumed a central place within CCP techniques of government.

The problem of *how* to govern was by no means a hypothetical question for the CCP before 1949. First in the Jiangxi Soviet, and later in Yan'an, Mao and his colleagues had to turn their minds not only to strategies of military struggle and revolution but also to the issues involved in the day-to-day governing of a sizable population.[42] The link between a mobilization strategy and economic development had been forged initially in the Jiangxi Soviet period, when Mao called on the party "to mobilize the masses in order to launch an immediate campaign on the economic front."[43] However, it was in Yan'an that the CCP fully developed the mobilization forms of political organization that were to become the foundation for the distinctive Chinese mode of socialist government.

The town of Yan'an in northwestern China was the seat of CCP leadership from late 1935, when the survivors of the Long March arrived there, until the Communist forces made a tactical withdrawal in March 1947. It is generally accepted by scholars that the policies and strategies developed during this period were absolutely instrumental both in carrying the CCP to victory in their struggles with the Japanese and Chiang Kai-shek's Nationalist regime and in providing an effective and influential model for the reorganization of China after the assumption of political power. Several commentators who have written on the *danwei* system reinforce the latter point by tracing the origins of the socialist *danwei* model to certain policies and practices instituted during the Yan'an period. While I cannot concede their exclusive focus on Yan'an, I do agree that this period occupies a significant position within the complex genealogy of the *danwei*. Yan'an saw the emergence of a range of policies and practices related to the organization of bureaucratic, social, and economic life that were to become crucial features of the socialist *danwei* system.

One key feature of the Yan'an model of social organization was the way in which it simultaneously embodied both centralization and decentralization. Scholars have often ignored the significance of the relationship between these two aspects. Whereas some emphasize the former and read CCP organizational structure as simply a tool for the realization of centralized state power,[44] others, like Selden, emphasize decentralization, focusing particularly on the CCP's apparent commitment to the promotion of mass participation and egalitarian distribution of wealth.[45] Both approaches, however, tend to be skewed toward extremes of either totalitarianism or egalitarianism.[46] Instead, if these organizational methods are considered under the rubric of governmentality—namely, in terms of their rationalities, strategies, and practices—it becomes possible to develop a more nuanced understanding of the relationship between the seemingly contradictory policies of centralization and decentralization. From this perspective, it is no longer necessary to assume the two to be oppositional; rather they can be read as fundamentally interconnected.[47]

Xiaobo Lü considers the development of this relationship between center and grassroots production unit during the Yan'an period as crucial to the emergence of the *danwei* system.[48] Indeed, according to Lü, the reason the *danwei* assumed so many social and welfare functions can be ascribed to economic problems faced by the CCP government in Yan'an after the GMD blockade began in 1939. Central control over funds and budget allocation had been instituted in the Jiangxi Soviet in 1932 by a decision of the Central Military Committee of the CCP. This financial system included provision of basic living needs—food, clothing, health care, housing, and so on—for all party, government, and military personnel. It was known as the "supply system" (*gongjizhi*) and, given financial limitations, operated *in lieu* of a wages system. The budgetary crisis in Yan'an after 1939, however, meant conditions were not conducive to the continuation of this centralized allocation. The solution to this financial dilemma was twofold, to decentralize management of production and to make each individual unit (*danwei*) responsible for its own upkeep. As a result of this, all organizational units had to engage in production in order to support themselves. This requirement included not only government, party, and military units but also hospitals, schools, and cultural organizations.[49]

The subsequent production drive resulted in a massive increase in industry and commerce in the base area, a region that hitherto had had very little in the way of industrial or commercial infrastructure. With the GMD blockade drastically reducing supplies of necessities like cotton, paper, and soap, the CCP government was forced to encourage local self-sufficiency in such products and established factories and production cooperatives accordingly.[50] The results of this policy were rapidly apparent; for example, between 1938 and 1942 the proportion of cotton cloth produced locally increased from 5 percent to around 50 percent of the total demand.[51] More important, however, were the implications of this new strategy for the development of organizational relationships between the center and the grass roots.

Decentralization of production saw a change in the way the supply system operated. Where central authorities had previously allocated provisions and other daily necessities for party, government, and military personnel, now each grassroots production unit took responsibility for the livelihood of its own members, including those cadres who had been "sent-down" (xiafang) from central organizations.[52] Moreover, when a unit produced more than was required for its own upkeep, it was permitted to retain a part of this extra revenue to invest in expanded production. Many units used this freedom to establish their own shops, co-ops, and even trading companies.[53] In this way, they came to constitute a realm of collective life quite distinct and relatively autonomous from central government. The distinction was officially recognized with the term xiaogongjia ("little public family") used to designate this sector, as opposed to dagongjia ("big public family") of central government. According to Lü, the assets controlled by grassroots units came to be known as jiawu, which he translates as "collective assets," but which could more literally be translated as "family assets."[54]

Lü suggests that these developments were significant because they led to the establishment of grassroots organizations whose economic interests were separate from those of the central authorities.[55] According to this analysis, the primary interest of the newly self-sufficient unit became the protection and expansion of its own assets and the provision of welfare and benefits for its members. If grassroots units could control a large proportion of their own assets, then they were potentially able to pursue activities independent of the directives or wishes of the center. For Lü, then, what was most crucial about the emergence of the danwei system was that it instituted a bifurcation of interests and priorities between the center and the unit. In other words, this dual structure established the material basis for an ongoing power struggle between the state and the danwei.

However, in portraying the relationship between the center and the unit as a bipolar oppositional struggle for power, Lü occludes a number of important factors from his analysis. In particular, he does not attempt to account for the specific form of organization that the grassroots unit adopted and the implications this had with regard to the question of subjectivity. Furthermore, in characterizing the relationship between center and unit as one of competition, he neglects to consider the productive potential of this relationship as embodying a distinctively new style of government. There seems little doubt that the emergence of the grassroots unit reflected a deliberate and planned shift toward a new style of mobilization government. An examination of the logic behind this move and the specific micro-level practices through which it was implemented is crucial to reaching a full understanding of how developments in Yan'an influenced the formation of the *danwei* system.

Subjectivity in Yan'an

So far as Lü is concerned, the rise of the *danwei* as a repository of sectional economic interest can be ascribed to an accident of history, that is, to the financial hardships faced in Yan'an after 1939, which forced the CCP central authorities to decentralize production and distribution. This analysis is plausible to the extent that it identifies a practical problem that had to be addressed through some form of reorganization on the part of the CCP. What this approach cannot account for, however, is the question of why this reorganization gave rise to the particular socioeconomic formations that emerged as the *danwei* system.

In my view, Lü's arguments could have been strengthened if he had paid more attention to the etymologies of some of the terms his research uncovered. While he does point to the important distinction implied by the terms *dagongjia* and *xiaogongjia*, he takes the analysis no further. Because of this, Lü fails to recognize that the terms themselves may be read as lexical signposts to the connection between the collective social structures that were emerging in Yan'an and the notion of "family" (*jia*). To be fair, Lü is simply following convention in translating *gongjia* as "public." Yet, in the same way that the standard rendition of *guojia* as "the state" does not adequately account for the *jia* in *guojia*, so the term "public" is unable to embody the complexity that underlies the notion of *gongjia*.

The character *gong* itself is normally translated as "public" or "common" but also can mean "just," "fair," or "impartial." According to the classical *Shuowen Jiezi*, the top part of the character means "to divide," while the bottom half means "private property." Hence, *gong* is literally "to divide that which is private." In its early usage, *gong* was associated both with property that belonged to the emperor or local feudal lord and with property shared within a local community or clan.[56] Later, *gong* came to be associated with the idea of government property in general but by the mid-Qing dynasty had taken a more specific usage, referring to property, accounts, and business at the local "public" level, that is, at the county or district level.[57] This designation of local-level public activity as *gong* was further enhanced in rural areas during the late Qing and early Republican period, where *gonghui* (1), or "public associations," were formed to manage communal land and enterprises which had formerly been in the hands of village temple associations. In many places, the *gonghui* also established and ran new Western-style schools and were even given powers to tax their local population.[58] This period also saw the emergence of political discourses urging democratic reform in which *gong* was employed, through terms such as *gongmin* to denote the concept of public participation in the political process.[59] Rowe and others have built upon this historical transformation in the uses of *gong* to suggest that it connotes the emergence of a public sphere during the late Qing and the Republican period. In this analysis the public sphere, *gong*, stood between the realms of the state, *guan*, and the private, *si*.[60] Yet, if their reading of the lexical evidence is correct, how does one account for the appellation of the character for "family" (*jia*) to *gong*, as in the term *gongjia*?

Within the tripartite model of state, public, and private, the family is clearly located within the realm of the private. In the term *gongjia*, however, this neat separation of realms is upset. The concept of family has not remained confined to the private but has migrated across into the public realm. Thus, *gongjia*—"the public family"—suggests quite a different notion of the "public" than is implied in the mainstream discourses on the "public sphere." The usage of *gongjia* in Yan'an affirms the problematic nature of the tripartite model, for in the emerging socialist society the *gongjia* did not denote a social realm separate from the private realm of the *jia*; it was in fact the new *family* to which the revolutionaries belonged. As the traditional *jia* provided comfort, protection, and security to family members, so too the *gongjia* took up a wide range of collective welfare and security functions. The central distinction within this new model of society was not between a public and private sphere, but rather between the "big public family" and the "little public family." The "big public family" referred to the central administration and its various departments, committees, and institutions, while the "little public family" was the grassroots unit, or proto-*danwei*, which provided the basic framework for the practical operation of the new society. As in traditional China, where the nation with its patriarchal emperor was considered to be simply a larger version of the archetypal Confucian family, so in Yan'an a familial metaphor signified the link between the grassroots "family" unit and the government as "family."[61]

While the family metaphor crossed both micro and macro levels of society in Yan'an, it was within the grassroots *danwei*, or "little public family," that the implications of the familial genealogy become particularly apparent.[62] In a number of crucial areas, the traditional *jia*, the extended Confucian family, informed the structure and functions of the new *danwei*. The most important aspect of this appropriation was the reaffirmation of the sense of collective identity and duty of care to members of the group that was a feature of traditional family life in China. Thus, as the *danwei* became a fully fledged, tightly knit community, it bestowed upon its members a similar sense of collective identity that had been the hallmark of traditional familial relations.[63] The grassroots *danwei* became the *jia* of socialist China, albeit a *jia* transformed in crucial ways.

While the collective mode of subjectivity that structured the emerging *danwei* in Yan'an derived from a traditional heritage, the new collectivized formation modified the Confucian family model to reflect revolutionary practices and goals. Confucian hierarchy and sense of moral duty to elders and ancestors were replaced by a more egalitarian structure in which loyalty had been transferred to the CCP and its military and revolutionary aims. Thus, where the new *jia* turned upon a collective identity, it was a collective that no longer looked purely inward to focus solely upon its own order, advancement, and perpetuation—as had the traditional family. Instead, its collectivity was constructed as part of a larger whole with a clearly defined set of common aspirations and goals. In short, the "little public family" (*xiaogongjia*)—the grassroots proto-*danwei*—became part of a larger *jia*, namely the "big public family" (*dagongjia*)—the central government. The way the relationship between the two was mediated in Yan'an formed the basis of a unique type of governmental rationality.

Yan'an and Governmentality

When Foucault first proposed "governmentality" as a new field of research, he framed the problem as an investigation into the rationale and operational strategies behind the emergence of liberal government in Europe. Since then, almost all the studies that have been undertaken around the concept of governmentality have been concerned with the rationalities and practices of Western liberal government.[64] One commentator even contends that governmentality is a uniquely Western phenomenon.[65] Nevertheless, if we consider the basic conceptual parameters around which the literature on governmentality has been articulated, there is no reason to suggest that it can only be applied to the liberal paradigm; on the contrary, I believe it can usefully be turned to the analysis of socialist government in China. For liberalism is only one of many paradigms within which various societies have been subject to long and complex processes of "governmentalisation."[66]

The work of Peter Miller and Nikolas Rose is perhaps the best known for having engaged with Foucault's preliminary work on the concept of governmentality and its particular liberal manifestations.[67] In the first place, Miller and Rose argue that the term *governmentality* indicates a shift in the way government was both thought about and operationalized after the overthrow of absolutist monarchies in the eighteenth century.[68] From that time, a new form of government emerged that was concerned principally not with the maintenance of absolute power but rather with "attempts to know and govern the wealth, health and happiness of populations." Efforts to achieve this have seen the proliferation of a whole range of techniques, institutions, and fields of knowledge related to the practice of government and to understanding the nature of the population that was to be governed.[69]

It is not difficult to see that this Western trend is equally apparent in the emergence of socialist forms of government under the CCP in China. Beginning in Yan'an, under Mao's leadership, Communist government took an increasingly active interest in the development of techniques aimed at both knowing and governing the population and the economy.[70] Although the genealogy of this form of government in China can no doubt be traced back much further, the establishment of the Shaan-Gan-Ning Border Region Government in late 1937 saw a particularly dramatic increase in the scope of governmental interest. CCP-led government rapidly expanded its scope of operation and intervention to encompass a wide range of fields, from defense and public security, to rural land management, taxation, and industrial production, as well as health, education, arts, literature, and newspapers.[71] This expansion of governmental interests was manifested not only at the central level, with the proliferation of bureaucratic offices and departments, but also at district and grassroots levels, where government and party cadres were charged with the implementation and popularization of government policies.

The emergence of socialist government in China apparently led to a process of "governmentalisation" similar, in terms of broad operational logic, to the rise of liberal governmentality in the West. However, to explore the particular mode of governmentality that emerged in socialist China, and to differentiate it from liberal governmentalities of the West, it is necessary to undertake a more detailed analysis of both. I will build this analysis around the four interrelated realms of governmental activity that, according to Miller and Rose, constitute the scope of governmentality: political rationalities, programs of government, technologies of government, and the role of expertise and knowledge in the operationalization of government.[72]

Political rationalities, according to Miller and Rose, are the features of political discourse that establish a moral framework around which the ideals, principles, and justifications of a particular form of government are articulated. Furthermore, political rationalities construct their own epistemological systems that promote particular frameworks for the understanding of reality. This is supported through the development of a distinctive language for the representation of reality, such that problems of government are rendered thinkable in ways amenable to the particular mode of government practiced.[73]

This analytical framework is directly applicable to the study of Chinese socialist government. The CCP was founded according to the political rationalities of Marxism-Leninism, which saw socialist revolution as an inevitable outcome of the historical process. The party justified its central role in the revolution according to Leninist principles, whereby an enlightened proletarian vanguard was required to organize and lead the revolutionary struggle. Also from Lenin, the CCP adopted the notion of central planning as the fundamental principle of governance. Moreover, principally through the writings of Mao, the party constructed a view of Chinese reality based on a Maoist interpretation of Marxist class analysis applied to Chinese sociopolitical circumstances. During the Yan'an period, these rationalities found systematic and coherent expression through a revolutionary discourse promulgated through the various study meetings, educational institutions, and newspapers under the organization of the CCP. As Apter and Saich suggest, this discourse was crucially important in constructing a unified revolutionary community with a shared epistemology such that concerted collective action could be readily rationalized and operationalized.[74]

Rationalities of government form the foundation upon which programs of government can be articulated.[75] For example, the way in which problems are identified and measures are adopted to address them depends upon the rationalities that underpin a particular governmental regime. The possibility for the development of such programs of intervention is also dependent upon the assumption that the current state of affairs can be altered and improved. To achieve this, programmatic forms of government rely upon a whole range of knowledges and conceptual frameworks through which reality can be studied, quantified, made knowable, and hence programmable. Thus governmental programs do not simply represent the desires or hopes of governments for positive change; more significantly such programs infer a mastery over the field to be transformed, supported both by an accumulation of knowledge and by an assumed legitimacy to intervene in the name of improvement.[76]

The form of socialist government developed by the CCP in China clearly adopted an interventionist and programmatic mode. From the foundation of the CCP there were programs for revolution and social change. Under Mao, initially in the Jiangxi Soviet and later in the Shaan-Gan-Ning Border Region, detailed programs were developed on issues such as land reform, economic development and productivity, education, and social organization. These programs were based in part upon certain epistemological assumptions derived from Marxist-Leninist theory, but also upon detailed research and analysis of the socioeconomic circumstances of the region that the CCP sought to govern. The importance of this was emphasized in 1941 when the Party Central Committee issued a directive, drafted by Mao, on the establishment of specific research and investigation organs at every level of government.[77] The directive begins by complaining of the paucity and poor quality of the CCP government's knowledge base. Mao posits a number of reasons for this shortcoming, including the assessment that "many comrades . . . still don't understand that systematic and thorough social investigation is the foundation for determining policy."[78] The directive then outlines an extremely wide scope for official investigation and research—covering almost all areas of military, economic, political, cultural, and social life—and stipulates that all information collected should be submitted to central authorities.[79]

The degree to which knowledge was accumulated and deployed to justify and bolster governmental programs is also demonstrated by Mao's detailed analysis of the Border Region economy in the study entitled *Economic and Financial Problems*. This lengthy report was presented to the Senior Cadre's Conference held in Yan'an from October 1942 to January 1943, where it was promoted as the definitive analysis of the economic situation. It became the main platform for the Great Production Movement of 1943 and was based on the notion that goals of revolutionary mobilization should be linked closely to economic strategy.[80] These examples clearly illustrate that the systematic gathering and processing of knowledge became instrumental to the development of the programs that underpinned socialist government in China.

Programs of government are rendered into practice through the intercession of various strategies, techniques, and procedures, or technologies of government, as Miller and Rose refer to them.[81] Technologies are not mechanisms for the direct implementation of the ideals expressed in government programs. Rather they are the means through which complex interactions between authorities and subjects are negotiated. The effective prosecution of governmental programs depends upon an ability to recruit and mobilize subjects to act in certain ways and toward certain ends. This can seldom be achieved successfully through coercion; rather it relies upon the construction of lasting networks, often formalized around established institutional formations such as the school, factory, family, or other structured social groupings. Factors such as architecture (or more broadly, the organization of social space) and the deployment of specific modes of discourse also tend to contribute to establishing norms of behavior among a population within a given sphere of governmental activity.[82]

The CCP and the socialist governments it led placed a great deal of emphasis upon strategies to recruit and mobilize broad sections of the population under its jurisdiction. Wide-ranging networks were established through the organization of campaigns for land reform, production, and military struggle, as well as through the establishment of schools, shops, cooperatives, and self-help brigades and through sending thousands of cadres down to the villages and townships to organize, train, and assist the local population. Mao's famous "mass line" leadership policy epitomized the mobilization strategy that formed the core of CCP governmental technology.

Technologies of government could never be operationalized without the mediation of a vast array of experts whose authority derives from their specialized knowledge in a particular aspect of the social, the economic, the technical, or the psychological. Miller and Rose point out that the expert plays a crucial role under liberal modes of government, precisely because of the distance that liberal forms of reasoning posit between the political and the private.[83] The role of experts is to establish links between the two. They engage with the problems posed by government, systematize and analyze these problems through the development of specialized fields of knowledge, and propose and enact measures to bring about solutions.[84] At the same time, they develop relationships with the population, bringing their specialized skills to bear upon the myriad problems of everyday life, suggesting, for example, ways to better manage business, finance, or family life. In short, the very possibility of liberal government depends upon the ability of vast numbers of experts to establish norms of behavior for the whole range of everyday activities engaged in by the population.

The role of the expert was just as vital to the operation of socialist government in China. However, the socialist expert, or cadre, was directly, rather than indirectly, linked to the operation of government. That is to say, where the liberal expert occupies a relatively neutral position between the realms of government and individual, the cadre owed a direct loyalty to the party and its political program. According to the well-known Maoist dictum, the cadre was required to be *both* red *and* expert. Mao repeatedly stressed the importance of this role and the need to train a corps of dedicated and effective cadres in order to achieve the goals of CCP government policy. In one of his many comments on the subject, Mao favorably quoted Stalin as having stated that "cadres decide everything."[85] As the link between government and the population, and as an authority in areas of specialized knowledge, the cadre performed an analogous role to that of the liberal expert. Yet, because the cadre's role also demanded a political commitment and direct participation in the revolutionary mobilization of the population, it is in the area of expertise that the Maoist form of governmentality differs most markedly from the Western liberal forms described by Miller and Rose.

Toward an Analytic of Chinese Socialist Governmentality

The foregoing discussion suggests that under CCP rule society in the Shaan-Gan-Ning Border Region underwent a high degree of "governmentalisation." Naturally, many specific practices and techniques of CCP government differed from those employed by liberal governments in the West; nevertheless, the basic conceptual parameters of governmentality can be applied to productive effect in the examination of socialist government in China. In this section I develop a more detailed elaboration of the logic, programs, and operational practices that constituted Maoist-style governmentality. In particular, I argue that the emergence of the *danwei* and the practices that informed it were absolutely integral to the formation of Maoist governmental strategy.

I suggest above that the *danwei* emerged as a key institution within CCP governmental practice as a result of developments in the Shaan-Gan-Ning base area from around 1939. These developments were partly dictated by financial and military necessity resulting from, respectively, the withdrawal of GMD aid and the escalation of the Japanese war offensive.[86] Policies pursued by the CCP in the early 1940s, like the campaign for "crack troops and simple government," the "to the villages" movement, and the "Great Production Drive," all aimed, on the one hand, to reduce central government costs, and on the other hand, to improve productive and military capacity in the border region. Nevertheless, the organizational, managerial, and administrative techniques that emerged through these developments cannot simply be attributed to historical necessity, but rather reflected a definite political and strategic response to the particular problems that arose. What emerged then was a particular mode of governmental rationality, one that aimed to address problems of production, mobilization, and political education while simultaneously attempting to avoid the dangers of overcentralization and bureaucratization. This mode of rationality was epitomized by slogans such as "centralized leadership, decentralized management" and "the mass line," and many of the practices that contributed to the formation of the *danwei* system arose out of the attempt to operationalize it at the grassroots level.

The rationality that informed CCP-led government turned largely upon mainstream Marxist-Leninist principles. The need for social revolution and a redistribution of wealth in favor of the masses of working people, both urban proletariat and rural peasant, was considered to be self-evident, as was the assumption that such a revolution had to be led by a well-organized revolutionary party. Of course, there had been considerable debate within the CCP, since its formation in 1921, of the correct strategy for leading the revolution, but by the early 1940s Mao's view that the peasantry should be the major force for revolutionary struggle had become dominant. Moreover, and in contrast to the Russian revolution, which had been won in a very short period, the Chinese revolution involved a protracted struggle over many years during which the CCP controlled quite large rural areas. This meant that the CCP found itself not simply leading a revolutionary uprising but also governing large territories and populations for extended periods. Long before their final victory in 1949, the CCP had to deal with the problem of how to govern a revolutionary society.

Under conditions of protracted war, both against the Japanese invaders and the GMD, the primary role of the revolutionary government was to secure the necessary funds required to maintain the military struggle. In the long term, particularly after the GMD withdrew its financial assistance, the CCP and the Red Army had to depend upon the local economy to supply these funds. At the same time, the logic of socialist revolution demanded that, within the areas under its military control, the CCP overthrow the existing class order and its inherently exploitative economic structure. A revolutionary realignment of social and economic forces within the local region would not only realize the CCP's fundamental goals for social change but also secure the support necessary for extending the revolution to an ever greater area. Revolutionary government was not simply an end in itself, but more importantly a strategy that laid the groundwork for an envisaged takeover of the entire nation.

In order to secure these military, economic, and social aims, the CCP adopted a predominantly mobilization form of governmental practice. That is, it developed specific techniques of organization aimed at recruiting as much of the local population as possible to participate in the campaigns for production, land reform, and army support. In addition to centralized policy and planning organs, such a mode of government required a network of sophisticated grassroots organizations through which local populations could be contacted and mobilized. The central problem, then, became the question of how to manage the relationship between the central government and the grass roots. Attempting to get this relationship right was an ongoing concern of Mao's and occupies a significant place within his writings of the period. While he clearly supported the concept of strong unified central leadership, he was equally concerned with the possibility of overcentralization and dangers of bureaucratism and dictatorial leadership. These concerns came to a head in the early 1940s through the campaign for "crack troops and simple government" and the movement to send cadres "to the villages" and were distilled into a theory of revolutionary leadership which came to be known as "the mass line."[87]

The mass line is most commonly associated with the slogan "from the masses, to the masses," an injunction for leaders to take ideas from the masses, develop them into systematic policies, and then take them back to the masses to put into practice.[88] It is generally forgotten that mass line leadership also emphasized the necessity for grassroots unit leaders to ensure that general policy was translated into specific practices that related to the needs of the particular local situation. This was to be a matter of initiative for the local cadres, as Mao demanded "that comrades in all localities will themselves do some hard thinking and give full play to their own creativeness on the basis of the principles here set forth."[89] The mass line established two basic principles of leadership: local leaders had to be close to and responsive to the masses, and they had to use initiative to adapt general policy to local circumstances.

In short, the mass line was the operational creed of CCP governmental rationality. It was through the various practices that grew out of the mass line that CCP policy was able to connect with the masses and mobilize them in large numbers to participate in military, economic, and social programs. Moreover, in devolving operational autonomy to the grass roots, the mass line aimed to circumvent the dangers of overcentralization and bureaucratism. In this respect, the mass line was an enabling strategy, since it opened up space at the local level for spontaneous activity and autonomous operation, while at the same time circumscribing the degree to which central governmental organs could intervene in day-to-day local organizational affairs.

The mass line emerged fully during the second half of 1941, when the campaign for "crack troops and simple administration," coupled with the "to the villages" movement, saw the CCP institute a more decentralized, grassroots mode of government. To accompany this move and to ensure that mass line principles and party policy were properly followed, the party retrained its corps of cadres through "rectification" campaigns that ran throughout 1942–44. But the full importance of these developments was only realized with the advent of the Great Production Campaign of 1942–43, which was underpinned by a strategy to promote local self-sufficiency and initiative in economic development. To bolster this strategy, the CCP reformulated the mass line concept into the slogan "centralized leadership, decentralized management." It is out of this conjunction, between the mass line and the economic push, that the grassroots unit, or *danwei*, emerges as an important, and comparatively independent, component of socialist governmental practice. The CCP effectively endorsed the formation of the *danwei* as a solution to the twin problems of bureaucratism and production.

Although the *danwei* was allowed a degree of operational and economic autonomy, it was still a unit of CCP governmental planning and was required to function as a transmission belt for central policy in areas such as education, politics, and culture. To achieve this commonality of general purpose, the party relied heavily upon the abilities of trained experts—namely, the *ganbu*, or cadres who were responsible for leadership at the grassroots level. Mao reiterated the important role played by party cadres when he commented, "It is on these cadres and leaders that the Party relies for its links with the membership and the masses."[90] The renewed emphasis on local mobilization ensured that the role of the grassroots cadre became increasingly important.[91] And as mobilizational momentum built up over a succession of campaigns through the early 1940s, the specific functions of the grassroots cadre were defined and standardized. In short, the cadre was expected to embody three distinct roles: the exemplary, the pastoral, and the technical.

First, the cadre was required to possess and display all the attributes and principles of the ideal socialist revolutionary. In his educational treatise *How to Be a Good Communist*, Liu Shaoqi argued that party members must engage in constant ideological self-cultivation so as to "temper themselves to become staunch and utterly devoted members and cadres of the Party who make constant progress and serve as examples for others."[92] Through a process of study, self-cultivation, and devotion to the party, the communist cadre was required to possess the following basic attributes: a high communist morality, great revolutionary courage, a good grasp of Marxism-Leninism and the ability to apply it in practice, sincerity and honesty, and a high degree of self-respect and self-esteem.[93] In striving to attain these attributes, a communist cadre aimed to become "a living embodiment of the general interests of the Party and the proletariat and to merge his personal interests completely in their general interests and aims."[94] By practicing this selfless devotion to the revolutionary cause, the grassroots cadre, it was hoped, would inspire the support of the local people among whom he or she worked. Although Liu emphasized the concept of "self-cultivation," it was clearly intended to be a closely guided course in "self-cultivation"; according to Apter and Saich, the majority of the fifty-thousand-odd cadres holding government and party positions in the 1940s had undergone at least some training at the various party-run educational institutions in Yan'an.[95]

The cadre not only was required to be an exemplary figure, but was also expected to actively intervene in society at the local level to transmit party ideology, as well as organize and mobilize the local population to participate in the revolution. In pursuing these objectives, the cadre was asked to fulfill what can best be described as a kind of pastoral role. Foucault argues that the pastoral practices of Western Judeo-Christianity paved the way for the emergence of a modern form of individuating power that he terms bio-power. Bio-power alludes to the numerous public and private institutions that have emerged in modern states to govern the health, welfare, security, and productivity of populations. More specifically, the term refers to the various techniques deployed by these institutions for surveying, recording, and intervening in the biological functions of individuals in an attempt to produce normalized subjects.[96] According to Foucault, pastoral power was a kind of "government of souls" in which knowledge was utilized in an organized way so that the pastor might bring his flock to salvation.[97] With the decline of the church and the rise of the modern state, the techniques of pastoral power "spread and multiplied outside the ecclesiastical institution," leading to the formation of bio-power.[98] In my view, a similar argument can be made in relation to China. That is to say, the more complex institutional forms of power that emerged with the development of the post-1949 socialist state are greatly influenced by the form of revolutionary pastoral power, centered on the cadre and the *danwei*, that arose during the Yan'an period.

According to Foucault's analysis, pastoral power embodies four central characteristics: its primary aim is salvation; it encourages individual sacrifice for the sake of the "flock"; it promotes the individual care of each member of the community; and it is premised upon an ability to reach into the minds and souls of the "flock."[99] It is beyond the scope of this chapter to explore the origins of pastoral power within the Chinese revolutionary context; suffice it to say that the organizational and political choices made by CCP leaders resulted in the development of distinctively pastoral modus operandi. This was reflected first in the fact that the cadre brought to those among whom he or she worked the promise of salvation in *this* life—if only the revolution could be won and communism established. In promoting this form of worldly salvation, the cadre had an advantage over the Christian pastor insofar as being able to point to the Soviet Union as an example of a place where socialist salvation had apparently been achieved. A firm belief that the successful prosecution of their revolution would bring about ultimate salvation for the Chinese people was central to the cadre's own motivation and ability to mobilize others.

The preparedness to sacrifice all for the party and the people in achieving victory in the revolution was another central tenet of the cadre's brief. According to Liu Shaoqi, "it is the worthiest and most just thing in the world to sacrifice oneself for the Party, for the proletariat, for the emancipation of the nation and of all mankind, for social progress and for the highest interests of the overwhelming majority of the people."[100] This ethic was further bolstered by the CCP nurturing a cult of martyrdom. The Monument to the Revolutionary Martyrs, erected in the center of Tiananmen Square in the early 1950s, symbolizes the centrality of the ethic of sacrifice within CCP culture. But the cadre did not only demonstrate sacrifice through a martyr's death; in his day-to-day life, too, the cadre was required, as a matter of duty, to sacrifice all other interests in the cause of serving the party and the masses.

In addition to a belief in salvation and a commitment to self-sacrifice, the communist cadre was also charged with the task of mobilizing and leading the local population to contribute to the revolutionary goals. Through this task the cadre became responsible for both the activism and the welfare of the community under his or her guidance. In my view, this aspect of the cadre's role was also pastoral, in the sense elucidated by Foucault, yet at the same time, both the aims and techniques of this "pastoral" intervention differed from those associated with Christian pastoral care. The Christian pastor cares for each member of the "flock" individually, both because each "sheep" is equal in the sight of God and because each has the potential to achieve his or her own individual salvation, regardless of the other members of the "flock." Thus, the pastor intervenes in order to facilitate the direct relationship between the individual "sheep" and God. The communist cadre, on the other hand, intervenes among the "masses" in order to promote a form of salvation that can be achieved only through collective, mass effort. Communism can be realized only when all people are liberated from the economic and political relationships that oppress them. This objective of a collective salvation, however, did not mean that the cadre dealt with the people only on a mass level. On the contrary, much of the cadre's work depended upon establishing and fostering intimate relationships on an individual level, since the success of collective action relied upon recruitment of individuals to the cause. A critical aspect of cadre work, then, was to recruit individuals to the revolutionary cause and to foster their participation through ongoing dissemination of party and government policy. Furthermore, implementation of the mass line policy demanded that grassroots cadres maintain close relationships with the masses, both in order to be better able to popularize policy and also to gain access to the creative and practical ideas of the masses themselves.

Finally, Foucault argues that pastoral power depends upon the ability of the pastor to reach into people's minds and souls. This ability is crucial, since true salvation can be achieved only if each individual "soul" truly believes in the cause. Within the party, the communist cadre was trained using techniques designed to reach into and remold their minds and souls. Hence, as I have already illustrated, considerable emphasis was placed on study, self-cultivation, criticism, and self-criticism. Through participation in intense education campaigns, such as the Rectification Movement of 1942–44, the party aimed to mold the minds and souls of its cadres to promote the abnegation of all other interests and commitment to the collective communist cause.[101] Once trained in this manner, the cadre relied upon similar techniques in the mobilization of local populations. This was carried out primarily through the various mobilization campaigns prosecuted by CCP leadership from 1942, the first of which was the Mass Movement for Rent and Interest Reduction. In such campaigns the first task of the cadre was to identify potential activists within the local community and cultivate them through education. In his instructions to cadres preparing to launch this movement, Liu Shaoqi gave specific guidance on how this task was to be approached:

We should carefully prepare a talk, the gist of which might run: Who created the world? The workers and peasants did. Where do our food and houses come from?

They are created by the workers and peasants. . . . The experiences of peasant struggles in other places and the success of the revolution in the Soviet Union should be used to drive home the point that the workers and peasants should become masters of society. Once they appreciate this truth, they will be in high spirits and will raise the demand to turn the existing world upside down and wipe out the landlords altogether. . . . When they first became politically awakened, many peasants in central China were so excited that they could hardly sleep at night. They approached the work teams, asking all sorts of questions. In this way, the peasants acquired revolutionary ideology or, to use their expression, "had a new head" placed on their shoulders. This type of stimulation is what we mean by Marxist-Leninist education of the peasants. It is an enlightenment campaign of a new form—class education. If it is carried out successfully, the peasants will follow us and will not have misgivings or waver when things are not going smoothly.[102]

Liu's directives called upon local cadres to reach into the minds and souls of the local population. The objective was no less than "putting a new head on their shoulders" and thereby ensuring a high level of loyalty and commitment to the difficult tasks of the revolution. Liu's comments further illustrate the degree to which the CCP depended upon grassroots cadres in enabling effective government of the revolution. In popularizing the communist program as the salvation for China, in promoting an ethic of selfless sacrifice, in recruiting individuals to the revolution, and in transforming the minds and souls of the masses, the local cadre was required to build very close relationships with and an intimate understanding of the people within his or her local community. This called for a distinctly pastoral mode of operation, through which the cadre could disseminate CCP policy as well as attend to the spiritual and material welfare of the local population. The cultivation of this method of mobilizational leadership contributed greatly to the transformation of the grassroots organization into the proto-*danwei*.

Beyond assuming the pastoral role, cadres were also called upon to be leaders in the field of production. To this end, cadres were required to undertake training in technical as well as organizational aspects of production. In an internal party directive, dated October 1943, dealing with tactics for a renewed mobilization campaign, Mao declared that all "leading personnel in the Party, government and army organizations and in the schools should master all the skills involved in leading the masses in production."[103] These skills were to be gained by attending training courses on practical aspects of daily life such as "vegetable growing and pig farming, and on the preparation of better food by the cooks," and by studying "the model methods of work used by some of the agricultural labor heroes" of the base area.[104] According to Mao, it was particularly important that party cadres "attain a full grasp of all the principles and methods of organizing labor power" so as to be able to maximize the potential for productivity.[105] This new emphasis on technical expertise placed an extra burden upon the cadre, who was now expected to be able to combine technical know-how with political expertise and onerous pastoral functions.[106]

In summarizing the role of the cadre, it is important to bear in mind the ways in which the Chinese socialist form of governmentality differs from that which emerged in the West. While the cadre filled an analogous position to that of the expert, insofar as he or she functioned as a link between government programs and everyday practice, the cadre did not subscribe to an ethic of political neutrality as was expected of the expert in the Weberian mold. On the contrary, the cadre was both deeply committed to and intimately involved in the ethos and program of the revolutionary government. Moreover, whereas the expert is generally a specialist within a single field of expert knowledge and confines his or her activities to the accumulation of knowledge and development of practices within that field, the communist cadre was expected to be schooled in many areas of social, political, and economic knowledge, as well as being required to develop an intimate familiarity with a particular local community.

Charged with exemplary, pastoral, and technical functions, the local cadre was the focal point of CCP grassroots operation. It was around the cadre, and as a result of the various mobilization campaigns and the push for more guided and efficient production, that distinct organizational units, or proto-*danwei*, emerged at the local level as the basic unit of CCP government. With the policies of decentralization and promotion of local initiative and self-sufficiency that were pursued by the CCP in the early 1940s, the grassroots *danwei* became an increasingly important institution in the lives of its members, taking on responsibility for the distribution of resources as well as mobilization for the war effort. The emergence of the *danwei* system gained impetus from the broad economic policies adopted by the CCP as well as from the specific style of grassroots leadership practiced by the local communist cadre. Moreover, it represented the appearance of a distinctly socialist mode of governmentality that would form the foundation for governance after 1949.

Conclusion

In this chapter I charted the emergence of the proto-*danwei* through two disparate genealogical strands. First, I examined the forms of labor and social organization that emerged out of the industrialization of Chinese cities. Through reference to the work of a number of scholars of the Republican period, I demonstrated how traditional forms of social organization were adapted to the requirements of cities in which a new mode of industrial production was rapidly emerging. Underworld gangs, trade guilds, and neo-

Confucian corporations came to dominate, respectively, the organized labor of skilled workers, unskilled workers, and middle-class professionals. The common factor that united these social organizations was that each embodied aspects of the traditional collectively oriented Confucian family structure, albeit recast into new forms. These new social formations maintained collective-oriented practices as well as some of the ethical proclivities of the Confucian tradition, thereby illustrating the dangers inherent within universalist modernization discourses which see modernity as a passage from collective to individual forms of subjectivity. Clearly, in the Chinese case, modernization and the development of new industrial modes of production did not result in the wholesale destruction of traditional social forms and the atomization of the individual.

Second, I focused on the Shaan-Gan-Ning Border Region, centered on Yan'an, where the CCP honed the specific practices that were to inform the organization of the *danwei* system in urban China after 1949. I argued that the *danwei* emerged, primarily during the later Yan'an period, as the principal operational locus of Chinese socialist government under circumstances that demanded the mass mobilization of the population to meet the economic and military requirements of a revolutionary war. While the grassroots unit was certainly part of a centralized political and economic structure, it was also invested with a significant degree of local operational autonomy. This autonomy was in part the outcome of economic pressures faced by the border region government after 1940, which led to a call for all units to become self-sufficient. It was also an outcome of Mao's famous "mass line" leadership strategy, which was designed to maximize mobilizational potential as well as avoid the problems of bureaucratism and over-centralization. Implementation of the mass line at the grassroots level depended heavily upon the party-trained cadre, who was called on to perform the roles of exemplary revolutionary, pastoral caregiver, and technical expert. Because of this, the cadre was absolutely instrumental in the formation of local populations into proto-*danwei*. As I have shown, these *danwei* were much more than simply units of production; they were tightly organized living communities organized along collectivist lines. They were "small public families" (*xiaogongjia*) which operated to guarantee the livelihood and welfare of their members, as well as to contribute to the revolutionary program of the entire border region, the "big public family" (*dagongjia*).

In many ways the factories and corporations of urban Republican China and the revolutionary *danwei* of the Shaan-Gan-Ning Border Region were worlds apart. Yet, as I have shown, these two vastly disparate settings produced forms of production-based social organization which both centered upon a collectivist ethos of community based around the ethical model of the "family." The guilds, gangs, and corporations of the Republican cities each invoked the Confucian family and its ethical underpinnings as their model. The Yan'an revolutionaries rejected the Confucian heritage, instead developing an alternative collectivist ethic based around the idea of a "public family." From 1949, with the CCP takeover of the cities, these two models of "family" were momentarily brought together. While it was the latter "public family" model which would prevail, the common collective orientation ensured that the transition to socialism resulted in less social upheaval than many predicted.

CHAPTER 4

From the Government of Space to the Spatialization of Government

The Emergence of Revolutionary Spatial Practice

Our world, like a charnel-house, is strewn with the detritus of dead epochs. The great task incumbent on us is that of making a proper environment for our existence, and clearing away from our cities the dead bones that putrefy in them. We must construct cities for today.

Le Corbusier, 1929[1]

We are not only good at destroying the old world, we are also good at building the new.

Mao Zedong, 1949[2]

Within ten years of assuming political control, the CCP-led government had effected a dramatic transformation over the face of urban China. A huge program of industrial development had seen the once cramped and squalid cities of low-rise housing and narrow lanes overtaken and dwarfed by vast expanses of factories, bureaus, schools, and institutes arrayed neatly along the wide avenues of a constantly expanding modern socialist suburbia. Although it seems a world away from the themes discussed in the previous chapter, appearances can be deceptive. For each factory, bureau, school, and institute was of course a *danwei* and, thus, much more than merely a place of work, study, or research; each constituted a distinct unit of social, economic, and political organization—in short, the basic building blocks of the new planned economy. In organization, management style, ethos, and orientation, if not appearance, they reflected the developments discussed in the previous chapter; they were organized according to the mobilizational principles devised in Yan'an, managed by cadres trained in the "pastoral" methods of Maoism, underpinned by the welfarist ethos and strict ethical ordering characteristic of the workplaces of Republican China, and structured through a distinctly collectivist orientation within the daily regimes of production and social interaction.

Appearances are important too, and in one respect the newly built *danwei* of socialist China recalled something from the past—for each was surrounded by a high enclosing wall producing a compound form that resembled, at least superficially, the walled courtyard residences of premodern times. The walls, of course, demarcated the space of the *danwei*, as in the past they defined the realm of the traditional family. But as soon as we move within the walls, we realize that the space itself is arranged quite differently than in the past. Instead of being inscribed with the cosmological and hierarchical order of the Confucian family, *danwei* space appears to be ordered according to a strictly functionalist and productive logic; the workshop (or bureau), dormitories, auditorium, canteen, kindergarten, and sports grounds are all arranged conveniently within a neatly symmetrical space—everything is at hand to provide for the daily needs of a modern working community. All this may seem entirely straightforward and self-evident, but concealed within the compound of the modern *danwei* lies a crucial and as yet unexplored element of its genealogy: namely, the distinctive rationale of modern spatial practice. There is nothing natural, obvious, or commonsense about the spatial arrangement of the *danwei*—it derives from a Western tradition of revolutionary spatial practice that sought to produce and manage forms of space that would facilitate a radical reconstruction of society. It is a tradition that was transmitted to China primarily via Soviet experts (architects and urban planners) who played a critical role in the early phase of socialist development. In order to understand the implications and logic of *danwei* space more fully, we must first trace the emergence of Soviet spatial practice. This chapter, then, takes us on a journey far from China.

I begin by considering how urban spatial forms came to be seen as a legitimate concern of modern government and how the discipline of urban planning emerged as a means through which government could conceive and plan methods for transforming the spatial environments within which people lived. Drawing once more on the concept of "governmentality," I suggest that urban planning as a technique of modern government first took shape with Georges-Eugène Haussmann's "regularization" of nineteenth-century Paris. After Haussmann, urban planning became one among many standard techniques within the repertoire of modern liberal government. At the same time, however, it offered a range of other strategic possibilities to those who wanted to attempt the radical reorganization of society.

Spatial planning as an agent of revolutionary transformation first appeared with the "utopian" socialists, Robert Owen and others, who devoted considerable effort to the design of spaces appropriate to their vision of socialism. The transformative potential of spatial design gained a further boost with the rise of the modernist movement in architecture. Le Corbusier, for example, devised many radical new urban forms in the belief that they would transform society. While Le Corbusier's plans remained largely unrealized, the Russian Revolution of 1917 brought with it the first genuine opportunity for theories of revolutionary urban design to be put into practice. With the implementation of centralized planning, modern techniques of government were combined with the radical objectives of socialism, leading to important innovations in the standardization of housing and urban design. On a more controversial front, the "social condenser" emerged as a radical new architectural formation in which production, proletarian culture, and everyday social life were combined within a single collective space. It was this heritage of revolutionary spatial practice, passed on to China in the 1950s by Soviet experts, which had a major influence on the spatial formation of the *danwei*.

Toward a Genealogy of Urban Planning

In recent historical work, the emergence of modern urban planning is generally associated with the fairly sudden appearance of a public social consciousness in the late nineteenth century.[3] The catalyst for this perceived "awakening" was a heightening perception of the social, moral, political, and sanitary dangers that the growing urban slums posed to the maintenance of social order.[4] Urban planning is seen, then, as an attempt to redress these dangers through intervention at the level of the urban environment. It sought to devise systematic strategies for transforming a chaotic urban environment that had resulted from the rapid unplanned urbanization of the industrial revolution. In short, urban planning is seen as part of a larger social reform movement in the late nineteenth century that sought both to ameliorate the lives of the poor and to improve their moral and productive capacities.

Yet in reading the rise of urban planning as a response to socioeconomic conditions, mainstream urban historians neglect the importance of other vital elements. In endeavoring to mark out a distinct historical space for their discipline, such scholars tend to overlook the relationship between urban planning and the development of the other human sciences. While the historical viewpoint posits urban planning as a unique and innovative field of expert activity, it avoids the broader theoretical problems related to the production of knowledge and to the emergence of strategies whereby such knowledge enabled positive intervention within the social realm. Clearly urban planning is both a field of knowledge and a set of practices. As a field of knowledge, it attempts to constitute the urban as an object that can be known and understood; as a system of practices, it aims to intervene in and transform the urban environment. The origins of urban planning, therefore, should be sought not only within the specific realm of urban problems, but also within the broader history of the production of modern fields of knowledge, as well as with the emergence of a logic which allowed for the systematic, programmatic, and optimistic intervention by governments in the everyday lives of their subjects.

Historians who do link the rise of urban planning to developments in other areas of the human sciences generally provide no satisfactory explanation for the connection. Françoise Choay and Peter Hall, for example, both point to links between a new interventionist urban consciousness and the appearance of studies in urban health, crime, and housing conditions.[5] Yet both portray the nexus between knowledge and institutional intervention as a natural and transparent development. The emergence of a field of knowledge concerning urban "problems" is presented, in unproblematically positivist terms, as the extension of scientific reason into new frontiers. According to this viewpoint, once the "problems" have been "discovered," it is only "natural" that authorities intervene and attempt to solve them. Such an approach not only fails to problematize the production of these new knowledges, but also makes no attempt to address the processes by which these forms of knowledge are employed as both resources and justifications for intervention in the social.

While the specific social problems addressed by early urban planners are obviously worth consideration in any historical study of urban planning, a genealogical approach must first examine the process by which forms of social knowledge came to be represented in ways that made government intervention in the social both a possibility and a necessity. In this respect modern urban planning is the product of a more general historical trend, a "complex interweaving of procedures for representing and intervening,"[6] through which a particular form of relationship between institutional knowledge and action emerged. The genealogical origins of urban planning must then be sought in the rise and formation of this modern rationality of government.[7]

Governmentality

Colin Gordon suggests that Foucault's interest in the question of government arose in response to critics who pointed out that his focus on the micro physics of power and disciplinary regimes failed to account for the political relationship between society and the state.[8] Yet in meeting the challenge of this broader question of power, Foucault refused to return to the conventional conception of the state that underpinned the comments of his critics. This was because Foucault saw the state not as a massive unitary repository of power but rather as a complex web of rationalities, strategies, and practices. What interested him was how the interplay of these relationships made the conduct of government possible. In particular he was concerned with investigating the ways in which the idea of government could be rationalized and how strategies for its operation could be put into practice. Foucault maintained that questions such as these, which ultimately concerned the government of populations within societies, could be studied through the same genealogical method he had employed to study the effect of disciplinary regimes upon subjects within institutional settings. The concept of "governmentality" emerged as a result of this shift from an emphasis on "the subject" to an emphasis on "population."

According to Foucault, a modern form of government began to emerge in the latter part of the eighteenth century as the result of a number of complex interrelated developments. First there was the movement from an "art of government" preoccupied with the question of sovereignty and its exercise to a "science of government" founded upon a growing wealth of statistical knowledge of peoples and things. Second, and closely related, there was a shift in the understanding of economy from one based around the model of the family to one concerned with the wealth of the population and nation in general. Finally, there was the transition from thinking about government in terms of the legalistic concepts of sovereignty to thinking about it primarily in terms of political economy.[9]

Two major consequences flowed from these trends: an explosion in both the quantity and the variety of knowledge related to human social and economic activity, with authorities actively sponsoring the work of social scientists; and, subsequently, the formulation of strategies for government intervention in the economic and social operation of society. Whereas formerly authorities intervened in society on a relatively ad hoc basis, primarily in order to preserve sovereign power within the territory they ruled, the age of governmentality ushered in a mode of governmental intervention based upon the notion that it was possible to improve and perfect the manner in which society operated, or as Peter Miller and Nikolas Rose put it, "that reality is, in some way or another, programmable."[10] The ultimate aim of this rationality for intervention was, according to Foucault, "the welfare of the population, the improvement of its condition, the increase of its wealth, longevity, health, etc."[11] Henceforth, those engaged in the practice of government saw their role as one of positive intervention and guidance made possible by an increasingly "complete" and scientific understanding of every aspect of social and economic activity.

Paul Rabinow suggests that the new science of biology provided the conceptual framework for an emerging governmental concern with human welfare. According to Rabinow, physiological epistemology and vocabulary

were readily transferable to the realm of social relations as soon as human society itself came to be viewed metaphorically as a social "body." Fueled by a
growing archive of statistical data, this new approach resulted in the objecti-
fication of human social interactions. Society thus became open to scientific
study and experiment. As with the human body, where internal laws could
be discovered, so too weaknesses and illnesses could be diagnosed and cured.
From the moment society came to be seen in these terms, it followed that
social problems must be remedied not through "treatment" of individual er-
rant subjects (as had been the mission of moral reformers up to the nineteenth century), but rather through positive intervention by the authorities
at the level of the social environment itself.[12]

This is not to say, however, that the rationalities and practices of modern
government are concerned only with society as a whole, or that they tend
toward totalization rather than individuation. This is only one side of a
complex double movement. Moreover, to consider it alone would return us
to the conventional view that posits the relationship between the state and
society in simple binary terms. Foucault specifically rejects this formulation,
asserting instead that the relations of power of which the state is a part are
both totalizing *and* individualizing.[13] This is because the modern rationality
of government turns upon *two* interrelated notions, namely the government
of others *and* the government of self. Thus, while modern government is
concerned with maximizing the wealth and welfare of the population as a
totality, this can be made possible only through a complex array of micro-
level practices of self-governing which center upon the individuation of
subjects.

The population census provides a good example of this double movement. From the governmental perspective, the primary function of the census is to provide data through which a generalized picture of the nature and
requirements of the population can be formulated. This is achieved by con-
densing a massive volume of information relating to individuals into a totalized view of society. In turn, this totalized information becomes the knowledge base upon which governments develop plans for the social body as a
whole. At the same time, however, the practice of census collection depends
upon the ability of each participating individual to reflect in detail upon
their own individual lives and circumstances. In addressing the questions put
by the census, each respondent must engage in a process by which his or her
own individual experience is standardized according to the categories provided. Through this process the census tends to produce an individuating effect, not because it fosters a notion of abstract individuality, but rather because its framework constrains individual subjects to think of themselves
within specifically defined parameters of individuality. Considered in this
light, the census can no longer be seen as a neutral technology for the gath-

ering of information. Rather, at the same time as it aggregates data on individuals, it disseminates notions of individual subjectivity. In this way the practice of census collection clearly produces effects that tend toward both totalization and individualization.

Many scholars have utilized the concept of governmentality in recent years to reexamine fields such as policing, economic management, accounting, statistics, insurance, welfare, education, medicine, and sanitation. In each case, modern practices have been linked to an interventionist and programmatic governmental logic that took shape primarily during the nineteenth century.[14] While some of these projects touch upon aspects of governmental interest in urban space, none deals with the specific emergence of urban planning or its role within this new mode of government.

The rise of modern urban planning as a technique of government is exemplary of the shift from paternalistic to programmatic forms of governmental rationality outlined by Foucault. The policing of urban spaces has always been a particular concern of government; however, the emergence of a new rationality of government in the nineteenth century marked a significant shift in the logic of how such an objective was to be achieved. It was the notion that the good government and welfare of the population could be furthered through the transformation of the urban environment, which made possible the development of a repertoire of knowledges and practices which would come to be known as urban planning.

Foucault has noted this important shift in ways of thinking about urban spaces:

The point, it seems to me, is that architecture begins at the end of the eighteenth century to become involved in problems of population, health and the urban question. Previously, the art of building corresponded to the need to make power, divinity and might manifest. The palace and the church were the great architectural forms along with the stronghold. Architecture manifested might, the Sovereign, God. Then, late in the eighteenth century, new problems emerge: it becomes a question of using the disposition of space for economico-political ends.[15]

As the result of this development, by the mid-nineteenth century a clearly programmatic and interventionist attitude toward the management of space had become predominant. Moreover, as noted above, new attitudes toward space were closely linked to newly emerging governmental concerns with the health, welfare, and policing of populations. This connection is very clearly illustrated by the work of Haussmann, the father of modern urban planning, in his grand project to "regularize" the spatial organization of Paris during the second half of the nineteenth century.

The Rise of Urban Planning: Haussmann's "Regularization" of Paris

Haussmann's transformation of Paris during his term as prefect of the Seine in 1853–69 is often portrayed as simply a strategy to facilitate the rapid deployment of Louis Napoleon's troops throughout the capital in case of disorder.[16] No doubt this was one effect of the project, but as Choay points out, such a limited interpretation misses almost entirely the more significant aims and implications of this urban transformation. Haussmann's great innovation was to treat the urban agglomeration as an organic whole and to see its primary function as promoting the circulation of goods and men.[17] Clearly any improvement in "circulation" would facilitate troop movements; nevertheless, to emphasize this factor alone is to mask a far more important innovation—namely, a fundamental shift in the way government treated questions of urban order.

Haussmann's strategy to facilitate the "natural flow" of goods through urban space was influenced by contemporary liberal understandings of how the capitalist economy operated. Both the vocabulary and the techniques used by Haussmann demonstrate the way in which biological concepts informed the understanding of economic processes. Thomas Osborne points out that in nineteenth-century discourse the regulation of health and sanitation, including such measures as the installation of drains and sewers, was explicitly linked to questions of "nature" and "economy."[18] Informed by classical liberal conceptions, this mode of governmental practice saw intervention in urban space almost purely in terms of facilitating the operation of the supposed "natural" economic order.[19] Haussmann adopted the term *regularization* to describe his work because he believed that his interventions would restore the city to its "natural" order.

The large-scale demolitions and public works undertaken by Haussmann were designed to bring all parts of Paris into contact with each other through a vast circulatory network of major thoroughfares. In this manner the old quarters of Paris were to be opened up, traversed, and brought within a larger organic whole. The aims that informed this urban transformation were not only economic, for if the flow of goods constituted the lifeblood of the capitalist system, respiratory and sanitary systems were also essential to maintain the organism in a state of health. To this end, regularization required the clearing of open spaces to promote ventilation and the instillation of water and sewerage networks to facilitate sanitary needs.[20]

In viewing the city as one gigantic organism, Haussmann was able to develop a completely integrated grand plan for the entire city of Paris. The plan itself was meticulously plotted through the use of elaborately detailed scale maps, the production of which had been Haussmann's first task on taking up his post.[21] The scale and detail of the project necessitated gathering huge archives of information about the city, since it could only proceed once a complete understanding of the existing city structure was achieved. Haussmann's project was the first urban plan to be based so profoundly upon the new scientific commitment to the collection of data. Indeed, what made Haussmann's project so significant in the rise of urban planning as a strategy of governmental intervention was the way in which exacting technical and statistical practices were combined with the visions of a transformed spatial environment.[22]

In his study of modern French planning, Paul Rabinow plays down the significance of Haussmann, arguing that his methods did not establish the link between spatial forms and social norms that exemplified later urban planners.[23] According to Rabinow, this was because Haussmann did not conceive of the city as a social environment, but rather saw it simply as a technical object upon which to work. It is true that the logic of planning employed by Haussmann assumed the city to be an organic whole and gave little consideration to its inhabitants as distinct social groups or social actors. However, it is also important to recognize that regardless of the logic behind the formulation of the plan, its implementation necessarily had a great impact upon the social life of Parisians. Moreover, since the plan itself aimed to bring a regular and standardized order to the urban structure of Paris, it was likely that its implementation would tend to have a normalizing effect on social and economic life.

Haussmann may not have shared the social awareness of later urban planners; however, some of his interventions in the physical form of the city brought about crucial transformations in micro-level social practices. For instance, the provision of clean piped water and a reliable sewer system for each individual household, a major innovation achieved under Haussmann's planning, had a profound effect on the urban pattern of life.[24] Not only did these developments improve the general standard of sanitation; they also contributed to a trend that saw everyday life confined, to an increasingly greater degree, within the individual dwelling. Haussmann's planning was crucial to the process whereby the urban family home was gradually transformed into a realm of privatized social space. Urban historian Josef Konvitz underscores the importance of the technical innovations developed by Haussmann: "The gradual internal transformation of houses and apartments involving heating and ventilation, cooking facilities, bathing and lavatories, and lighting represented on the micro scale what was happening to the city at large; within the house, as within the city, greater specialization of spatial uses depended upon the availability of certain common services."[25] Specialization of spatial organization was critical in the production of a new moral order and discipline within the population, particularly, as Foucault has pointed out, within the working classes: "We see this illustrated with the building of the cités ouvrières, between the 1830s and 1870s. The working-class family is to be fixed; by assigning it a living space with a room that serves as kitchen and dining-room, a room for the parents which is the place of procreation, and a room for the children, one prescribes a form of morality for the family."[26] Even if Haussmann did not explicitly link the planning of urban forms to ideas of social normalization as Rabinow contends, his technical innovations tended to produce spatial forms that facilitated an increasing normalization and individuation of urban subjects.

Haussmann's influence on the practice of urban planning was immense. In the latter third of the nineteenth century, many of the old cities of Europe adopted, with varying degrees of success, Haussmann's model of circulation and ventilation in order to redress the problems associated with crowded and decaying urban centers.[27] Even greater success on this front was achieved in the New World, where new cities could be planned from the beginning according to Haussmann's principles of regularized urban form. The far-reaching application of this planning model was no doubt due to its intimate relationship with the rise of capitalism; since it successfully addressed the problems of overcrowding and disease that the industrial revolution had produced, but in such a manner as to promote rather than hinder the further development of capital "flows." Haussmann, and those who followed him, saw planning as a technique for removing the blockages that impeded the "natural" flow of goods and men. For them the objectives of urban planning were not to bring about the transformation of society; rather they were to produce a "regularized" urban spatial form that reflected what they assumed to be a natural capitalist socioeconomic order.

Whereas Haussmann considered social questions as epiphenomenal to the perfection of "natural economy," later practitioners of government were forced to deal with the realization that despite the ever-increasing "circulation of goods and men" and productivity of industry and commerce, social problems persisted and even multiplied within the urban environment. Ongoing social upheavals led to numerous urban uprisings in the latter part of the nineteenth century, including the revolt in Haussmann's Paris that saw the foundation of the Paris Commune. While Haussmann's regularization ultimately failed to secure the order and prosperity that had been looked for, both his commitment to the science and practice of planning and his belief that the transformation of urban space was central to the improvement of society remained central to many subsequent reformist and revolutionary programs. The remainder of this chapter will trace developments in the revolutionary rather than reformist school of urban planning, as it is this tradition that most influenced spatial practice in China after 1949—especially in regard to the *danwei*.

Revolutionary Spaces

Revolutionary ways of thinking about space actually preceded Haussmann-style urban planning. While the latter arose out of a nexus between liberal governmental practice and the operation of the capitalist market, revolutionary discourses of planning emerged precisely in opposition to this prevailing economic governmental order. Marx was, of course, a strident critic of the "bourgeois" order, but he also opposed as premature any attempt to plan the actual form of an alternative socialist order.[28] Other socialists, like Robert Owen and Charles Fourier, however, were not so reticent and devoted considerable energy to the formulation of blueprints for ideal socialist communities.[29] Although ridiculed as "utopian socialists" by Marx and his supporters, Owen and the others believed themselves to be engaged in a "science" of social relationships that would form the basis for building model egalitarian and productive communities.[30] They sought to bring a kind of Newtonian order to the social sphere through the elaboration of a new "scientific" model for society. Crucially, for the purposes of this study, they believed a scientifically ordered society had to be underpinned by new forms of spatial arrangements.

Although a very successful and wealthy industrialist in the cotton spinning industry, Owen was disturbed by what he saw as the shocking social cost wrought by the early phase of the industrial revolution.[31] As a result, he came to see the capitalist factory system and the laissez-faire economic structure that supported it as the primary source of social disharmony and poverty. For this reason his plans to transform society focused upon alternative methods for the organization of labor and the distribution of wealth. Owen's first move was to reject the doctrine of self-interest that dominated economic orthodoxies of the day and adopt instead the communitarian principle of "mutual-cooperation" as the rationale for a new social order.

Owen's vision for a new society based upon cooperation and equality emerged out of his involvement in managing the model industrial village of New Lanark located near Glasgow.[32] New Lanark was one of a number of model factory towns built in the late eighteenth and early nineteenth centuries that became laboratories for social experimentation.[33] Owen was influenced initially by a group of benevolent industrialists who argued that improved factory conditions not only were beneficial for employees but also led to increases in productivity and profit. Through experimentation they aimed to discredit the conventional view that profit could be maximized only through a harsh regime of low wages and iron discipline.

These progressive industrialists believed that environment rather than innate character was most crucial in the social formation of human subjects. Where conventional opinion held that the working class was inherently degenerate and that labor discipline could be instilled only through punishment and fear, the progressives believed that discipline and order were best influenced through improving working and living conditions. At New Lanark, Owen introduced reforms such as shorter working hours, increases in pay, the provision of decent housing, and access to medical care and education.[34] Through his firsthand experience of such innovations, Owen's conviction of the direct relationship between environment and human character deepened. In particular, Owen came to believe education was the most important influence over social conditions. As a result, he established a factory school, known as the Institute for the Formation of Character, funded entirely out of company profits.

Most of the texts on Owen focus on his innovations in the areas of education, economics, and science.[35] What they tend to overlook is the spatial question and the way in which Owen developed specific spatial arrangements to order daily life, labor, and education. When Owen began to set out his blueprint for a new society, he not only designated economic relations, social structures, and educative methods, but also made clear and precise instructions as to the spatial order that would best serve his aims.[36] While his experiments began in New Lanark, Owen hoped to establish new communities elsewhere founded on agriculture. His ideas, however, were not animated by nostalgia for traditional rural life or by an attempt to reclaim some lost moral universe; Owen envisaged a radical rearrangement of rural society along communitarian and cooperative lines. Crucial to this model was a new scientific and logical spatial order that would reflect and at the same time bolster the operation of his "rationally" constituted community.

Owen adopted the square, or parallelogram, as the basic spatial form for his new society. He argued that this provided the "most simple, easy, convenient and economical arrangement for all the purposes required."[37] The four sides of the square contained apartments for the adult members of the community, dormitories for the children, storerooms, warehouses, guest rooms, and a hospital. In the center of the square was the school, communal kitchens, and dining rooms, as well as a church or other places of worship.[38] While Owen considered this design to represent "a well devised association of human powers for the benefit of all ranks,"[39] it also articulated in clear spatial terms his philosophical commitment to the centrality of collective endeavor. Individual space was to be located on the periphery of the community, while collective space was situated at its very heart.

The overall spatial configuration of Owen's ideal community also reflected the importance of science and order within his philosophical system. The geometrical design and the symmetrical distribution of buildings within the square were intended to impart an exact gridlike order to social life within the community. Individual quarters were to be of a standard form,

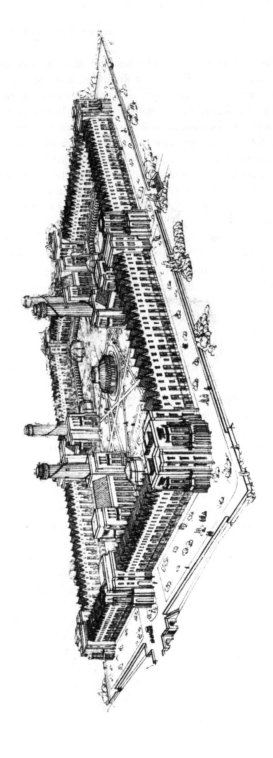

FIGURE 4.1. Design for an Owenite community at New Harmony, Indiana.
Source: From a rendering by Stedman Whitwell, ca. 1826 (held by the New York Historical Society), reproduced in Françoise Choay, *The Modern City: Planning in the 19th Century* (New York: George Braziller, 1969), fig. 56.

one sleeping apartment and one sitting room. This would afford ample individual space since children would be accommodated in dormitories and social life was to take place in the various public buildings provided. No individual kitchens were envisaged, since food preparation would be centralized and the community would "eat together as one family."[40] Even heating and cooling would be taken care of through a centrally planned ventilation system.[41] In short, all basic needs were to be provided for through the application of logic and science to the principle of communal living. Space within the community was standardized and regularized so as to bolster the ordered regimen of collective activity that formed the basis of Owen's system (see Figure 4.1).

His belief that education was the foundation for social improvement was reflected in the central location of the school in Owen's design. Experiments in New Lanark had convinced Owen that education was crucial both in forming the character of the young and in reforming the character of those who had gone astray.[42] To put this conviction into practice, Owen devoted considerable effort to the development of a new style of education. According to Harrison, Owen-style education aimed to produce subjects who identified their own interests and happiness with the interests and happiness of society as a whole.[43] Hence the school performed a vital function in binding the new community together through constant reinforcement of communitarian moral principles. The prominent positioning of the school within the community compound reinforced its central role.

In addition to fostering a commitment to community, Owenite education also emphasized practical schooling in the skills of labor.[44] If Owen's communities were to be founded economically on cooperative labor, then the education process needed to train students not only in communitarian values but also in the practical business of collective production. Such education was not restricted to children within the community, since at both New Lanark and New Harmony, Indiana, adults were also required to attend regular lectures.[45] Ongoing participation in education was clearly one of the major unifying elements of everyday life in an Owenite community. In this manner, education at once contributed to the dissemination of Owenite principles of cooperation while at the same time fostering a greater sense of community through participation.

Owen's attempts to build model communities based upon cooperation ultimately proved disappointing.[46] However, in bringing together collective labor, communal living, and universal education within a purpose-built architectural space, he provided an innovative model for the achievement of social transformation. Indeed, despite the derision with which his ideas were treated by Marx and Engels,[47] it was so-called utopian socialists like Owen who first proposed that social revolution ought to be accompanied by a revolution in the organization of social space. Where Haussmann recognized that spatial formations could be designed to improve society functionally (through the promotion of hygiene, fostering certain forms of economic interaction, etc.), Owen theorized that space could serve a much greater goal—namely, that it could contribute to the production of a new type of person, a new breed of enlightened, principled, and collectively minded subjects. Although its origins are seldom acknowledged, the conception that space is central to revolutionary transformation was taken up again almost a century later by the radical theoreticians, architects, and urban planners of the Soviet Union.

Socialist Space

According to Marx and Engels, the big error of the utopian socialists was their failure to grasp the importance of class struggle, since no kind of socialist transformation could even be contemplated until the capitalist class order had been overturned through a revolutionary seizure of political power. Marx and Engels argued that unless this revolutionary precondition was met, any attempt to establish socialist-style communities would be piecemeal and doomed to failure.[48] It must be said that the sorry record of the Owenites and others in maintaining viable communities for any period of time lends weight to this critique. In 1917, however, with the victory of the Bolsheviks in the Russian Revolution, it appeared that the political and economic prerequisites for building a new socialist society had finally been met. The problem faced by the new regime was precisely how to approach this massive task.

Lenin saw the key advantage of socialism over capitalism was its potential to establish a scientifically planned economic system capable of fulfilling the genuine needs of society. In contrast, capitalism was largely unplanned and driven by the desire to maximize profit; it produced an economic system that was highly unpredictable, prone to booms and busts, and which failed to meet the needs of major segments of society.[49] According to Leninist logic, socialism required coordinated central planning, which in turn necessitated the creation of a large bureaucratic apparatus of state dedicated to the mechanics of economic planning. It is with the emergence of centralized bureaucratic planning that utopian socialist ideals are wedded to modern techniques of government. Out of this marriage a new form of governmentality was born, one informed both by the ideals of revolutionary transformation and by the belief in the efficacy of governmental intervention. The sciences of government that had been developed under liberal administrations in the West were now to be adapted to the task of socialist construction. Indeed, with a commitment to central planning as the basis of socialist government, the role and scope of governmental intervention was to increase dramatically. The practice of urban planning in the Soviet Union reflects this trend.

Urban reformers under capitalism had always faced two major obstacles to the achievement of their aims—namely, private property interests and lack of government commitment—indeed, the two were usually closely connected.[50] Under socialism the situation was to be fundamentally different. On 18 February 1918, the Soviet government passed a law to nationalize all land, and on 20 August of the same year it was decreed that all urban property must be handed over to state or local authorities.[51] With the private ownership of land and property dissolved, the path was now clear for central planners and designers to begin a radical reconfiguration of social space to meet the needs of the new society.

If the establishment of the first socialist state saw a hitherto unprecedented marriage of the apparatus of government to goals of radical social transformation, the strategies that were to form the basis of a revolutionary practice of urban planning were themselves adopted and adapted from techniques already prevalent in parts of Western Europe and the United States. Cognizant of the relative backwardness of technology and industrial management in Russia, Lenin argued that the very success of the revolution depended upon "combining the Soviet government and the Soviet organization of administration with the modern achievements of capitalism."[52] In particular, Lenin admired capitalist management practices such as the meticulously systematic approach to the labor process developed by Frederick Taylor in the United States.[53] Given Lenin's respect for capitalist managerial techniques and practices, it is hardly surprising that the Soviet Union's first urban planning regulations were adapted directly from French legislation and required that all medium to large towns produce twenty-five-year development plans.[54] In this manner, techniques of urban planning first systematized by Haussmann in Paris were reemployed as the foundation for a new socialist urban practice.

While Soviet industry borrowed many practical techniques from capitalism, Soviet urban planners and designers were greatly influenced by trends in Western planning theory. The first two decades of the twentieth century were formative and exciting decades in the development of modern architecture and planning. According to design historian Reyner Banham, modern architecture emerged during this period through the convergence of three major trends: first, the notion that the architect should feel responsible to society, most exemplified by the philosophy of the Deutscher Werkbund, founded in 1907; second, the articulation of a structural approach to architecture, as promoted by Viollet-le-Duc and Auguste Choisy in France; and third, the practices of academic instruction for which the École des Beaux-Arts in Paris was best known.[55]

If such institutional developments formed the bedrock for the discipline of modern architecture, it was the fields of industry, mechanics, and engineering which provided both an aesthetic and a technical inspiration. Rapid development in these areas around the turn of the century introduced new materials and processes that were seen to offer enormous potential for the design and construction of distinctly modern buildings. Le Corbusier's famous dictum that "the house is a machine for living in"[56] is the clearest expression of the "machine age" aesthetic. The key schools of this new architectural movement included the Futurists in Italy, the Bauhaus in Germany, the De Stijl group in Holland, as well as Le Corbusier in France.[57] Particularly worthy of note is the apparent affinity that existed between this architectural movement and socialism, as several leading proponents of the new architecture visited the Soviet Union in the 1920s.[58] But, whereas the practitioners of the new architecture met much resistance from conservative forces within their own communities in the West, the new socialist state welcomed their radical ideas and the potential these innovations offered for the revolutionary renewal of urban life.[59] Architects and planners in the Soviet Union absorbed much from these interactions and adapted what they learned to the task of planning spatial forms appropriate to the new society. These developments in turn generated considerable interest among the more radical architectural and urban theorists in the West.

Three principles derived from modern architecture were particularly influential for Soviet architects and planners: standardization of forms, the application of time and movement studies to the planning of spaces, and the employment of new materials to enable the mass production of architectural components and fittings. Le Corbusier was undoubtedly the most outspoken advocate for the deployment of these techniques in the practice of architecture.[60] His aim was to transform the urban and architectural environment into one of pure, simple, and functionalist spaces appropriate to the new machine age. More specifically, Le Corbusier believed that the main task of the new architect was to design standardized living units which could be mass-produced as clean, efficient, and above all functional housing for the workers of the machine-age city.[61] Le Corbusier's objective was to overcome the disjuncture he saw between the modern workplace and the home; the former was characterized by the latest principles of industry and management employed under the direction of industrialists and engineers, while the latter he derided as "old and rotting buildings that form our snail-shell."[62]

If the home environment could be redesigned according to the same modernist principles that were applied to industry, Le Corbusier argued, urban life would be transformed without the need for a social revolution. Such was his conviction on this point that he concludes his famous architectural treatise *Towards a New Architecture* with the lines "Architecture or Revolution[?] Revolution can be avoided."[63] For Le Corbusier, technology itself would be the agent of change; so long as it was applied logically to every aspect of the human environment, then social harmony and progress would be ensured.[64] Le Corbusier believed that all the problems of the modern world could be resolved through attention to the design and construction of lived spaces. Although the emerging architects and planners of the new socialist state were influenced greatly by Le Corbusier's commitment to the industrialization of urban space, they could not accept his functionalist view of technology, wherein technical solutions operated as an alternative to revolution.[65]

The birth of the socialist state fundamentally transformed the relationship between humans and their environment. For architecture and planning, there were three key implications. First, the overthrow of capitalism made possible the abolition of bourgeois private land tenure, thus providing an unprecedented opportunity for the planned redesign of urban space—a possibility that was unimaginable under capitalism. Second, the course taken by the revolution averred the primacy of politics over technology. The success of a socialist revolution in a country whose technological development was still in a relatively undeveloped state seemed to support Lenin's view that technology was essentially a neutral factor, a tool which inevitably served the interests of the ruling class. With the overthrow of capitalism, the same technologies that served the capitalist order could be redeployed in the service of socialism. Hence, technology could play a positive role in the building of a new society, but only when deployed under the guidance of a socialist government.[66]

Finally, unlike Le Corbusier, Soviet architects and urban planners saw themselves as technicians in the service of a primarily political project, rather than as the vanguard of social transformation.[67] As they saw it, their task was to design spaces, buildings, and cities that would reproduce and reinforce the political, social, and productive relationships demanded by socialism. This is not to suggest that they saw architectural form as unimportant. In contrast to Le Corbusier, who held that architectural design of itself could bring about social transformation, the Soviets recognized that spatial design could only have a transformative effect when applied in concert with political and social change. Thus, although they adopted many of Le Corbusier's design principles (particularly taking up the call to industrialize architecture), Soviet architects and planners rejected his politics. On the question of the relationship between proletarian politics and technology, they were far more influenced by Soviet theoretician A. A. Bogdanov.

Bogdanov, Proletarian Culture, and "Social Condensers"

A. A. Bogdanov was a contemporary of Lenin, and although now largely forgotten, was very influential in the period leading up to and following the revolution.[68] Lenin repudiated Bogdanov's ideas in the early 1920s, but by then they had already become embedded within revolutionary practice in a number of cultural and technical disciplines, including architecture and planning. The vehicle through which this had occurred was the Organization for Proletarian Culture, or *Proletkult*, which Bogdanov founded in 1918 to lead the revolutionary push in the cultural sphere.[69] According to Lenin's famous formula, socialism would be realized through a combination of "soviet power plus electrification." Bogdanov, however, believed that the revolution could be successful only if it saw the establishment of a new proletarian way of life to accompany the new political and economic regime. Thus, while Lenin concentrated on strategies for consolidating Bolshevik power and establishing an organizational basis for industrialization, Bogdanov mobilized *Proletkult* propaganda teams to initiate what he hoped would be a sweeping cultural revolution.[70]

Proletkult reached a peak of activism in 1920, when its membership numbered over five hundred thousand, but had virtually disappeared by 1922 after coming under sustained attack from Lenin for supposedly promoting an independent and "un-Marxist" cultural line.[71] Despite the briefness of its operation, however, the theories and practices which informed *Proletkult* remained influential for at least another decade, that is, until the intellectual avant-garde were finally silenced by Stalin in the early 1930s.

The central aim of the *Proletkult* movement was to forge a new form of revolutionary culture through the radical combination of science, industry, and art. The bearer of this new culture was to be the industrial worker, and the primary locus for its development and practice was to be the site of collective production—the socialist factory. The factory was crucial, since it was there that the most advanced forms of science, technology, and organizational method met. According to Bogdanov, the worker who participated in highly mechanized factory production would inevitably be affected by the logic, discipline, and creativity of the industrial process and hence undergo a cognitive transformation.[72] If social and cultural life were also centered on the factory, the transformative effect would encompass not only the labor process but also every aspect of the worker's life. A new mode of life would emerge in which industry, art, and collective life would be combined within a radical proletarian culture.

Popularized through the *Proletkult* movement, Bogdanov's theories came to have a great influence upon Soviet architects and planners of the 1920s because they provided an apparently logical justification for the development of a new proletarian science of space.[73] Indeed, it was no coincidence that the term Bogdanov adopted to describe his new science, *tectology*, was taken from the Greek word "to construct," and that the architectural style developed during this period was known as "constructivism." Both terms signaled the privileged role technology and the "machine aesthetic" would play in the construction of a new proletarian society.[74] The role of the architects and urban planners was to design spaces that would wed technology and advanced industrial production to the process of everyday life. Through this they would contribute to the socialist transformation of the working class and its lifestyle.

The architectural movement that promoted these views was at its height in the seven years between 1925 and 1932. Prior to 1925, civil war and the desperate economic situation did not allow for a great deal of new construction to be undertaken. After 1932, however, Stalin and his supporters suppressed the movement, along with other elements of the radical avantgarde. The most influential group of architects during this period was the Association of Contemporary Architects, or OSA, which formed in 1924 primarily in response to the pressing need for a solution to the housing shortage.[75] OSA participated in competitions for the design of housing and public buildings while using every opportunity to promote the merits of prefabrication, industrialization, and standardization in the construction industry.[76]

OSA devoted considerable effort toward developing prototype residential units for communal living. Finally, in 1928, the government responded to the urgent need for action on the housing situation by establishing a research group to explore the possibilities of housing standardization.[77] The designs which emerged out of this group, known as the "Stroikom units,"[78] sought to reflect a need for economy as well as providing workers with a modern, efficient, and comfortable living space. In addition, according to the decision of the Construction Committee, "the new types of housing must give the workers maximum free time and energy for their social and cultural activities, must place at their disposal suitable leisure opportunities and facilitate the passage from an individualistic concept of housing to more collective forms."[79] The intention, then, was to produce new housing not simply to meet the urgent demand for shelter but also to promote the development of workers' cultural life and collective consciousness. The standardized designs would provide a blueprint for achieving cultural and social transformation, as well as a technical foundation upon which to industrialize the construction process.

Most of the residential units designed by Stroikom were of a fairly conventional form, providing self-contained apartments for nuclear family groups. However, they did include one design for a fully collectivized resi-

dential unit, in which food preparation, child care, laundries, and other social activities were organized communally.[80] Yet the designers were cautious
in regard to the possibility of establishing collective lifestyles immediately.
Because of this hesitation, a kitchen alcove was designed that could be removed at a later date when the expected collective facilities had begun operation. Moses Ginzburg, leader of the design team, envisaged a gradual transition to communal living and saw the design of the residential units as
encompassing an educative element. According to Ginzburg, the design
team "considered it absolutely necessary to incorporate certain features that
would stimulate the transition to a socially superior mode of life, *stimulate but
not dictate*."[81] But whereas this group saw social transformation as a gradual
process, other architects were anxious to push for much faster change.

In 1928 a conference of OSA proposed the design and construction of an
entirely new form of collective living unit, which they called the "social
condenser." The adoption of this term again illustrates the profound influence of the machine age on architectural innovation. Just as the electrical
condenser concentrates the electric current that passes through it, so the social condenser was intended to concentrate the nature of social interaction
among the human subjects who passed through it.

One of the principle advocates of the social condenser was the architect
T. Kuzmin. After surveying working-class housing in many of the newly
emerging industrial districts, Kuzmin found living conditions to be both un-
hygienic and socially regressive. He saw little qualitative change since the
revolution and complained that "the new man, the public man, has no
chance of development in the petty-bourgeois and restrictive atmosphere of
the home."[82] Kuzmin declared the situation completely unacceptable, as the
status quo seemed to offer no possibility for the development of a new proletarian lifestyle.

Grounded in the principles of the *Proletkult* movement, Kuzmin and the
other advocates of the social condenser were convinced that socialism implied more than simply state ownership of industrial complexes. For them,
socialism had to encompass a transformation in the lifestyle of the working
class. The social condenser would be the vehicle to create a new collectivized environment suited to the ideals of socialism. The goal these radicals
set themselves, then, was to design spaces in which the industrial labor process could be wedded to the formation of proletarian culture. Hence, the social condenser would be a living space designed around sites of large-scale,
scientifically advanced mechanized production. The spatial form of these
new institutions was intended to promote a communal lifestyle and foster
workers' participation in collective production. This would provide spatial
reinforcement to the ideal of labor collectivity while apparently strengthening the potential transformative effect. Living in a social condenser, workers

would no longer leave collective life behind when they clocked out after work; instead, their whole life would be circumscribed by communal modes of social interaction. The social condenser was designed to extend the revolution in labor organization brought about by large-scale machine-age industrial production to the practices of everyday life. In this regard, it was envisaged that they would carry the process of proletarianization to its logical conclusion (see Figure 4.2).

Through its communal style of organization, the social condenser was intended to replace the family as the basic unit of society. Hence, within the social condenser workers were to sleep in dormitories, eat in collective canteens, socialize in public recreation areas, and attend lectures and discussion groups in communal meeting halls. The population was to be divided into groups according to age rather than family ties. Adults were grouped together while children were divided into a number of different age groups. Each of these groups was to live "in quarters specially equipped for and adapted to its particular activities."[83] Under these conditions every aspect of daily life was to be given a collective context and undertaken within a space that had been specifically designed to bolster that very principle of collectivity. At every turn the communal values of socialism were to be reinforced in lived practice.

Previously, Soviet architects had spatially segregated different aspects of daily life; there had been factories for work, workers' clubs for recreation and education, and communal apartment houses for accommodation. With the advent of the social condenser, the functions of the factory, workers' club, and communal house were unified in one spatial form. Through this conjunction, it was hoped that social condensers would produce both material wealth—through improving labor productivity—and cultural wealth—through creating model proletarians. To help facilitate this transformative process, the social condenser combined a collectivized spatial form with a regularized schedule of collective activity. Kuzmin, for example, developed a military-style timetable to accompany his architectural plans and to demonstrate how daily life within a social condenser might have been organized.[84]

In juxtaposing regularized systems of space and time, Kuzmin appears to have created what Foucault terms a "disciplinary regime."[85] At first glance, the social condenser seems remarkably similar to Bentham's Panopticon, insofar as it establishes a coordinated regime of space and time built around minutely detailed disciplines of training and regulation. Like Bentham, Kuzmin aimed to produce a certain form of disciplined human subject; or to put it another way, both the Panopticon and the social condenser are machines for the production of subjectivity. However, the mode of subjectivity implicit within each of these spatial devices is quite different. Whereas the Panopticon operated to produce a self-reflexive, individualized subject, the

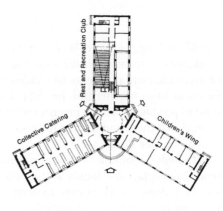

GROUND FLOOR
Collective Facilities

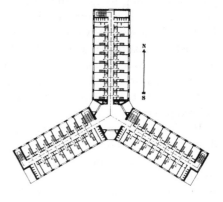

ACCESS FLOOR

FIGURE 4.2. Design for a communal
house, or "social condenser" (K.
Ivanov, F. Terekhin, and P. Smolin),
overall floor plans (*this page*) and
cross-section and floor plan of an
individual living unit (*opposite*).
Source: Anatole Kopp, *Town and Revolution: Soviet Architecture and City
Planning, 1917–1935*, trans. Thomas
E. Burton (New York: George
Braziller, 1970), 146–47.

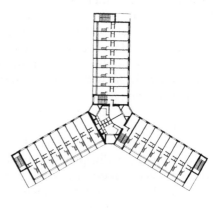

LIVING UNITS
Upper and Lower Levels

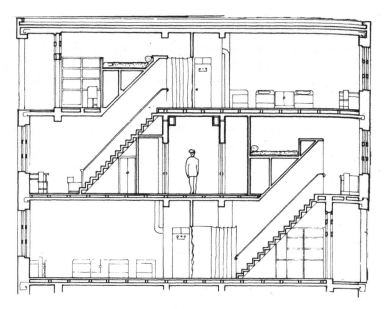

РАЗРЕЗ И ПЛАНЫ ЯЧЕЕК

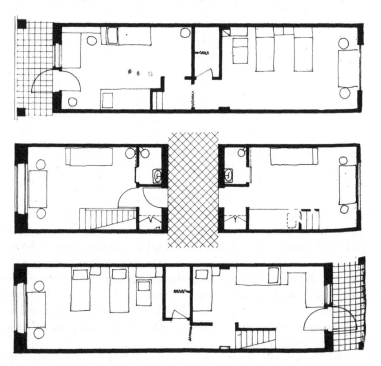

social condenser was designed to foster the emergence of a collectivized proletarian subject. This is reflected in the very different manner in which the disciplinary gaze operated within the two institutions. Within the Panopticon, surveillance was centered upon the individual alone inside his or her cell. The (potentially) ceaseless gaze directed at the individual reinforced the necessity for constant self-policing and self-reflection. The social condenser, on the contrary, was designed to enforce a regime of surveillance around participation in organized collective activity. Through this mechanism, collective subjectivity was bolstered via the intercession of mutual, or group, policing.

Stalinism

The concept of the social condenser was considered extreme even among the radical avant-garde in the Soviet Union. This, together with the economic and political situation of the time, ensured that the idea was never fully realized. A strong undercurrent of popular opposition to the imposition of this kind of "super-collectivity" helped justify Stalin's crackdown on the entire avant-garde in the early thirties. This suppression began with the assertion that its architectural and urban design projects were "utopian" and showed a lack of understanding of Soviet reality. According to Kaganovich, a close ally of Stalin's and a chief critic of the architectural avant-garde, it was entirely unnecessary to design new socialist urban spaces, as the cities were already socialist. Kaganovich put a stop to further debate by declaring that "our cities became socialist from the very moment of the October Revolution, when we expropriated the bourgeoisie and socialized the means of production."[86] This pronouncement epitomizes the interpretation of socialism that prevailed under Stalin. Socialism was henceforth read in largely economistic and nationalistic terms, embodied in the doctrine of "socialism in one country." For Stalin and his supporters, cultural change was seen as subordinate to economic development. Thus the cultivation of proletarian culture did not require a radical reordering of social space; instead it would occur as an inevitable outcome of the process of state-managed industrialization. This did not mean architecture and urban planning were to be abandoned completely; nor did it mean that new forms of urban space would not arise. What it did mean, however, was that architecture and urban planning were to be shorn of their radical and transformative content and afforded a merely technical and decorative role. The link between architectural form and revolutionary politics that had been forged by the radical Soviet designers was thereby broken.

With the suppression of the avant-garde and their theories, a new state-sponsored architectural form emerged. The new official style, commonly referred to as "pillars for the people,"[87] was neoclassical and monumentalist. The architecture, now termed "stalinist," that emerged out of this new orthodoxy was clearly not intended to be a foundation for a new way of life or new cultural form; rather it was supposed to represent the might of Soviet power and the dominance of the masses (embodied by the state) over the individual. Instead of becoming a site for the production of new proletarian culture, as the radical architects had hoped, the Soviet city rapidly became a city of monuments and grandiose state buildings.[88]

Stalin's government explicitly repudiated the idea of collective or communal-style housing, with a decree passed on July 14, 1932, specifying separate family apartments as the standard for all new housing units.[89] In practice, however, ongoing housing shortages meant that several families usually occupied apartments intended for a single family; each family occupied one room with kitchen and bathroom facilities shared.[90] Circumstances thus resulted in a de facto form of communal living being forced upon a large majority of the population without the benefits that planned communalism might have provided.

While this kind of communal living was by no means an intended outcome, Stalinist planners consciously appropriated other aspects of the radical architectural program. An example of this was the policy to site new housing within close proximity of the factories and industrial complexes where the occupants were to work. The expressed reason for this was to minimize the length of the journey to work.[91] The effect of this principle, however, was to focus social and cultural life around the workplace, thus in part reproducing a central tenet of the radicals' program. This outcome was further augmented by the involvement of individual enterprises in the provision of housing.

The reconstruction of Moscow as envisaged under the First Five-Year Plan, which ran from 1929 to 1933, included blueprints for the construction of enough new housing to meet the demands of industrialization. However, as Kenneth Straus reveals in his case study of a Soviet factory during this period, the population increased much faster than had been allowed for and state-funded housing fell far short of demand.[92] Added to this problem was a drastic shortage of labor, which made it very difficult for enterprises to retain an adequate workforce. Under these conditions, enterprise management found it necessary to provide housing, both to make up for the state shortfall and to encourage workers to stay at that particular enterprise. According to Straus, roughly 60 percent of all housing construction undertaken in Moscow during the First Five-Year Plan was carried out by individual enterprises.[93] Similarly, chronic food shortages and inadequacies in the supply system led to factories taking on responsibility in this area as well. Canteens were set up at workplaces to supply meals for workers, and "closed" grocery stores were provided for the exclusive use of factory employees. To guarantee supplies, factories also established direct relationships with state farms.[94] According to Straus, the combination of a chaotic supply system, lack of infrastructure, and shortage of labor led to enterprises taking on these extra-economic activities. Only later did the authorities recognize and approve this role for enterprise management.[95] In this way, the tendency for daily life to be collectivized around the workplace appears to have emerged more or less inadvertently, rather than as the result of deliberate planning.

Straus also suggests that this move toward collectivization can in part be attributed to the agency of the workers who formed the new factory communities. Many of the workers who made up the industrial workforce were rural migrants who had left the countryside to find better jobs. Initially they worked as laborers in the construction of new industrial complexes and then stayed on as workers in the new factories. As new migrants to the urban areas, these workers had no other resources, social ties, or networks and depended almost entirely upon the factory to supply their daily needs. In return, they committed themselves to life in their new communities, raised families, and contributed to the formation of a new social structure.[96]

The analysis provided by Straus shows that despite the official repudiation of the social condenser and its utopian notions of communal life, a combination of other, unplanned factors meant that within the new industrial estates a form of communal-style life emerged. Moreover, as Kopp explains, the Stalinist period saw continued rapid industrial development under a regime which although culturally conservative nevertheless remained committed to principles such as planning and standardization.[97] And while Soviet urban planners never returned to the concept of "super collectivity," they did recognize the utility in providing housing and other facilities for daily life within easy reach of the factory. In the decade preceding the Second World War, this principle was gradually formulated into the concept known as the "super block"—a group of apartment buildings (housing a thousand to fifteen hundred inhabitants) arranged around a quadrangle that shared facilities such as shops, kindergartens, and meeting halls.[98] These units were to form the basis for industrial urban development in the period of reconstruction after 1945, thereby retaining at least some aspects of urban collectivism within the socialist city.

Conclusion

My objective in this chapter has been to trace the emergence of socialist spatial practices. Understanding these practices and the logics that inform them is crucial to understanding the genealogy of the *danwei*, in particular, the ways in which the *danwei* came to combine revolutionary social practice with spatial forms. I have also aimed to highlight the fact that, although the *danwei* is in many ways a distinctive product of Chinese socialism, significant aspects of its complex genealogy derive from sources far removed from the Chinese world. Indeed, one of the reasons the *danwei* is so fascinating is because of the way in which it brings together a range of diverse practices within a discrete institutional setting.

I began this chapter by showing how the emergence of urban planning was linked to the rise of a new form of "governmentality" founded upon the belief that economies and populations could be both better known and better managed through direct planned intervention. Under Haussmann, urban planning was deployed in the service of capitalism, as a strategy to "regularize" urban space, so as to better facilitate the "natural" circulation of goods and men. The work of "utopian" socialist Owen, however, showed that spatial interventions could also be deployed for more radical purposes, namely to foster the transformation of social relations. In later years, others built upon this insight and developed radical new strategies for spatial intervention that combined the technical developments of modern urban planning and architecture with a revolutionary social program. This movement was most influential within the Soviet Union, reaching its peak during the 1920s and early 1930s.

The most significant innovation of the radical Soviet planners was the attempt to create new communal living environments that combined daily life with collective labor. These new sociospatial arrangements were designed not simply with the aim of increasing labor productivity, but rather they were seen as the foundation for revolutionary social and cultural transformation. Indeed, these new living environments were envisaged as playing a major role in the forging of new proletarian subjects. As the term "social condenser" suggests, radical planners believed that spatial forms could operate like machines for the transformation of human subjects. Through living and working within the social condenser, bourgeois values and ways of life would inexorably be stripped away and replaced by a collectivized daily practice appropriate to the principles of socialism.

Although Stalin's repudiation of the radical avant-garde ensured that the social condenser was never fully realized, the principle of planned urban development was retained, albeit subordinated to questions of economic construction. At the same time, the ad hoc communalism brought on by the urban housing shortage and the partial collectivist nature of the postwar "super block" suggest that radical ideas for socialist transformation were by no means entirely dead. This was the spatial heritage China inherited from the Soviet Union in 1949. Yet, as I will show in Chapter 6, the idea of the social condenser found far more fertile ground for realization within the Chinese context than it ever did in the Soviet Union.

CHAPTER 5

Governing Urban China
Labor, Welfare, and the *Danwei*

> There occurred a subtle process, which we must seek to reconstruct in its particulars, through which the science of government, the recentering of the theme of economy on a different plane from that of the family, and the problem of population are all interconnected.
>
> Michel Foucault, 1978[1]

> Factories are not built to produce commodities. They produce the united-working-class-body. . . . They result in a deficit of goods, but an overproduction of symbolic meanings. . . . Labor is a ceremony begetting the communal body of the working class.
>
> Vladislav Todorov, 1995[2]

When the Chinese communists arrived in the cities, following their victory over the Nationalists, they brought with them a well-developed organizational structure and a strategy of governance based on grassroots mobilization. Yet in the cities they were faced with quite a different range of problems than those they had dealt with in the remote rural base areas. The intricacies of social and economic organization in urban China were largely outside the knowledge of most party cadres, and senior officials were all too aware of the steep learning curve that faced them in mastering its operation. Nevertheless, the new CCP-led government moved swiftly to consolidate urban rule and initiate an ambitious program of centrally planned industrial development. In this they followed closely the path to socialist transition already established by the Soviet Union.

Such was the success of the new regime in remaking and reorganizing urban China that by 1957 over 90 percent of the urban population already belonged to a socialist *danwei* of some kind.[3] Within eight short years the *danwei* had been cemented as the dominant social, economic, and organizational unit of the Chinese city. It was the foundation of urban management and the basis for a distinctly socialist strategy of governance. At the same time, it played a crucial part in mobilizing labor to transform "consumer" cities into "producer" cities and in the process create a large new working class. The aim of this chapter, then, is to trace the "subtle process" through which the *danwei* system came to underpin a new revolutionary "science" of population and economy and to explore how the new technologies of government came to structure and regulate everyday life within the city.

Accordingly, this chapter will examine the emergence of a range of governmental strategies and techniques that served to consolidate and define the *danwei* system. It is worth reiterating here that my approach in undertaking this analysis differs from other scholarship on the *danwei* system. I do not propose to interpret the *danwei* either as the seamless extension of so-called party/state power or as a center of localized power engaged in an ongoing struggle with the central state. Rather, I read the *danwei* as both a product of and an enabler of centrally determined policies and strategies. The *danwei* was the site at which policy and strategy imperatives came face to face with complex social and cultural practices. It was in the context of this encounter that the new CCP-led government faced the dilemma of how to govern an urban population. The rationale of government which the CCP developed was necessarily influenced by several factors: first, it reflected the CCP's previous experiences of government, especially those of the Yan'an period; second, it sought to embody the goals that had been set for socialist industrialization; and third, it had to contend with complex existing social and cultural practices.

At a conceptual level the "art of government" is an intellectual, imaginative, and fundamentally utopian undertaking. In actual practice it is far messier, and even the best-planned policies can unravel when faced with realities of implementation. The CCP-led government had a very clear idea of what it wanted to achieve and a basic "toolbox" of governmental techniques, mostly inherited from the Soviet Union. But in striving to achieve its objective to create "producer cities," many original policies had to be adjusted, compromised, and even abandoned in the face of adverse conditions. The outcomes of governmental intervention, then, reflect an ongoing process of negotiation between a core set of rationales and a complex set of contingencies. In Yan'an, the CCP had prided itself on being good at adapting the principles of Marxism to the realities of the Chinese situation. In the cities after 1949, it was, of course, forced to adapt again to quite a different set of circumstances. One of the most significant results of its efforts was the creation of the *danwei* system. In this chapter I focus on political, economic, and social factors that led to the consolidation of this system. In the following chapter, I explore the all-important spatial dimension of the question.

Baoxialai: *The Emergence of a Social Guarantee*

When the CCP assumed political power over all of China, the question of how to govern the cities was foremost in the minds of its leadership. In his address to the Central Committee in March 1949, Mao declared that imminent victory would signal a shift of focus in party work from the countryside to the cities and a shift in emphasis from military struggle to economic construction. According to Mao, the major task of this new urban–centered strategy was to bring about a transformation in the nature of the Chinese city. As Mao urged his colleagues, "From the very first day we take over a city, we should direct our attention to restoring and developing its production. . . . Only when production in the cities is restored and developed, when consumer-cities are transformed into producer-cities, can the people's political power be consolidated."[4] Thus, while the urgent short-term goal was to restore production, which had been severely affected by the war, the longer-term objective was to turn the cities into net producers instead of net consumers of wealth. This reflected a common view among CCP leaders that Chinese cities were characterized by a predominantly wasteful and decadent bourgeois lifestyle.[5]

Since the cities were to play the leading role in the twin push toward industrialization and socialism, it was urgent that they be brought under central CCP control as rapidly as possible. According to Bo Yibo,[6] Mao proposed a two-pronged strategy to facilitate the takeover of the cities: organs of Guomindang (GMD) political power—government departments and offices, the police, the military, taxation bureaus, and the like—were to be stripped of power, disbanded, and replaced by appropriate new CCP-led organs; on the other hand, economic units—factories, shops, electricity plants, transport companies, and the like—were to be consolidated in their existing form so that production could be restored as rapidly as possible.[7] While this strategy seemed straightforward enough in its conception and spoke to the obvious need to restore urban production as rapidly as possible, its implementation posed numerous difficulties. In both the political and economic sectors, the CCP immediately came up against a range of challenges that resulted in a far higher degree of governmental intervention than had been initially envisaged.

One prong of Mao's strategy called for disbanding GMD government organs. The immediate impact of this move was to put thousands of former GMD functionaries out of work. Naturally this led to considerable resentment and opposition from those who had suddenly lost their positions, status, and source of material support. In response to this problem, CCP leadership determined to provide former GMD employees with basic subsistence—food and a living allowance equivalent to 60 or 70 percent of their previous salary—on the proviso that they participate in reeducation and retraining programs. Through reeducation the CCP hoped to win over the political allegiance of the former Nationalist officials, while through retraining they sought to transform this group into productive members of the new society. The strategy to provide a basic material guarantee and a place in the new society for agents of the former regime came to be known simply as *baoxialai*, which translates as "to bring under a guarantee," or "to take care of."[8] It signified that the new government would take full responsibility for the livelihoods of the employees of the former regime; they were to be "enveloped" (*bao*) within a system of comprehensive material support similar to that enjoyed by party members through the revolutionary supply system.[9]

Much of the literature on the takeover of urban industry after 1949 centers on the temporary alliance the CCP forged with the so-called national bourgeoisie. Central to Mao's concept of "New Democracy," the strategy required eliciting cooperation from the existing factory managers and technical experts in order to ensure the restoration of industrial production.[10] Because of this focus, scholars have paid comparatively little attention to the policy rationale and practices of *baoxialai*. By providing former GMD functionaries with basic living requirements, the new government aimed to bring them under CCP influence. According to Bo Yibo, Mao saw the issue as one of decisive political importance, particularly after the dispersal of twenty-seven thousand former GMD employees in Nanjing, Shanghai, and Hangzhou had resulted in major social unrest. Addressing this problem, Mao is reported to have said, "We've smashed the big stove of the Nanjing GMD government; if we don't feed people they'll build their own stoves (*ling qi luzao*)."[11] In Chinese political usage, to "build one's own stove" is a metaphor for establishing a separate power base. Traditionally, all family members ate from the same stove; when a family split or divided property, each new family unit would eat from its own stove. The new CCP government provided food and other material support to functionaries of the overthrown GMD regime not only in order to forestall the possibility that they would pursue independent means of survival and oppositional politics, but also to provide a powerful symbol of the strength and unity of the new government.[12]

Initially the *baoxialai* policy was rationalized as a strategy for ensuring the success of political transition. However, before long *baoxialai* also came to play a significant role in achieving the other major task undertaken by the new CCP regime, that of economic restoration. As has already been mentioned, in taking control of economic units, CCP policy called for a moratorium on managerial change in the interests of restoring production as rapidly as possible. Army and party units were required to maintain the existing structures within any enterprises they "liberated," and where possible they were also called upon to retain the original management and technical staff.[13] This would allow for the rapid resumption of operation that was essential to the practical functioning of the new government. To achieve this outcome, however, a great deal of organizational work was required on two major fronts. First, economic relationships had to be reestablished between the enterprise in question and its suppliers and distributors, since most of these economic connections had broken down or been dramatically affected by the war. Second, the new regime had to mobilize a workforce that was generally very dispirited as a result of the exploitation, mismanagement, corruption, economic chaos, inflation, and hardships of war that they had suffered during the period of GMD rule.

The process of mobilization was known as *zuzhiqilai*—literally, to "get organized." Owing to a lack of ready financial resources, it depended much more on moral persuasion than on material benefit. Yet precisely because of the new regime's inability to provide any significant level of financial reward, the most basic material necessities had to be provided for workers at the workplace.[14] In short, the newly "liberated" enterprise was required, by default, to adopt the *baoxialai* policy as part of its operational survival strategy.[15] It was largely as a result of necessity that two of the core organizational characteristics of the socialist enterprise were established at a very early stage. The ability to successfully mobilize—*zuzhiqilai*—the workforce for productive labor was predicated upon a commitment entered into by authorities to provide the workers with at least a basic level of material guarantee—*baoxialai*.

Many of the benefits and services that later came to be considered integral components of the *danwei* system began as "temporary measures," adopted during the immediate postliberation period as part of the *baoxialai* strategy. A number of these measures were first set out during the Sixth National Labor Congress, convened at Harbin in August 1948. The key document passed by this congress dealt primarily with strategies for the management of industry in the areas of the country that had already come under CCP control.[16] In particular, it called for the urgent adoption of measures to improve the situation in labor protection and workers' welfare. Under the so-called temporary measures, responsibility for labor safety, health care, welfare, culture and education, and financial support for those in need was officially devolved to each individual enterprise.[17] According to the document, the "temporary measures" were intended for use only until the new government was able to establish a fully nationalized and unified system of social insurance. As it turned out, however, a nationalized system never materialized, and the "temporary measures" became permanent features of urban life in socialist China.

The "temporary" decision to make the enterprise responsible for provision of urban social welfare was a decisive moment in the history of urban

China and was one of the critical steps that resulted in the transformation of the urban workplace into a socialist *danwei*. The decision also showed that despite the much-vaunted shift from a rural to an urban policy focus, many operational practices adopted by the CCP after 1949 bore a remarkable resemblance to governmental strategies developed during the Yan'an period. Just like the latter years in Yan'an, numerous aspects of everyday social, economic, and political management in the newly socialist cities were to be entrusted to the grassroots-level *danwei*.

Zuzhiqilai: *Urban Mobilization*

The organizational strategy *zuzhiqilai* also derived from policies developed in the border region.[18] Organization was undoubtedly one of the CCP's fortes, since without the ability to establish and maintain tight disciplined organizations, the CCP would never have defeated the superior GMD forces. As I demonstrate in Chapter 3, CCP organization was founded upon a comprehensive form of grassroots mobilization that combined an idealistic and utopian morality with concerted education and pastoral-style leadership. These strategies, which aimed to mobilize large numbers of people to the CCP cause, had proved enormously successful prior to liberation; so it was not surprising that they were adapted to the urban situation after 1949.

As in Yan'an, the primary objectives of postliberation *zuzhiqilai* were to foster political loyalty and promote production. It was hoped that productivity would be achieved not through the use of coercion or force, but rather through reliance upon moral persuasion and education. According to CCP labor authorities, the *zuzhiqilai* strategy required that urban workers receive educational instruction on the new political situation and on the (CCP version of) events that had preceded the Communist takeover.[19] The purpose of this educational instruction was to raise the political and class consciousness of workers, apprise them of their historical status as members of the working class, and instruct them in their new role as masters of their own workplaces and of society in general.[20]

Having alerted urban workers to their newfound status, the party was quick to point out that this position carried with it certain crucial obligations—namely, "responsibility for industrial development." This responsibility required workers to exhibit a positive new attitude toward their labor.[21] Specifically, their new status meant that in the state sector workers had "both the right to participate in factory management, and the responsibility to labor enthusiastically in order to complete or even surpass the production tasks demanded of them by the state."[22] Workers employed in private industry were also charged with the responsibility to "supervise the capitalist managers in their implementation of government directives."[23]

The demands placed by the CCP-led government on urban workers evidently aimed to forge a strong link between economic goals and political mobilization. Not only were workers required to participate enthusiastically in production; they were also expected to participate in enterprise management and demonstrate a detailed understanding of government policy and its implementation. For the ordinary urban worker, the political ascendancy of the working class under a CCP-led socialist regime resulted in a heavier rather than lighter workload. Through active participation, the politically conscious worker was expected to play a positive role in the construction of a new socialist society. This entailed a commitment and level of awareness that began with workers' own labor and extended to an understanding of the political and economic fate of the whole country. Committed participation in all aspects of economic, political, and social life within the workplace thus became the central criterion by which an urban worker was judged.

According to the new logic, participation in productive labor became the primary determinant for the attainment of both political status and material benefit. In this way the industrial workplace was further privileged as the key site of urban social identification. This trend mirrored, in some respects, the role the workplace had played in the formation of urban worker subjects in presocialist urban China. However, in significant ways the socialist workplace was underpinned by quite a different rationale than had informed earlier forms of urban labor organization. As I demonstrate in Chapter 3, the workplace was also the locus of social life for the urban worker in Republican China. However, it was not the act of labor itself which determined a Republican worker's identity; rather it was his or her affiliation with a particular native-place-oriented guild or gang. The workplace was simply the site through which these traditional forms of group identification were channeled and reconstituted. CCP policy, on the other hand, invested the workplace itself with significance, precisely because it was the site of labor.[24] In short, a worker's political and social identity as a member of the working class was determined through participation in the act of industrial labor itself, rather than by place of origin, social affiliation, or particular trade.

During this period, of course, not everyone in urban China was a worker, and many did not belong to a *danwei*. In order to mobilize and organize urban residents who could not be reached through the workplace, the new government established Residents' Committees (*jumin weiyuanhui*) and a network of Street Offices (*jiedao banshichu*)—administrative outposts of the city or district government.[25] Although these organizations operated as a kind of parallel system to the *danwei*, they were designed as a temporary solution to an urban problem, and it was always assumed that they would whither away as the process of socialist construction progressively absorbed the remaining urban population into a socialist *danwei* of one sort or another.[26] From the government perspective in the early 1950s, then, it is very apparent that the workplace was seen as the ultimate organ of urban governance. This vision proved to be largely correct, as by 1957 just over 90 percent of the urban workforce already belonged to either a state-owned or a collective-owned *danwei*.[27]

As the *danwei* system solidified, the shift from the Republican period to the socialist period was underpinned by a critical shift in the framework of worker identity formation. A framework centered on a global notion of social class affiliation had replaced the traditional framework of localized, familial-style identity formation. Yet, despite this shift from an ostensibly traditional to an ostensibly modern framework, the continuation of the workplace as the basic unit of urban social organization ensured that worker identity was still formed within a collective rather than individual context. For although the workers of socialist China belonged to a large social class, their identity as subjects was formed through participation in collective labor within the *danwei* to which they belonged.

In the early days of its rule, the CCP-led government moved quickly to bring about and consolidate this shift in the basis of workers' identification. This task principally involved removing the various gang leaders, labor contractors, and guild officials, to whom workers had owed loyalty under the previous regime, from positions of influence within enterprises.[28] While the removal of such figures was crucial to consolidating the political power of the new government among the urban working class, it was only the first step. Of even more importance was the ability of the new authorities to establish an alternative grassroots support network within the factories to replace the networks operated by the gangs and guilds. In Chapter 3, I illustrate how these organizations played a significant role in providing social and material support for urban workers, particularly since most workers had been recruited directly from the countryside and had little access to other social networks within the harsh urban environment. Kenneth Lieberthal's study of the CCP takeover in Tianjin, for example, shows that the ability of the new government-sponsored trade unions to guarantee welfare support was very important in winning workers over from the gang bosses.[29] Henceforth, most of the organizational and welfare work undertaken within urban factories—*zuzhiqilai* and *baoxialai*—was carried out by the trade unions.

Organizing Workers: Trade Unions and the Danwei

From the outset, the role of the trade union in the new socialist state was quite distinct from the role trade unions have played within capitalist economies. The difference was based upon the principle that socialist ownership of the means of production eliminates the contradiction between workers and owners that characterizes the capitalist mode of production. Under these conditions, there is no longer any need for the trade union to take an adversarial role on behalf of the worker against the interests of the owner. Instead, the trade union was to be seen as an arm of Communist Party government; its role was to mobilize workers to serve the interests of the socialist state.

CCP authorities derived their understanding of the trade union's role under socialism primarily through reference to the experiences and practices of the Soviet Union.[30] The Soviet position emerged out of the "Trade Union Debate" of 1920–21, through which Lenin established the principle that socialist trade unions should operate as "transmission belts" between the party and the working class. Its task was to transmit party policy, decisions, and general wisdom to the workers, to provide political education, and to instruct workers in their duties toward socialist construction. In this respect, the trade unions would also be "schools of communism," training workers in the principles of communism as well as in the technical skills necessary for the management of production.[31]

The 1948 Labor Congress established a national trade union organization and passed a detailed resolution confirming its role in much the same terms as those developed in the Soviet Union. Central emphasis was placed on the role of the trade union to *zuzhiqilai*, namely to mobilize and organize workers to support the party and to restore production in the factories.[32] In addition, the trade union was to carry out education among workers in order to raise their political consciousness and enthusiasm for the new socialist system. The trade union also undertook to organize workers to participate in industrial management, in enterprises under public ownership, and in supervision over management in private enterprises. Finally, the trade union was charged with responsibility for the management of workers' welfare, including the establishment of a labor insurance scheme and provision of assistance to needy workers.[33]

Trade union organizations were established in urban factories immediately following their takeover by CCP authorities. Basing their approach on a model developed in the northeast during 1948, the new authorities sent work teams to each factory to manage the takeover.[34] Their first task was to establish a party branch made up of work team members, underground party members already within the factory and other activists identified within the workforce. Having set up this core leadership group, the work teams proceeded to establish a trade union branch to operate as a link between the party branch and the rest of the workforce.[35] The new party organization then established a factory management committee made up of party and trade union members as well as any of the original technical and management personnel who had remained behind and were willing to cooperate with the new authorities.[36]

The central objective of the new management committee was to restore production.[37] In this task the trade union played a very important role. A union official who worked in the industrial sector of Beijing reported attending a delegates' meeting of the Beijing trade union organization hosted by Peng Zhen in his capacity as president of the Beijing City Federation of Trade Unions. Peng informed the delegates that they had three principle tasks: "number one, production; number two, production; and number three, production." In order to develop production, the delegates were required to study Soviet documents on industrial production and labor mobilization and to launch labor competition campaigns modeled upon the Soviet Stakhanovite movement.[38] The objective was to foster competition among workers to set new productivity records as well as to encourage innovation in work practice that would increase productivity.[39]

The push to restore production and increase productivity was closely tied to the issue of proletarian education. As noted above, education of workers was one of the key tasks to be undertaken by the socialist trade union. The most common method adopted to pursue this task was the establishment of after-hours classes for factory workers at their places of work.[40] Such classes encompassed a range of topics: general political education (including the history of the labor movement in China, the history of the CCP, current policy, and general socialist principles), technical and management subjects, as well as literacy and culture.[41] Through education, workers were trained to become both politically enlightened and technically proficient, or in the parlance of the time, "both red and expert." Promoting a large number of "red experts" was considered a crucial precondition for achieving a transition to socialism; for only when the old bourgeois-trained experts upon whom the Communists had to rely in the early years of CCP rule were replaced would the crucial urban industrial sector truly come under socialist control.

If education was vital to securing working-class commitment to political and productive goals in the urban factories, the provision of a basic material safety net was another important factor in establishing legitimacy for the new regime in the cities. This was particularly significant where the new authorities had to fill a vacuum left after the destruction of the guilds, gangs, and labor bosses. One of the first welfare-oriented tasks taken on by the trade unions in newly "liberated" factories was to establish a labor insurance scheme.[42] It became the responsibility of each enterprise union to collect contributions regularly from both workers and employers. The funds were managed by the union at the enterprise level and distributed to workers in the case of injury, incapacitation, or other forms of material hardship.

The *danwei*-based welfare system, a "temporary measure" since 1948, was codified in February 1951 with the passage of national "Labor Insurance Regulations."[43] The regulations set out both the scope to be covered by the welfare system and the methods for funding it.[44] It included provision for the payment of medical expenses, disability pensions, funeral costs, and financial support for the families of workers killed in the workplace, retirement pensions, and maternity leave. The regulations also guaranteed the right of workers to utilize various collective welfare facilities run by the *danwei*, the city, the industry, and the trade union organization itself. These facilities included sanatoriums, kindergartens, homes for the aged, orphanages, institutions for the disabled, and holiday facilities.[45]

The benefits established under the new Labor Insurance regime were to be funded from two sources. First, each enterprise was required to contribute 3 percent of the total monthly wage bill into a Labor Insurance Fund. Thirty percent of these funds were remitted to the city trade union organization for the central management and provision of regional welfare facilities, while the other 70 percent was placed under the management of the enterprise trade union for use within that enterprise.[46] The Labor Insurance Fund was used to pay the various long-term pensions provided for under the regulations—namely, to the disabled, the incapacitated, the retired, and the families of deceased workers. The fund was also responsible for the four-yuan payment made to parents on the birth of a child and the payment of workers' funeral expenses. The financial responsibility for other benefits, such as medical expenses for injuries and illness, maternity pay, and reduced pay during convalescence lay directly with the enterprise itself. Resources for the provision of collective facilities within the enterprise, like hospitals, clinics, and kindergartens, were supplied jointly out of the enterprise management budget and the trade union–managed Labor Insurance Fund.[47]

Although it was promulgated on a national scale, the welfare system established in 1951 depended very heavily on each *danwei* to organize both the provision and the management of a fairly comprehensive social security net for its workers.[48] The implementation of this system not only required each *danwei* to provide funds to operate the various welfare programs, but also demanded that they construct the physical infrastructure necessary to service most of these welfare needs. The rapid construction of clinics, kindergartens, and other collective facilities to meet these demands only consolidated the process through which the urban workplace was transformed into a relatively self-sufficient community.[49]

Trade unions also became particularly active in the organization of consumer cooperatives as a way of providing workers with a reliable source of food and other necessities. At the time of the CCP takeover, the cities suffered from dire shortages of daily essentials as well as from runaway inflation, which had created enormous financial hardship for urban workers. To address this problem, the newly formed trade union organizations set about the development of alternative supply systems based around a network of consumer cooperatives.[50] Taking advantage of the purchasing power achieved through combining the financial resources of a factory's workers, the cooperative could purchase goods in bulk at lower prices. In addition, the trade union–run cooperative was able to use its political connections to establish direct relationships with agricultural and industrial producers, guaranteeing a fairly reliable source of supply.[51] The benefits in financial saving and convenience for their worker members were not the only useful purpose served by the consumer cooperatives. The day-to-day operation of these enterprise-based supply cooperatives bolstered the other mobilization strategies employed by the trade unions, helping to enmesh workers within the socioeconomic structures of the new regime.

While the specific benefits differed from those provided in pre-1949 factories, nevertheless the practice of investing the workplace with responsibility for a broad range of workers' needs was carried over from the former system to the latter. In this, the image of the family was again ever present. In Chapter 3 we saw how the internal organization and social practices of the guilds and labor gangs were modeled on the traditional Confucian family. While the Communist trade unions certainly rejected the rigid hierarchical differentiations embodied by the traditional family, they were often portrayed as being like a family for the workers. A cadre involved in the takeover of the Mentougou Coal Mine near Beijing, for example, ascribes the success of the transition to this factor: "the prestige of the trade union among Mentougou Coal Mine workers was very high; workers considered the trade union to be their own family."[52]

Where the CCP did not command the resources to establish a universal welfare system for urban workers, the preexisting practice of workplace-based welfare provision turned out to be readily adaptable to the initial goals of the new regime. The adoption of this policy did not imply a fundamental compromise in CCP principles. Indeed, one of the reasons the new regime was able to operate effectively within the urban environment was that in many important respects the collective-oriented social structures they found there were not dissimilar to the self-sufficient units that the CCP itself had promoted during the Yan'an period. Both were premised upon a strong identification with a social group centered on the organization of labor, and both sought to provide for and look after the interests of group members. To this degree, the two forms of social organization were built upon similar forms of collective-oriented subjectivity.

In pointing this out, however, I do not mean to suggest a direct continuity between presocialist and socialist forms of organization. Rather the similarities illustrate the ways in which certain practices and techniques of government can be redeployed within a new context and toward new goals. In this case, the CCP was able to successfully adapt aspects of the existing urban socioeconomic structure to serve its own strategic objectives for the mobilization and reorganization of the workforce. This strategy of adaptation contributed to the high degree of success the CCP leaders enjoyed in the early years of their rule within the cities. It also prepared the ground for the huge socialist development drive that was to come.

The Great Trade Union Debate: Implications for the Danwei

Despite, or perhaps because of, the early success of *baoxialai* and *zuzhiqilai* under the new *danwei*-based trade union organizations, conflict between unions and managers over their respective roles soon emerged. The outcome of this dispute was to have major consequences for the development and consolidation of the *danwei* system. The dispute arose because the respective roles of enterprise management and the trade union were not clearly defined. Documents from the 1948 Labor Congress were vague on the specific division of labor between trade union and management within an enterprise. This is particularly apparent in the provision that called for the trade unions to mobilize workers to participate in factory management.[53] It implied that the trade unions themselves would have some involvement in the actual management of the factory. Similar ambiguities existed in the provisions for the operation of certain welfare and safety requirements. Some duties were assigned to "the factory *or* the trade union," while others were made the responsibility of "the factory *and* the trade union."[54] Again, no specific instructions were provided for how to mediate the respective roles in carrying out these various tasks.[55]

In the light of this confusion, attempts were made to specify more clearly the division of duties between the trade union and the administration. For example, in 1951 the Ministry of Textiles and the Textile Workers Trade Union issued a document entitled "Joint Decision on Forging Closer Ties Between Administration and Trade Union."[56] Despite the title's allusion to "closer ties," the intention of the document was to set out distinct spheres of operation for administration and trade union within the enterprise. The administration was to be responsible for production planning, the management system, personnel deployment, safety and hygiene, and welfare infrastructure. The trade union was to be responsible for the organization of labor competition, worker education—including instruction in the areas of labor discipline and technology—and organization of workers to participate in economic accounting and factory management. Furthermore, the trade union was charged with the task of improving workers' daily life, and in this regard to both assist and supervise the management of production, safety, hygiene, and welfare infrastructure.[57] The document also directed both sides to co-operate fully in the implementation of economic plans, government policy, and party directives. Nevertheless, the overall tenor of the document—which utilized terms like *duifang* (the other side) when referring to the mutual relationship—was to establish two relatively distinct organizational structures within each enterprise. While the two sides were required to co-operate, they were also directed to supervise each other's work. Within this bipolar structure, the trade union by no means occupied a subordinate position.

The document reflected the views of the national trade union leadership on the role of the socialist trade union within urban enterprises. Li Lisan, vice president of the All China Federation of Trade Unions (ACFTU), was the main force behind this position.[58] In the critical theoretical debate that was to take place, his position was also supported by Deng Zihui, who headed trade union work in the CCP's Central-Southern Bureau, and Liu Shaoqi, who held the honorary presidentship of ACFTU and who wrote a detailed paper advocating a more independent role for the trade union which, for political reasons, was not published at the time.[59]

Despite eliciting the support of a senior CCP leader like Liu, ACFTU attempts to mark out a relatively independent role for the trade union came under immediate attack from another group of senior CCP figures led by Gao Gang and Chen Boda. The debate that followed centered upon two basic points of contention: first, whether there could be conflict between public and private interests within state-owned enterprises; and hence, second, whether the trade union and the enterprise administration represented different points of view.[60] Li Lisan and Deng Zihui argued that while the interests of the two were broadly the same, there were aspects of workplace management in which it was inevitable that differences between administration and labor would emerge. According to their view, the trade union should represent the interests of the workers when any such differences arose.[61] Liu Shaoqi fully endorsed this position, pointing out that working-class enthusiasm for economic construction could be ensured only if trade union officials remained close to ordinary workers and were seen to represent their interests within the broad goals set down by the state plan.[62]

Gao Gang and Chen Boda disagreed. So far as they were concerned, any suggestion of a divergence in interest between enterprise administration and workers once socialism had been established ran counter to Marxist-Leninist theory. In their view, trade union and administration simply represented different aspects of socialist enterprise management. The role of administration was to manage enterprise production, while the role of the trade union was to mobilize the workers to fulfill the production quotas set down under the plan. In performing these roles, both were required to cooperate fully under CCP leadership.[63]

This important debate was brought to a close at a national ACFTU conference held in Beijing over ten days in December 1951. The Li/Deng position was repudiated and Li Lisan forced to make three separate self-criticisms.[64] Li was charged with the anti-Marxist-Leninist "crimes" of "economism," "syndicalism," and "subjectivism," errors which were said to reflect the fact that he had followed a "social democratic" line, which had in turn resulted in negating the leadership of the party, losing contact with reality, and separating himself from the masses.[65]

The charge of economism related to the accusation that in his leadership of the ACFTU, Li Lisan had overemphasized the role of the economic sphere in the building of socialism, thereby underplaying the importance of central political leadership.[66] To be accused of syndicalism was perhaps even more serious, for historically the syndicalist movement had always rejected the need for leadership by a centralized party, instead supporting the principles of workers' self-management and "socialism from below."[67] This accusation implied that Li Lisan saw the leadership of the party as irrelevant to building socialism within the industrial workplace, indeed that in his leadership of the ACFTU he had attempted to undermine the importance of the CCP. Finally, the charge of subjectivism was tied to the CCP's belief that Marxist-Leninist doctrine represented objective, scientific truth. To be accused of subjectivism simply meant that Li had left what was taken to be the orthodox path and acted according to his own subjective views.

More specific charges made against Li Lisan included his apparent failure to emphasize party leadership enough in the Trade Union Law that he had been responsible for drafting; his perceived overemphasis of welfare and material benefits for workers, thereby promoting the short-term, sectional interests of workers over the long-term goals of national economic construction; and his alleged failure to place significant priority on the political education of workers.[68] For these alleged "crimes," Li Lisan was removed from his position at the head of the ACFTU and replaced by Lai Ruoyu.[69]

The purge of Li Lisan had major implications for the emergence of the *danwei* system. I have already shown how grassroots trade union work was organized around the individual enterprise, thereby tending to reinforce the position of the *danwei* as the locus of collective urban life. Within this framework, Li Lisan had attempted to establish a partially independent position for the trade union inside the enterprise, as well as building a strong national organizational network. While there is very little evidence to support the charge that Li had repudiated the leadership of the party, it is clear that a number of key CCP figures were very uneasy about what they perceived to be the development of an alternative power base, particularly when that base

was being established among members of the population who were supposed to be the core CCP constituency—namely, the urban proletariat.[70] In
this light it is apparent that the overthrow of Li Lisan was aimed at strengthening CCP control over the trade unions. It resulted in a substantial weakening of both the national organizational structure as well as the operational
scope of the enterprise-level trade union. Henceforth, within the *danwei*, the
trade union would be entirely subordinate to the party and administrative
structures.

This move to downgrade the operational role of the trade union organization was confirmed in the proceedings of the Seventh National Trade
Union Congress convened in Beijing in May 1953.[71] The new position was
outlined in the keynote speech made by the new trade union head, Lai
Ruoyu. Note that this congress was convened ostensibly to coincide with
the launch of the First Five-Year Plan. In this context, the purported aim of
the congress was to set out the role of the trade union movement under new
economic circumstances. Not surprisingly, the stated role coincided exactly
with that which had been articulated in the party's critique of Li Lisan.

In his speech, Lai particularly emphasized the central role of the party in
the leadership of all trade union work. Under party leadership the trade
union was to perform a range of functions: build and maintain close links
with the masses of ordinary workers; carry out political education among
workers so as to raise their political consciousness and organizational ability;
cement the worker/peasant alliance; mobilize workers to fulfill state construction plans; seek to gradually improve the standard of living for workers;
and promote the broad goals of industrialization and the transition to socialism.[72] More specifically, Lai called on the trade union organization to con-
vince workers that their interests should be seen as long-term and collective
rather than immediate or sectional.[73]

Most of the objectives enumerated by Lai were the same as those that had
been set down at the Sixth Labor Congress in 1948. There was, however,
one crucial omission from that original list—namely, the goal of promoting
worker participation in factory management. This is perhaps surprising,
given that the CCP, as a self-proclaimed party of the working class, had always included the principle of worker control within its revolutionary man-
ifesto. Clearly this position had changed to meet new political and economic
circumstances. With the commitment to a Soviet-style centrally planned
economy and the need for a disciplined workforce to meet the needs of
rapid industrialization, the party felt the need to reinterpret the nature of
worker participation. Where it had once been conceived in terms of direct
participation, workers' participation was now to be seen in a more indirect
way, as working-class control exercised not by workers individually and collectively within factories, but rather by their representatives—the Commu-

nist Party—through the various bureaucratic and technical mechanisms of government.[74]

In the light of this new interpretation, Li Lisan's attempt to promote worker participation in management through a strong and partially independent trade union organization was seen as detrimental to centralized party control. With the repudiation of Li Lisan, the trade union was reduced to an arm of enterprise management. Its primary role henceforth was to aid in the production of an enthusiastic, disciplined, politically conscious, and—above all—productive workforce. Its secondary role was to provide some basic services for workers, including the provision of emergency material aid and financial assistance, and the organization of cultural and educational activities.

The repudiation of an independent role for the trade unions was a crucial event in the emergence of the *danwei* system. Although the socialist trade unions had always been closely tied to management at the enterprise level and involved in the daily work and social lives of workers, the policies pursued under Li Lisan's leadership sought to provide a broad and independent network to support the enterprise-based grassroots union. This would have linked workers across the country into an organization that, at least potentially, represented their interests distinctly from those of the administration. It would have allowed the possibility that workers at any given enterprise had a strong external political force to call upon in the case of a dispute with their administration. The weakening of the trade union's role after 1951 meant that, although they maintained a city, provincial, and national organizational structure, they had no power to intervene on behalf of workers within an individual enterprise. The enterprise trade union in effect became wholly subordinate to the party and administrative organs within the enterprise and virtually indistinguishable from other arms of *danwei* management.

Central Planning and Technologies of Socialist Governance

Settling the question of trade union status was part of the CCP's attempt to consolidate and centralize governmental practices in preparation for the full implementation of the planned economy. The removal of Li Lisan and the realignment of trade union work coincided very closely with the launching of the "three antis" (*sanfan*) and the "five antis" (*wufan*) campaigns. The former targeted corruption, waste, and bureaucratism among party cadres, government officials, and administrative organs, while the latter targeted the urban bourgeoisie with a crackdown on bribery, tax evasion, fraud, theft of government property, and state economic secrets.[75] Together these two campaigns were designed to consolidate unified central leadership over the urban sector.

The *sanfan* campaign was intended to remove party and government officials, including former GMD functionaries, who had shown themselves unreliable in the implementation of government policy.[76] Unified planning required a loyal and dependable cadre, or as Mao commented in relation to the purpose of these campaigns, "Planned economy is impossible unless we are clear about the situation."[77] If the *sanfan* campaign signaled the CCP cleaning up bureaucratic ranks in preparation for the task of socialist construction, the *wufan* campaign signaled the end of the brief "New Democracy" alliance with the national bourgeoisie. By facilitating the formation of unified and loyal party-led regimes within each urban enterprise, the *sanfan* and *wufan* campaigns greatly strengthened the CCP's administrative and political control over urban industry.[78] This process further facilitated the transformation of bourgeois-run factories into socialist *danwei* in readiness for the shift to full-blown central planning.

CCP authorities closely followed Soviet practice in developing strategies for the implementation of central economic planning. Under Soviet guidance, the First Five-Year Plan focused predominantly on urban industrial construction,[79] the core of the plan being 694 key industrial construction projects (referred to as *jianshe danwei*), 145 of which were based on designs and technology supplied by the Soviet Union itself.[80] In addition to these major projects, another twenty-three hundred smaller-scale industrial construction projects were to be completed. Because of the priority given to these industrial construction projects, virtually all available capital was channeled into this sector at the expense of other sectors, especially agriculture.

The massive investment in urban industry naturally required the construction of social infrastructure and services to support the large new industrial workforce. In order to maximize coordination of resources within a very tight budget, planners decided that infrastructure and service provision would be attached directly to each individual project. Hence, within the budget for each new industrial complex, funds were included for the construction of housing, schools, canteens, and other services required by the factory workforce.[81] In this way, as part of the central plan, each new industrial enterprise was provided directly with the resources to develop and maintain its day-to-day operation as a viable working community. Housing development was the most notable example of this policy. According to Li Fuchun's report on the First Five-Year Plan, 33 million of a total 46 million square meters of new housing to be constructed during this period were directly linked to state-owned enterprises or government administrative departments.[82]

Linking investment in urban social services to each enterprise and institutional *danwei* in this way provided both financial and organizational benefits for CCP government.[83] For example, by making the individual *danwei* responsible for the construction and management of urban housing, planning authorities circumvented the need to establish a national housing bureaucracy.[84] Moreover, this strategy allowed for the provision of services to be targeted to those enterprises, and workers, who were considered to be most crucial to the industrialization process.[85] Project-based infrastructure funding greatly bolstered the connection between workplace and community that already existed in urban China and thereby further consolidated the role of the *danwei* system.

The regime of planning adopted by the CCP-led government ensured that the urban *danwei*, which had already become a basic unit of political organization, was rapidly transformed into the basic unit of economic planning as well as the primary site for the redistribution of resources. Through this process, the new urban *danwei* was fully subsumed within the grassroots organizational system that had long been practiced by CCP-led party, government, army, and mass organizations. In accordance with the principle of dispersed management that had emerged during the Yan'an period, most of the particulars of resource management were left to each *danwei* to arrange according to its own needs. The central government did establish universal national scales for wages and various kinds of monetary subsidy; however, because wage rates were kept very low, direct financial reward was only a small part of the overall package of material benefits provided to urban workers through their workplace.[86] Paradoxically, then, while the practices of central planning allowed for the implementation of certain universal production- and consumption-related norms at a macro level, it also reinforced the degree to which individual workers became dependent upon their *danwei* for material benefits and social services. This is reflected in other policies that became integral to the Chinese planning regime, such as the unified purchasing and marketing system (*tonggou tongxiao*), the unified job-assignment system (*tongpei*), and the household registration system (*hukou*). When combined with the investment provisions discussed above, these policies provided the individual *danwei* with control over most of the basic necessities of everyday life.

The unified purchasing and distribution mechanism, introduced by Chen Yun in 1953, was devised to guarantee the supply of grain to urban areas.[87] Under the system, rural producers were compelled to sell grain to the state at fixed prices. Government agencies then arranged for the grain to be transported and distributed to state employees in the cities.[88] For a growing number of urban residents, access to grain and other commodities was channeled through their *danwei*, and when rationing began, it was through the *danwei* that ration tickets were issued. The number of items subject to *tonggou tongx-*

iao increased rapidly to encompass a wide range of industrial as well as agricultural products.[89]

The *tongpei* job assignment system developed out of a unified job introduction system (*tongyi jieshao*) instigated in March 1950 following a meeting of national Labor Bureau heads.[90] The primary purpose of this system was to address the serious unemployment that afflicted China's urban areas. Under the new policy, labor bureaus were established in all urban districts to act as agents between unemployed workers and enterprises. Unemployed urban residents were required to register with their local labor bureau, while enterprises in need of workers had to submit their requests to the labor bureau. The labor bureau then introduced suitable workers to the relevant enterprise. In 1952 the State Council published its "Decision on the Labor and Employment Problem" aimed at further strengthening centralized control over labor deployment. The new policy empowered labor bureaus to investigate any request from an enterprise seeking to employ extra workers. If the request met with official approval, the labor bureau would then assign appropriate workers from the pool of registered unemployed. Enterprises were forbidden from directly hiring employees themselves and were also forbidden from employing students, workers who were already in employment, or migrants from rural areas. In addition, workers could be transferred between enterprises only if both were within the same administrative system and then only with the approval of the administrative department responsible for the enterprises.[91] Finally, the new regulations stipulated that in cases where an enterprise was closed down and its capital transferred to another *danwei*, then the workforce should be transferred also.[92] It is clear from this evidence that even from a fairly early stage in the emergence of the *danwei* system, the employment relationship between worker and *danwei* had already become extremely close.

With the launch of the FFYP in 1953, the focus of macro labor management shifted from the question of unemployment to the need for a rational deployment of labor power to meet the demands of socialist construction. Not surprisingly, it was in the construction industry where the need for a coordinated deployment of labor first became urgent. From 1954, state labor bureaus began to manage the recruitment and assignment of all workers in this industry according to a fully coordinated national plan.[93] As construction proceeded and the requirements for labor in other industries expanded, the system for the planned recruitment and assignment of labor was extended to include all enterprises in the industrial, mining, and transport sectors. The need for national coordination was particularly apparent in regard to the deployment of skilled workers and technical personnel. Naturally, skilled staff were concentrated in the well-established coastal industrial centers, whereas the newly developing inland industrial areas were desperately short of expertise. Achieving a rational deployment of skilled personnel was one of the main initial objectives of the coordinated labor assignment system.[94]

The task of rational labor deployment proved much more difficult than planners originally envisaged. The pressure to reduce unemployment soon overwhelmed the principle of rational assignment within the labor bureaus, and by early 1957 it was already clear that many enterprises and other types of *danwei* had been assigned considerably more staff than they required. Faced with this problem, the State Council ordered that any *danwei* with surplus staff should attempt to find other workplaces for them. If new places could not be found, however, the State Council stipulated that "they must not be retrenched."[95] To support this directive, *danwei* were warned that they would be investigated and punished if they attempted to dismiss any surplus staff.

As Yuan Lunqu points out, the effect of this decision was to greatly expand the scope of *baoxialai*. Henceforth, the social guarantee was to be provided for the entire state sector, including all state-owned enterprise (*qiye*) and institutional (*shiye*) *danwei*.[96] Labor policy now ensured that employment assignments in the state sector were jobs for life.[97] Moreover, regardless of the obvious overstaffing that existed in most state sector *danwei*, the labor bureaus continued to assign employment to all demobilized army personnel and graduates of urban high schools, colleges, and universities until the late 1980s. Widespread and perennial overstaffing within state sector *danwei* also meant that it was almost impossible for workers to transfer between *danwei*, since vacancies rarely appeared. As a result, each *danwei* maintained a very stable workforce over long periods of time. This phenomenon led to the popular quip in regard to state employment that "you can only get in; you can't get out" (*zhi neng jin, bu neng chu*).

Another critical factor in the low rate of mobility among China's urban labor force was the staff quota, or *bianzhi* system. The *bianzhi* linked the *danwei* budget to a staff quota determined by the central planning authorities.[98] Funds were made available according to a *danwei's bianzhi*. Thus, if the *danwei* employed extra workers above the level set by the *bianzhi*, it would not receive funding for these positions, nor for the other benefits provided to employees. The *bianzhi* system thus made it difficult for a *danwei* to recruit staff outside of the formal mechanisms of centralized planning and labor allocation. Moreover, it added another obstacle to labor mobility and strengthened the bureaucratic links that bound individuals to their *danwei*.[99]

The development of a national population register, the *hukou* system, placed further restrictions on urban population movement. While most scholars portray the *hukou* as a mechanism implemented in the late 1950s to stop rural workers migrating to the cities,[100] registration of the urban population had begun almost immediately after Communist victory in 1949. As Michael Dutton points out, within the cities, the *hukou* was underpinned by a much more positive logic—it produced practical knowledge about the urban population, thereby facilitating economic planning and the rational deployment of urban labor.[101] In principle, at least, the urban *hukou* was an enabling rather than a repressive technology; it enabled labor to be freed from the vagaries of markets, to be deployed in a rational manner, and it offered full employment for the urban population. Nevertheless, under the circumstances of perennial overstaffing in urban *danwei*, it also became another governmental practice that tied individuals to their *danwei*.

The *hukou* not only constrained the movement of workers between workplaces; it also played an important role in consolidating the dependence of workers on their *danwei*. There were two reasons for this. First, although the population register was primarily the responsibility of the local police station (*paichusuo*), much of the day-to-day work involved in maintaining and updating the register was delegated to the *danwei*.[102] Second, the *danwei*-based *hukou* register was utilized as the basis for the planned distribution of resources. In 1955 the government instituted a rationing system to facilitate the allocation of necessities such as grain, cooking oil, and cotton. Under this system, ration tickets were issued to urban residents on the basis of their *hukou* registration.[103] Management of the rationing system was also delegated to the *danwei*, thereby further strengthening the role of the *danwei* in the everyday lives of its members. Through its close involvement in administration of the *hukou* and in the distribution of rationed goods, as well as through its role in the provision of housing and welfare, the *danwei* became the primary source for the supply of most basic daily needs.

To augment the information provided by the *hukou*, each *danwei* was also required to establish a system of internal personnel files, or *renshi dang'an*. Where the *hukou* register contained fairly basic information, including facts such as a person's place of origin, ethnicity, cultural level, religious belief, and former places of registration,[104] the personnel file provided a much more detailed record of each individual's work history and social background, as well as assessments of his or her attitudes toward politics (*biaoxian*) and work performance.[105] These files were utilized primarily by the *danwei* when assessing personnel for promotion, reward, or redeployment and also for determining whether someone would become a target during political campaigns.[106]

The personnel file system was managed by the personnel department within each *danwei*, according to standardized guidelines set down by the central government.[107] The contents were secret, and under normal circumstances *danwei* members could not gain access to their own file. The file was crucial in another way, since, until quite recently, without it a *danwei* member could not transfer to another *danwei*.[108] Because the personnel file provided a detailed history of the individual *danwei* member, including details on work and political history, as well as comments on character, attitudes, family relationships, and so on, no *danwei* would accept a new member without having first viewed his or her file. Even if a second *danwei* agreed to accept a transferee, the original *danwei* could block the transfer by simply refusing to release the file. This further underscores the critical importance of the file to the life of *danwei* members; it determined their treatment and access to opportunities within their *danwei*, and it functioned as an indivisible part of their identity outside their original *danwei*.

The *hukou* register and the personnel file were technologies of government that transformed the individual worker into a knowable economic and political subject and fixed him or her visibly within the administrative and physical space of the *danwei*. Within the *danwei*, this knowledge was linked to a management regime that monitored production and authorized distribution. Together these practices produced a disciplinary environment in which the interests of the individual worker were tied closely to the interests of the *danwei* and its managers. While this system was designed to promote an orderly and productive socialist lifestyle, it could not guarantee against the possibility of disruptive antisocial and criminal behavior from the "enemies of socialism." To safeguard against this ever-present danger, a well-prepared security presence was necessary. From a very early stage, the national Public Security apparatus enlisted the participation of the *danwei* in policing urban social order.

The *danwei's* responsibilities in relation to security can be traced back to the emergence of policing organs within the party organization during the Yan'an period. In September 1949, this responsibility was extended dramatically with an order issued by the Social Department (*shehuibu*) of the CCP Central Committee requiring all *danwei* to establish their own internal security apparatus.[109] Henceforth, each *danwei* was to be held responsible for the behavior and activities of its population.[110] As a result of this decision and a range of follow-up regulations set down by the Department of Public Security,[111] each *danwei* set up its own internal security department, usually known as the *baoweike* or *baoweichu*, which was charged with basic policing duties within the *danwei*.[112]

Danwei security staff worked under the direct management of the *danwei* leadership but also liaised closely with local Public Security police units.[113] Moreover, the powers of *danwei* security staff were circumscribed by Public Security regulations; they were allowed to investigate and intervene in disputes and carry out surveillance but were not permitted to arrest, fine, or punish. In serious cases, where formal legal intervention was required, the local Public Security police were to be called in. Some large *danwei*, like universities and large-scale industrial complexes, were allocated their own police stations in addition to the internal security department. According to Public Security regulations, police stationed within a *danwei* were subject to *danwei* as well as Public Security leadership. More importantly, the pay, benefits, and facilities for police stationed inside a *danwei* were the responsibility of that *danwei*.[114]

The way in which grassroots security work was organized illustrates how closely the *danwei* was involved in policing the daily lives of its members. In carrying out its security functions, the *danwei's* involvement in the management of the *hukou* register and the personnel file ensured that it had access to a detailed source of information on its members and their families. In this way security strategies and bureaucratic techniques of knowledge were inextricably linked within the day-to-day operation of *danwei* management. While in principle this kind of regime delivered the ordered and disciplined workplace environment required to meet the onerous demands of socialist development, its implementation placed a very heavy burden on the grassroots *danwei* cadre. Mao, like Stalin, had long acknowledged the importance of cadres; however, the strategies of cadre work developed in Yan'an did not always mesh smoothly with Soviet methods of central planning.

Cadres and the Danwei

There were obvious reasons behind China initially adopting Soviet methods in industrial planning and management. However, in order to understand why many of these methods ultimately proved unacceptable and were abandoned, it is important to take into account the differences between the Soviet and the Chinese circumstances. Franz Schurmann argues that the key difference concerned the profile and educational background of the technical personnel in the two countries.[115] Stalin had introduced "one-man management" into Soviet industry in the early 1930s only *after* a corps of young technicians had emerged from the new specialized engineering colleges. This new technical elite were significant not simply because they had been equipped with the expertise to run modern industrial plants, but also because their education had inculcated an absolute loyalty to Stalin and his economic program. This new corps of Stalinist technocrats was then positioned to take over the tasks of industrial planning and management from the old prerevolutionary bourgeois-trained intelligentsia.[116] In China, the circumstances were quite different. Under Soviet guidance, moves to establish one-man management began only two years after the PRC was established, when the vast majority of competent technicians and managers were those who had been trained under the bourgeois education system of the

GMD regime. In this context, appointments to industrial management positions in urban China were determined primarily on the basis of technical rather than political considerations.

Schurmann's point is apposite but cannot entirely explain the strength of the opposition that emerged against Soviet management style in China. It was not just the class background of the industrial managers that caused resentment; it was also the fundamental logic of the one-man management system that loyal party cadres and many workers found impossible to accept. This was because the hierarchical "scientific" division of labor and the authoritarian rationale of the Soviet methods clashed directly with the practices of pastoral-based leadership that had emerged during the Yan'an period. The *danwei* organizational model that had developed in Yan'an operated according to relatively egalitarian and autonomous principles. Thus, when managers were instructed to adopt the hierarchical authority of the Soviet system, they met with considerable resistance from below, resistance which was formidable because it was embedded within the very system of social organization which had been adopted and which was characteristic of the distinctly Chinese form of socialism.[117] The prevailing ethos could simply not be reconciled with the new policy direction, since the latter appeared to negate the entire radical political project that the revolutionaries had trained, struggled, and fought for.[118]

After a period of debate during the mid-1950s, the policy of one-man management was formally abandoned at the Eight Party Congress in September 1956. In its place, a system of collective leadership was to be instituted. The new management strategy was known as "factory-manager responsibility under the leadership of the party committee." It was designed to counteract the kind of managers who "disregard criticism and suggestions from the masses" and who "sit behind closed doors and make up plans." This style of management was condemned as an example of "bureaucratism and subjectivism" because it ignored the creativity of the workers and damaged the relationship between the party and the masses.[119] In this light, it was clear that the shift in policy was not simply a move from individual to collective decision making at the managerial level; it also demanded a return to the mass line principle of close consultation between management and ordinary workers.

While the shift from one-man management to collective leadership was presented as a return to the Yan'an ideal of the mass line, it could never be a full return for the simple and obvious fact that circumstances were now vastly altered. Whereas in Yan'an the grassroots cadre as revolutionary "shepherd" was the direct and only link between government and masses, in the socialist state the work of the cadre was now mediated by a growing number of systematized bureaucratic practices. Everyday life for the population became increasingly regulated through the implementation of standardized wage systems, labor codes, production quotas, rationing measures, population registers, personnel dossiers, school curriculums, living spaces, and so on. In many respects this trend resembles the "governmentalization" of daily life that Foucault describes as marking the shift from pastoral power to bio-power in Europe.[120]

Nevertheless, the return to an emphasis on collective leadership and the mass line ideals of Yan'an, along with the continued reliance on the cellular-like *danwei* system of organization ensured that the governmentalisation of life in socialist China remained dependent on the pastoral-style interventions of the grassroots cadre. The Maoist developmental model that reemerged with the rejection of Soviet one-man management placed even greater reliance on the cadre—he or she was expected to mobilize the masses both for production and for participation in a whole series of political campaigns that lasted until Mao's death. Regardless of the type of unit we examine—be it urban factory, bureau, or school—we find the cadre working closely among their *danwei* members ("flock") in the mobilizational manner perfected during the Yan'an period.[121] In this way, the form of bio-power that developed in the PRC maintained a closer link to its pastoral origins than was the case in the modern West.[122]

The basic cellular structure of the *danwei* system helped to ensure the continued importance of pastoral power within urban socialist governance. Every *danwei* was staffed by a set number of cadres who were responsible for organizing and coordinating its various functions as well as mobilizing its members for production and political campaigns.[123] The grassroots cadre, then, had responsibility for the economic, political, moral, and social life of the people within his or her unit. Moreover, since the *danwei* system was rapidly institutionalized as the basic unit of urban governance, the pastoral techniques that characterized its internal logic emerged as increasingly standardized governmental practices.

I should admit at this point that the pastoral analysis I develop here does not accord with received scholarly wisdom on the nature of grassroots governance in China. While totalitarian models were influential in earlier periods, since the 1970s behaviorist, functionalist, and structuralist modes of analysis have become more dominant.[124] Out of this work a fairly widespread consensus appears to have emerged in which cadre/worker relations are characterized as "clientalist."[125] According to this model, the fact that the cadre controls access to numerous "life chances" (reward, punishment, promotion, party membership, housing, etc.) within the *danwei* implies that he or she becomes a powerful "patron" to which the "client" population must defer in order to access benefits. There is much evidence to support this approach, especially in relation to the privileges afforded activists and "model workers," and it seems clear that as the Maoist vision faded, instrumentalist uses of power and connections (*guanxi*) became ever more prevalent within the *danwei* system.[126]

Other commentators have challenged the clientalist paradigm, pointing out that the *danwei* system also gave rise to forms of power that tended to undermine the authority of the cadre.[127] For the most part, cadres did not have the power to dismiss or expel members of the *danwei*; moreover, they depended on the cooperation of the members in order to meet the production targets set by their superiors. Under these conditions, the cadre had to be very careful to maintain a good working relationship with those under his or her charge. In this light, the cadre's use of discretionary power over resources, assignments, and so on was constrained by the need to foster harmony within the group. This point is given further weight by the fact that when reformers came to critique the existing system in the mid-1980s, they singled out the weakness of management for special emphasis. So far as the reformers were concerned, the *danwei* system undermined effective management of production—their conclusion was that the cadre/manager needed *more*, not less power.[128]

The pastoral model I have adopted avoids the need to choose between the competing analyses sketched above. It seems counterproductive to take sides on whether the role of the cadre is primarily authoritarian and coercive or primarily constrained and submissive. Rather I want to suggest that the role demanded aspects of both modes and much more besides. The clientalist model is grounded in an instrumentalist view of relations within the *danwei* and thereby elides many other aspects of the cadre's role. If at times the cadre coerced workers to meet production targets, or to participate in political campaigns, he or she was also expected to nurture, to guide, and to teach—to lead the "flock" toward "salvation" through production. In addition, as explained earlier, the cadres were themselves subject to rigorous party discipline, including the frequent practices of criticism and self-criticism. It should never be forgotten that in the main it was cadres who were targeted in political campaigns. If the cadre had to guide, foster, and discipline the *danwei*, he or she also had to maintain the tightest discipline over him- or herself. Taking into account all of these factors, it seems to me that the pastor/flock analogy is more appropriate than the patron/client analogy.

While I argue that the pastoral model best illuminates the nature of power relations within the cellular structure of Maoist China, it was by no means the only form of power that operated under the socialist system. I have already alluded to the range of bureaucratic and institutional practices (household register, wage system, etc.) which had emerged as strategies of governance during the 1950s. Some of these practices could be subsumed by or could even strengthen the dominant pastoral relations of power. Other practices, however, especially those associated with an expanding central bu-reaucracy, came to undermine and challenge the prevailing relations of power and the role of the cadre. The demise of "one-man-management" by no means meant the end of the conflict between the mass line and central-ized bureaucratic power. The critique of Soviet methods of industrial man-agement was only the first in a whole series of political campaigns promoted by Mao, virtually until his death, which aimed to counter bureaucratic ten-dencies in order to sustain a revolutionary form of governance.

Conclusion

Despite the polemic that emerged against the Soviet model from the mid-1950s, it is clear that Soviet practices had an enormous influence on the so-cialist transition in urban China. The work of many scholars attests to this point. Andrew Walder's study of factory labor regimes and Deborah Kaple's analysis of management texts are but two of the better-known examples from this field. Broader examinations on the nature of socialism also suggest a common heritage among the states of "actually existing" socialism. Kather-ine Verdery, for example, draws out the similarities in many practices: the emphasis on production over consumption, the highly bureaucratic regimes of central planning, the role of the party cadre, the techniques of surveil-lance, the critical function of the personnel dossier, the scarcity of goods, and the strategies adopted by workers to subvert the cult of labor.[129] While the Chinese *danwei* shared much of this heritage, however, it was something more than just another socialist workplace. The socialist "sciences" of econ-omy and population were layered upon the pastoral methods from Yan'an and urban traditions of collectivist-oriented labor organization. It was the subtle and distinctive combination of these influences that created the *dan-wei* system of socialist China.

The practices I describe in this chapter built upon earlier formations to bring about a decisive shift in the degree of systematization, normalization, and calculation that came to inscribe the lives of urban workers within their workplace. The increasing attachment of the worker to the workplace after 1949 was not simply a natural extension of "traditional" Chinese tendencies to valorize the collective over the individual, nor was it due solely to a so-cialist privileging of labor productivity and the site of labor. While both of these factors contributed to the emergence of the *danwei* system, it was the juxtaposition of a whole series of everyday governmental practices within the confines of the *danwei* that provided the grid upon which a workplace-based collective identity was formed.

Before the CCP took control of the cities, identity in urban China was already tied to the workplace, through the guilds, gangs, and corporations of the late imperial and Republican periods. While retaining and building on certain aspects of presocialist practice, governmental strategies introduced by the Communists recast and transformed the role of the workplace and its relationship with the worker in many significant ways. Under socialism, identity was articulated in terms of class rather than through native place or lineage ties; thus it was the act of labor itself that determined subject identity. The basis of this premise, the direct conceptual link between economic activity and sociopolitical identity, ensured that the CCP placed great emphasis on the organization of labor in urban China. The practices discussed in this chapter show how the link between sociopolitical aims and the imperatives of economic development were achieved in the early years of socialist rule.

Two of the most important strategies adopted by CCP policy makers in urban China were the provision of a social guarantee, *baoxialai*, and workplace mobilization, *zuzhiqilai*. *Baoxialai* ensured the urban worker was guaranteed a lifetime means of material support, while *zuzhiqilai* sought to align the worker with CCP policy and ideology. Trade union organizations supported these strategies, acting primarily as welfare agencies and "schools of communism" within each *danwei*. The role of the *danwei* as principal source of material support for workers was strengthened by a range of policies associated with central planning—investment strategies, unified job assignment, unified distribution of grain and other necessities, the *hukou* household register, and the personnel dossier all functioned to focus economic activity within the *danwei*. Through these practices, workers were defined—both in the mobilization of their productive capacities and in the fulfillment of their material wants—as members of the *danwei*. But this is only part of the story, for the *danwei* was also underpinned by a distinctive spatial order that further bolstered the regulation of subjects and the practices of socialist governance. The emergence of *danwei* spatial forms and their implication for urban governance are the subjects of Chapter 6.

CHAPTER 6

Danwei *Space*

A revolution that does not produce a new space has not realized its full potential; indeed it has failed in that it has not changed life itself, but has merely
changed ideological superstructures, institutions or political apparatuses. A social transformation, to be truly revolutionary in character, must manifest a creative capacity in its effects on daily life, on language and on space.

Henri Lefebvre, 1974[1]

In the very last pages of his landmark work, *The Production of Space*, Henri
Lefebvre contrasts Soviet and Chinese approaches to space. The Soviet
model, he suggests, is an intensified version of capitalism and leads to the
concentration of resources at a small number of production "strong points,"
while the periphery regions are left to stagnate and fall ever further behind.
The Chinese approach, in contrast, "testifies to a real concern to draw the
people and space in its entirety into the process of building a different society."[2] This is achieved through a focus on the multitude of small-scale production units—industrial and agricultural—instead of on a few privileged
centers, and involves "not only the production of wealth and economic
growth but also the development and enrichment of social relationships."
The "Chinese road to socialism" is clearly more revolutionary, argues Lefebvre, because it seeks to eliminate uneven spatial development and because it
"will not result in the elevation of either the state or a political formation or
party above society."[3]

Like many left-wing commentators in the 1960s and 1970s, Lefebvre
somewhat overestimated the achievements and the potential of the "Chinese
road to socialism." Nevertheless, he was absolutely correct in highlighting
the differences between Soviet and Chinese spatial practices. For despite the
close contact between the two socialist states and the extensive technical

support provided by the Soviets to the Chinese—including in the fields of architecture and urban planning—it was obvious long before the split in 1960 that China was creating a distinctly different form of socialist space centered on the grassroots production unit.

In the spirit of the radical Soviet architects of the 1920s, Chinese architects and planners came to see socialist construction as an opportunity for reconfiguring social life through intervention in spatial forms. But, whereas their Soviet predecessors had been forced to bow to Stalin's narrowly deterministic and nationalistic interpretation of socialism, the more radical, antibureaucratic, and utopian bent of Maoism allowed Chinese architects and planners greater scope to develop and realize their plans for revolutionary spaces. The period of the transition to socialism (1953–56) and the collectivization leading up to the Great Leap Forward (1956–58) were the high points of this push for a spatial realization of socialism.

Many grandiose public buildings appeared during these years, especially as a result of the Great Leap Forward.[4] It was these buildings—railway stations, revolutionary museums, national and provincial meeting halls, sports stadiums, and the like—which provided the most obvious evidence of the scope of socialist construction. Yet, despite appearances, it was actually the mundane and ubiquitous *danwei*—the school, the hospital, the government bureau, and above all, the factory—that accounted for the vast majority of new urban construction. The *danwei*, which had already become the basic unit of urban social organization, was, through the process of socialist construction, to rapidly become the basic unit of urban spatial organization as well. As Yang Dongping and other commentators have observed, this factor was to bestow a unique character upon the cities of socialist China.[5] The Chinese city was to develop more as a collection of self-contained and spatially defined communities than as an integrated urban network.

The predominant urban spatial form that emerged out of the socialist construction drive of the 1950s was the *danwei* compound, invariably an enclosed space marked out by a high surrounding wall. This enclosed form brings to mind the walled family compounds that constituted the dominant spatial form of traditional China. Although the traditional family and the *danwei* clearly belong to vastly different social orders, the compound wall operates in both architectural formations as a marker of social space. In traditional China, the wall defined the realm of the Confucian family and the space within which the family patriarch ruled supreme. In socialist China, the wall marks the realm of the collective "production unit" and the space within which the *danwei* reigns. The predominance of walled spaces within socialist China, then, is not indicative of a certain cultural closure or xenophobia as some have argued,[6] but rather shows the way in which modern social formations have redeployed an old architectural technique. The wall operates as a positive technology for the production and bolstering of collective forms of social relationships and is therefore open to a broad range of appropriations. In this respect, it is the spaces produced by the walls, rather than the walls themselves, that are of primary analytical significance.

The socialist *danwei* compound borrowed more from the traditional family compound than just the enclosing wall. As I will illustrate in this chapter, *danwei* space (in its archetypal form), like the Confucian family home, was arranged according to a highly symbolic order. But whereas Confucian spaces were encoded to represent and reproduce the clearly defined hierarchical social relationships that underpinned the Confucian moral order, *danwei* space was designed to represent the centrality of collective labor and egalitarian social relationships that exemplified the socialist ideal.

While traditional spatial practices informed certain formal aspects of *danwei* space, other aspects of the new spatial order derived from utopian socialist traditions that had developed in Europe. Chinese socialist architects and planners borrowed substantially from this radical European tradition, particularly in attempting to bring about a synthesis, within *danwei* space, between the technical/functional and the symbolic. That is to say, in designing socialist spaces, they aimed to construct environments that promoted both productivity—through the application of modern technology—and appropriate modes of proletarian social interaction.

In this chapter I explore the ways in which various spatial influences converged within the design and operation of the socialist *danwei*. However, in order to chart the emergence of *danwei* space, it is first necessary to document how government policy contributed to the production of a particular spatial practice. I begin by providing an account of the debates, controversies, and political campaigns centered on issues such as conservation, waste, architectural style, and standardization and how these contributed to the emergence of a clearly defined set of spatial forms and practices synonymous with the *danwei* system. Finally, I will take up the spatial question more directly by analyzing a range of *danwei* plans and blueprints. In bringing together these diverse strands, my intention is not simply to describe the *danwei* as a spatial archetype, but rather to explore the way in which spatial forms bolster and reproduce social relationships. Specifically, I will argue that the spatial formation of the *danwei* has been crucial in the production and reproduction of a particular mode of collective subjectivity.

The Limits of Socialist Urban Planning

It is by no means inevitable that a transformation in social, economic, and political relations will result in an immediate reconfiguration of social space; after all, the reconstruction of space is a costly undertaking. It is far more likely, rather, that a new regime will adapt existing spaces to its own uses. In postrevolutionary Russia, for example, the severe housing shortage was solved in part by expropriating the homes and apartments of the wealthy and partitioning them into tiny apartments for workers and their families.[7] Given the budgetary situation in post-1949 China, it was inevitable that similar kinds of spatial appropriations were practiced. On "liberating" the cities, PLA and CCP units took up residence wherever they could find space, in many cases taking over the traditional-style compounds that had housed the various organs of GMD government.[8] The decision for CCP senior leadership to take up residence in Zhongnanhai, former residential and recreational compound of the imperial family, constituted an exemplary case of this phenomenon.

The reuse of existing spatial forms, however, could only go so far, and it wasn't long before economic construction began to transform the urban environment. The massive construction project set out in the First Five-Year Plan (FFYP) and launched in the mid-1950s called for the development of hundreds of new industrial plants, the majority of which were to be constructed in and around the existing major urban centers. This resulted in the dramatic expansion of cities and the emergence of new forms of urban space. It is out of this process that the *danwei* compound came to dominate urban spatial organization.

The most characteristic feature of socialist construction in the PRC, as in the Soviet Union, was the degree to which it was coordinated and planned through central government agencies. While the primary focus of central planning was the rational deployment of economic resources, the principles of planning were extended into all areas of governmental activity. With the rapid expansion of urban territory that resulted from the socialist construction drive, it was inevitable that rationales of planning be applied to the spatial ordering of the newly emerging urban environment. It was in this context that theories and strategies of urban planning, which had emerged over a century of practice in the West and over three decades in the USSR (as described in Chapter 4), were deployed and adapted to the cause of socialist construction in China.

In urban planning, as in other areas of governmental strategy, it was the Soviet Union to whom the Chinese turned for initial guidance. The first group of Soviet urban planning advisers arrived in Beijing as early as September 1949 to oversee the development of plans for the socialist transformation of the capital and other major urban centers.[9] However, it was not until 1953, with the shift from renewal and consolidation to full-scale economic construction, that a draft plan for the urban development of Beijing was put forward. It is worth examining the debates that emerged around the planning of Beijing, as their outcome was instrumental in establishing the principles for further urban development.

The 1953 plan emphasized that Beijing should not only become a political, economic, and cultural center, but should also become a major base for industry, technology, and science.[10] In order to bring about this kind of transformation, the nature of the city itself had to undergo radical change. While the plan acknowledged that certain positive features of the ancient city fabric could be retained and preserved, it also called for the destruction of those aspects of the old city structure that limited and constrained development. Through elimination of the outdated and outmoded, the old way of urban life was to be effaced as the new authorities aimed at "turning the capital into a socialist city suited to a collectivized lifestyle."[11] However, it was around the issue of what to retain and what to demolish of the old city that a major debate emerged.

This debate was prompted in the first instance by a group of architects, led by Liang Sicheng,[12] who argued that the old walled city of Beijing should be preserved for its historical and architectural significance.[13] While they were keen to save the heritage of the ancient capital, Liang and his supporters did not oppose modernization and industrial progress per se. Rather, they argued that new development should occur on the land outside and adjacent to the walls of the old city. In this vein, they suggested that the needs of the new government be met by constructing a new administrative center immediately outside the western walls of the city.[14]

On the other side of the debate was a group led by the Soviet advisers who argued that for reasons of time and economy, government administrative headquarters should be established within the old city walls through the utilization and, where necessary, the renovation and rebuilding of existing structures.[15] For this group, preservation of an ancient architectural heritage was of secondary consideration to the immediate needs of the new regime. Although the construction of a wholly new and modern administrative center would no doubt have been preferable, they believed such an endeavor to be outside of the financial means available at the time. After some debate, CCP leadership accepted the advice of the Soviet experts.[16] In this way it was determined that the ancient spatial grid of the capital was to be adapted to the requirements of the new socialist regime.

While this decision may have seemed inevitable given the circumstances, it was of great symbolic significance for the future development of Chinese cities and is therefore worthy of analysis. The dispute between Liang's group and the Soviet group has generally been portrayed as purely a debate over preservation. In recent accounts, Liang tends to be valorized as a kind of lone defender of ancient Beijing, struggling against the philistines of the CCP who were intent on transforming the imperial capital into a Stalinist factory town.[17] In polarizing the debate in this manner, however, such readings miss the deeper layers of significance inherent within the dispute. Liang and his supporters did not propose that Old Beijing serve as the new capital, but rather that a new city be built beside the old to serve the requirements of a new and fully modernized industrial state. The key point to their proposal was not their call for the preservation of Old Beijing; instead it was the notion of establishing a clear demarcation between the old and the new. In this respect the Liang group were architectural purists rather than classicists. They saw value in both ancient and modern urban forms but sought to keep the two separate so as to maintain the character and integrity of each.[18]

The decision to utilize and modify the old city to the needs of the new regime was not, therefore, simply the result of a reassertion of CCP power at the behest of Mao, nor was it the triumph of socialist modernization over bourgeois classicism. Rather it was a victory of pragmatism over utopian architectural purism. This decision was crucial because it implied that the new regime would be constructed on the bones of the old. No doubt this resulted in the erasure of much of the past, yet it also ensured that important spatial memories of the past would be imprinted upon the architecture of the new. It is within the interstices of this layering of new upon old that the *danwei* compound emerges; for while the *danwei* was in many respects a new spatial form that grew out of the massive industrial construction program, it also bore the birthmarks of a traditional sociospatial heritage.

Despite rejecting the concept of a new administrative center for Beijing, planning authorities remained committed to the principle of urban planning and proceeded with the development of a coordinated plan for the city. This plan, and others like it, which were drawn up for all major cities, leaned heavily upon the experience and knowledge of the Soviet urban experts. Under the planning structures set down by the central government, all major urban centers were required to establish organs to oversee the design of comprehensive plans for future urban development.[19] In September 1952 the first national conference on urban construction was held. As well as formalizing the relevant administrative organizations, this conference set down the guiding principles for urban development. "To appropriately meet the needs of large-scale economic construction, urban construction must proceed according to the long-term plans of the state. . . . New construction and rebuilding should be carried out step by step in a planned manner; we must strengthen planning and design work and strengthen unified leadership, and we must stop acting blindly."[20] In March 1953 the Bureau of Urban Construction within the Ministry of Building and Engineering established the Department of Urban Planning (*chengshi guihuachu*) to put these principles into practice. Soviet experts were invited to lead the design work, and numerous graduates and planning personnel were recruited to begin the vast systematic design work required by the urban construction drive of the FFYP.[21] Based on advice from the Soviet experts, the Urban Planning Department set out to delimit the range of interventions appropriate to the work of urban planners. At the macro level planners were to determine the nature, future population, and developmental strategy for each city and would also decide upon land usage and the division of cities into districts and zones. On a more practical level, they would be responsible for developing road and transportation systems and for fixing the location of parks, city centers, town squares, train stations, ports, airports, and so on. The planning brief naturally covered the provision of urban infrastructure including water supply, sewerage, flood control, power supply, transport and communication infrastructure, as well as systems for civil defense, emergency services, and environmental protection. In addition, planners would be expected to master strategies for rehabilitating old city districts and preserving historical and cultural monuments.[22]

Based upon this comprehensive listing it is clear that urban planning authorities saw their role in very broad terms. They were to oversee planning for every conceivable aspect of the urban environment and even take control over management and supervision of the construction industry. Despite these grandiose intentions, however, the actual effect of urban planning intervention on the city environment was constrained by a number of factors. First, planning objectives were subject to financial limitations. It was one thing to develop comprehensive plans, but quite another matter to implement them. As I demonstrate in the previous chapter, funding for industrial development tended to be organized on a project-by-project basis, and infrastructural investment in areas such as housing, roads, and power, was tied to each individual project rather than channeled through a general urban development fund. This was primarily due to a shortage of funds and the need to prioritize key projects. Hence, while individual industrial and institutional *danwei* were provided with a direct source of central funding for their various requirements, city governments were starved of funds for investment in broader urban infrastructure. In this way many state-owned *danwei* became virtually independent of the city in which they were situated.[23]

This phenomenon reflected the overall governmental organizational model established by the CCP, which was known colloquially as the "strips and chunks structure" (*tiao-kuai jiegou*).[24] The "strips" (or "branches") are the administrative hierarchies established by central government ministries and bureaus with state-owned *danwei* at the lowest end, while the "chunks" (or "areas") represent the territorial domains of regional, city, and district governments. Under this system, all centrally funded construction projects came under the jurisdiction and control of the relevant central ministry or bureau ("strip") rather than under the local city authorities ("chunk").[25] As a result, city-level government often had no control over, and very little input into, the development of large-scale industrial and institutional *danwei* within their city. In some cases the city mayor could even have a lower administrative rank than the manager of a large state-owned enterprise located within the city. Because of this system, it was always very difficult for city authorities to maintain the integrity of an overall city plan.

Finally, the intervention of radical political campaigns contributed significantly to the failure of the urban plans. The first major political intervention into the arena of urban planning and construction began in late 1954, when Premier Zhou Enlai publicly criticized the construction industry for "wasting the limited resources of the state."[26] Through 1955 this campaign gained momentum as it targeted a number of key figures accused of adhering to extravagant standards in architecture, building, and urban planning. While much of the debate centered on questions of architectural style,[27] there was also criticism of norms and standards set by the Soviet advisers in the areas of housing and urban planning. Critics argued that while these standards may have been suited to the Soviet Union, they were too high for China given its inferior economic circumstances. The antirightist campaign that closely followed in 1957 heightened the attacks that had begun during the antiwaste campaign, ensuring that most supporters of earlier urban planning standards were removed or demoted from positions of influence.[28]

The campaign against waste also resulted in a further reduction in the funds made available for general urban infrastructure development. The only spending that could be justified in this new climate of frugality was for infrastructure that directly served the needs of key industrial enterprises. With the end of the FFYP and the accelerated push toward collectivization and increased productivity—soon to become the Great Leap Forward—industry and production were increasingly prioritized over other needs. As a result, less and less funding was made available for general community and social infrastructure. Under these conditions, it was the basic-level production unit itself—the *danwei*—which became almost totally responsible for providing the social infrastructure required by most urban residents.

Following the disastrous Great Leap Forward, many economic and developmental policies that had been overturned by that movement were revived during the first half of the 1960s. Policies relating to urban planning, however, were not reinstated. Instead, at the National Planning Congress held in November 1960, authorities decided that because of the dire financial situation "no urban planning would be undertaken for three years."[29] After three years, some efforts were made to reestablish urban planning organs. However, the launch of the Cultural Revolution in 1966 put a sudden and dramatic halt to these developments. From the second half of 1966 until the fall of Lin Biao in 1971, according to the authors of *Urban Construction in Contemporary China*, urban development was brought to a virtual standstill. The central bureaus of urban planning, construction, and design were closed down, as were the planning offices at provincial and city levels.[30] After 1971 the administrative structures of urban planning were gradually reestablished and staff returned to their former positions. However, given the continued policy domination by the Cultural Revolution leftists, urban planning was still considered to be a field tainted by bourgeois ideology and therefore remained largely starved of funding. It was not until the beginning of economic reform in the late 1970s that urban planning and its various concerns with the coordinated development and management of urban infrastructure regained the support of central authorities.[31]

As we have seen, the failure of urban planning during the Maoist period was due to a combination of funding shortages, deliberate policy strategy—namely, privileging key individual projects over general urban development—and the intervention of far-reaching political campaigns. Given the high expectations for a rational and coordinated approach to urban development that had accompanied the advent of socialism and central planning, it seems somewhat paradoxical that the outcomes were largely piecemeal, uneven, and uncoordinated. On closer analysis, however, this outcome is probably not so surprising. From the previous chapter it is clear that the *danwei* was delegated responsibility in a number of vital areas of social, economic, and political organization (including areas such as the provision of welfare, material support and housing, management of trade unions, employment and worker education, etc.). Given the role played by the *danwei* within the overall strategies of urban governance, it is less surprising that it would also become the locus of urban infrastructure. The fate of urban planning in Maoist China, then, helped to bolster the significance of the *danwei* among the inhabitants of the socialist city.

Standardization of Spatial Forms

Although attempts to establish a unified and centralized urban planning regime suffered major setbacks and remained largely unfulfilled, urban construction did not proceed in an entirely ad hoc fashion. While the management of much urban space was devolved to the *danwei*, there were some aspects of spatial planning where it proved possible to develop a high degree of centralization and uniformity. One important area in which this was achieved was in architectural design. Because it operated at a more theoretical and abstract level among a relatively small number of technical experts, architectural design was well suited to the logic of central planning, and a high degree of standardization was achieved in the area of design codes and construction regulations. Indeed, this factor accounts for the considerable uniformity in appearance and spatial configuration found among *danwei* of different types and different regional locations. It was precisely because the majority of urban *danwei*, particularly large-scale *danwei*, were established through direct central government funding that the central authorities could maintain tight control over norms for design and construction. The development of national blueprints based on standardized architectural forms was of great significance to the formation of a distinctive *danwei* spatial order and to the types of social practices that were produced there.

The notion that spatial forms could and should be standardized was by no means new. As early as the beginning of the nineteenth century, the so-called utopian socialists, Owen and Fourier, had proposed standardized spatial forms as the basis for their ideal communities. But it was the rapid development in building techniques and the industrialization of production methods around the turn of the twentieth century which provided architects with an efficient means of applying methods of standardization to the design and construction of living spaces.[32] Although the rise of Stalinism in the Soviet Union saw the repudiation of the modernist international style in favor of a neoclassical nationalist style, the principle of standardization in design and construction was retained. This became particularly evident with the advent of a massive urban reconstruction drive after the Second World War, when Soviet authorities ordered that all urban construction must follow authorized designs. To facilitate this regulation, the Soviet Academy of Architecture was commissioned to draft a series of standardized plans to be utilized in the construction of housing and public buildings throughout the nation.[33]

In 1953, when the CCP was ready to launch its own socialist construction drive, Soviet experts were on hand to pass on the results of many years' experience in design standardization. The Soviet design experts dispatched to China arrived with a full set of recently completed design standards and specifications covering every facet of urban construction, from designs for industrial plants and power stations to standardized plans for housing units, workers' clubs, and exhibition halls.[34] These Soviet blueprints, and the design principles that lay behind them, were to form the foundation for the development of design practice in China.

The first national design organization established in the PRC was the Central Design Company (*zhongyang sheji gongsi*), set up in May 1952. The decision to establish this company was made by the Central Committee in the wake of the *sanfan* (three antis) campaign, which saw the central government strengthen its control in many areas of government. In February 1953 the Central Design Company was shifted into the new Ministry of Construction and Engineering, which had been founded in the preceding August, and its name changed to the Design Institute of the Ministry of Construction and Engineering (*jianzhu gongchengbu shejiyuan*).[35] Subsequently, with the establishment of subordinate design offices in many provincial capitals and other major cities,[36] the name of the central organ was changed to the General Design Office (*sheji zongju*).[37]

When planning and design work for the FFYP began, the various design offices operated under the guidance of Soviet advisers. Twenty-one Soviet experts were invited to work in the General Design Office, where they not only led the design work but also played a major role in the training of Chinese industrial designers and architects. Other Chinese trainees were sent for "on-the-job" training under Soviet technicians attached to the 156 industrial plants then under construction with Soviet aid.[38] In this way, a corps of young Chinese architects, engineers, and industrial designers were trained in all aspects of Soviet-style socialist construction. Through this training process, they not only learned modern technical and scientific method, but were also schooled in the principles of design deemed appropriate by the Soviet Union for the spatial realization of socialism.

Centralization and standardization of the design processes were favored because they allowed for the coordinated and efficient deployment of technical resources. Centralization meant that design expertise could be concentrated and design tasks coordinated so as to achieve finished designs as efficiently as possible. The advantage of standardization was that it ensured that identical design standards could be applied throughout the nation. Thus, once designs had been formulated centrally, they could simply be distributed around the country wherever required. In this way, one basic design could be utilized in the construction of dozens of factories, offices, or schools. For example, the FFYP called for the construction of thirty-one tractor factories, each to be located at key points throughout the country to serve regional agriculture. All were built according to the same standard design developed by the General Design Office in consultation with the First Ministry of Machinery.[39]

Another prominent example of standardization during this period was in the design of institutes of higher education. Working with the various central and local design offices, the Ministry of Education coordinated designs for a large number of new universities and colleges. As early as 1956 the ministry published a complete set of design standards to guide construction in this sector.[40] The many campuses that line Xueyuan Road in the northern suburbs of Beijing provide excellent examples of the high degree of standardization in architectural and spatial design that emerged during the mid-1950s.

The importance of standardization was perhaps most pronounced in the area of urban housing. Naturally there were many different types of factory and institution, and each required a certain degree of specialization in design. However, the housing that was to be built alongside the factory or institution need not be specialized and could conform to universal national standards.[41] Economy and standardization in housing design was also an area on which the Soviet Union had placed great emphasis and for which the Soviet experts could provide detailed blueprints. With the FFYP calling for the construction of 46 million square meters of housing, the potential benefits from standardizing design and systematizing the construction process were readily apparent.

The basic principles developed by the Soviet Union for the construction of urban housing centered on economy, simplicity, and the industrialization of the construction process. In practical terms, this translated to the design of simple standard housing units that could be reproduced in large numbers as rapidly as possible. Whereas, in the past, housing construction had been a small-scale, artisan-based industry reliant upon methods that had developed little over centuries, under socialism the housing industry was to become a large-scale, highly systematized industrial process based upon new developments in science and technology. In China, the advent of the FFYP saw a dramatic shift in the rationale and form of urban housing. The apparently organic and chaotic expanses of traditional single-story residential compounds were no longer seen as appropriate. Instead, they were to be superseded by large planned developments of three- or four-story housing blocks clustered in ordered formations around the rapidly emerging urban industries in which the growing number of urban workers would labor.[42] These industrial/residential estates were to be the centerpieces of the new socialist society.

From the Soviet experience in design and construction, Chinese construction authorities adapted and developed two basic forms of housing suited to mass production: the first was a simple dormitory style consisting of individual rooms opening off long corridors with shared toilet, washing, and cooking facilities; the second was apartment style—two or more rooms forming an independent residence—designed in units, or *danyuan*, consisting of a set of apartments sharing an entrance and stairwell (see Figures 6.1 and 6.3). These units could be reproduced side-by-side as many times as required for any given housing development.[43] The dormitory form was ideal for institutions such as schools, colleges, and the military, as well as for any enterprise that employed large numbers of unmarried workers. Each room in such dormitory buildings would generally house more than one person, often as many as eight to twelve students at a high school, university, or college. The apartment form was intended for the housing of family groups.

Housing design was affected considerably by the campaign against waste in the construction industry. As already mentioned, this campaign began in late 1954 in the wake of Zhou Enlai's unfavorable report to the first NPC.

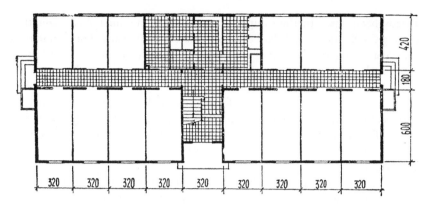

FIGURE 6.1. Floor plan for a dormitory building.
Source: Chengshi jianshe zongju guihua shejiju, "Comments on the Plans Selected by the National Planning Standards Selection Conference and Explanations of the *Danyan*," *Journal of Architecture* 2 (1956): 72.

However, Zhou's criticism was not the only origin of the reappraisal of design standards and architectural styles, for around the same time Soviet authorities themselves began to challenge some well-established practices. In
late November 1954, the Soviet government convened a national conference
of architects at which a major critique was launched against wasteful, extravagant, and overly "artistic" tendencies in design and construction. Architects were accused of promoting aesthetic concerns over those of economy,
practicality, and efficiency. Further, they were charged with having abandoned the principles of industrialization in the design and construction process.[44] This conference was one of the early signs of the shift away from Stalinism that was to be dramatically confirmed with Khrushchev's secret
speech to the Soviet Party Congress in 1956. In architecture, de-Stalinization
was to mean rejecting extravagant monumentalism that was the hallmark of
the "nationalist" style. Instead of flaunting the might of the state, Soviet architecture was henceforth to concentrate on more practical and immediate
concerns, such as addressing the urban housing crisis that had become increasing critical in the latter years of Stalin's rule.

A Chinese delegation attended the 1954 architecture congress in Moscow
and on its return recommended that a conference be convened in China to
discuss the implications. As a result, the Ministry of Construction and Engineering convened a national work conference for the design and construction industries in Beijing on 4–24 February 1955. The criticisms that had
been made at the Soviet conference reinforced many of the issues that had

already been raised by the campaign against waste in China. As a result, the Beijing conference focused on criticism of architectural and design practice, particularly targeting several established architects, including Liang Sicheng. Liang and several colleagues who had been at the forefront in the development of a Chinese "national style" to represent the new regime, were now accused of practicing "bourgeois formalism" and attempting to launch a "classical revival" in the guise of "nationalist style." In more general terms, the conference concluded that, given the state of the national economy, aesthetics could only be considered secondary to the principles of economics and utility.[45]

The attack on Liang and others focused primarily on the question of architectural style and was premised on the assumption that erroneous style was underpinned by incorrect ideology—in this case, bourgeois ideology.[46] Yet despite this overtly political focus, the antiwaste campaign also led to reappraisals of more mundane issues such as the standards adopted in design and construction. In June 1955 the CCP Central Committee issued a range of directives concerning measures to be adopted in order to reduce the costs of the construction industry. Construction costs were to be slashed in both productive and nonproductive construction projects.[47] In 1954 the government had already demanded that every project reduce its construction costs by 10 percent. The new directive called for an *additional* 15–20 percent to be taken off the construction cost. On 19 June 1955 the *People's Daily* reported that costs for construction of nonproduction-related buildings would be reduced even further. The cost per square meter for construction of offices and university classrooms was to be reduced from 100 yuan to 45–70 yuan, while that for housing was to be reduced from 90 yuan to 20–60 yuan.[48]

The demand for a dramatic reduction in costs and standards called for a thorough rethink of design criteria, particularly in the area of urban housing, which was, in terms of total construction outlay, the largest sector to be affected. A rethink of design principles was also required because of a range of problems that had emerged out of the employment of Soviet design standards within China's different social context. According to reports made in the press and also raised at the Beijing architecture conference, new housing based on Soviet standards did not meet the requirements of its occupants for three reasons. First, apartments tended to have one or two large rooms rather than a number of smaller rooms. This meant that three generations or more were often forced to sleep in the one room. There was also a lack of variety in apartment configuration to account for the varying needs of families of different size. Second, residents complained that not enough consideration had been given to providing suitable facilities for everyday needs such as cooking, rubbish disposal, and space for hanging washing and parking bicycles. Finally, the rent (based on construction costs) was too expensive for many ordinary workers.[49] On the basis of these criticisms, it was declared that the Soviet-influenced designs were "both uneconomic and impractical" and that, while they may have been "rationally designed," they could not be "rationally utilized."[50]

Chinese architects and designers, then, were confronted in 1955 with a two-pronged problem: how to design urban housing units that met the financial constraints demanded by the government and at the same time fulfilled the needs of urban residents. A partial solution was found with the decision to reduce the design standard for per capita living space by more than half—the nine square meters advocated by Soviet advisers was reduced to four square meters.[51] This new design standard naturally resulted in dramatic reductions in the size of rooms. The number of multiroom apartments was also reduced, such that according to the new standard, 70 percent of households occupied only one room and multiroom apartments accounted for only 20 percent of total room numbers.

In addition, it was determined that space could be further economized by the sharing of cooking and toilet and washing facilities among several apartments. The standard adopted for these services was two to three families per kitchen, and four to five families per toilet.[52] Finally, and most noticeably from an architectural perspective, significant economies were achieved through the abandonment of all internal and external ornamentation. Roofs that had previously been designed with traditional eaves and gables were flattened, balconies were dispensed with, and arches were eliminated.[53] The resultant buildings were severely austere in appearance and provided visual proof of the relentless shift of resources from consumption to production that marked this period. It was a physical embodiment of the slogan "production first, life later" (*xian shengchan, hou shenghuo*), which came into use at this time and reverberated for more than two decades.

Throughout 1955 and the first half of 1956, a long series of design meetings, competitions, and debates were undertaken in order to produce a full set of blueprints that reflected the new austerity standards. In 1956 those designs deemed most suitable were collected, published, and distributed to design and construction offices throughout the country.[54] In this way the new design standards and ready-made plans for most kinds of buildings were disseminated throughout the country. It fell also to the construction bureaucracy to ensure that all new construction projects met the strict requirements of the new standards (see Figure 6.2).

The move to reformulate construction standards played a significant and hitherto unexplored role in the formation of the *danwei* system. For although standardization in the built environment had been advocated consistently through the early 1950s, it was only after the antiwaste campaign of 1955 that it came to be seen as vital in political as well as in economic terms.

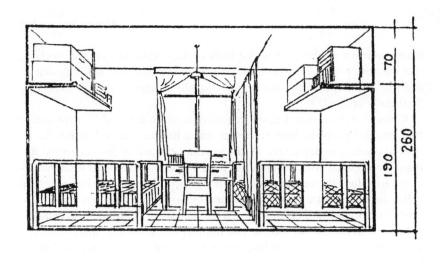

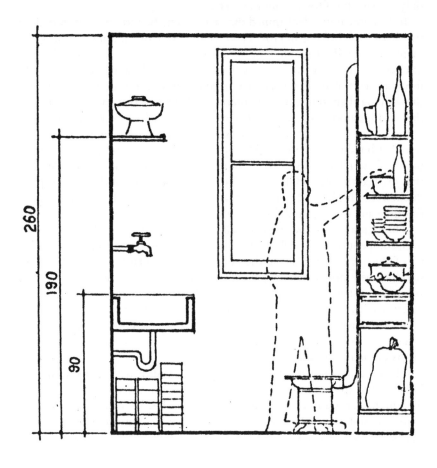

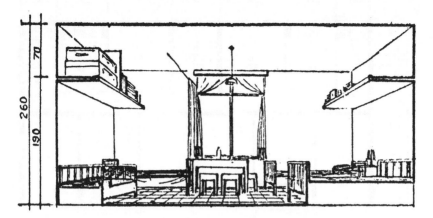

FIGURE 6.2. (*Opposite and above*): Internal layouts for standardized residential units.
Source: Ye Zugui and Ye Zhoudu, "On Further Explorations into the Design of Small-Scale Residences," *Journal of Architecture* 2 (1958): 30–31.

It was politically important because unity and standardization in architecture was seen as reflecting an overall unity in ideological stance. Politically the new standards also reflected an increasingly explicit commitment to the ideals of socialist collectivization. As noted above, criticism of design practice had not focused purely on the wasteful use of materials and inappropriate architectural styles; it had also pointed to practical problems faced by residents of the newly designed buildings. In this respect, the demands for austerity neatly dovetailed with the political push for collectivization. Smaller apartments and more public facilities not only reduced construction costs but also promoted the collectivization of daily life.

These trends in design practice brought about a crucial transformation in the nature of the basic housing unit, or *danyuan*. Initially the *danyuan* was simply a collection of independent apartments that shared an entrance and stairwell. During the mid-1950s, however, political and economic developments resulted in the *danyuan* becoming an integrated collectivized residential unit. In this process Chinese architects moved away from the purely technical emphasis of the Soviet architectural advisers to embrace a more explicitly political design ethos that was much closer in spirit to the radical Constructivist school of Soviet designers of the 1920s. From around 1956–57, the design literature began to focus much more on strategies for promoting the collectivization of daily life, and architects started to advocate "going down among the masses" as the best way to gain a better under-

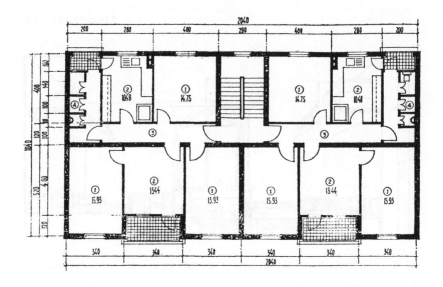

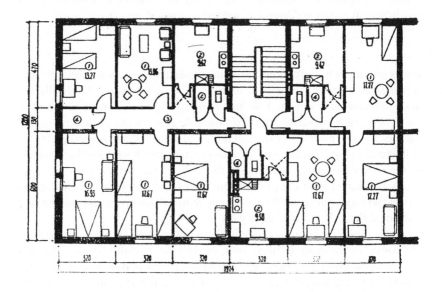

FIGURE 6.3. Apartment-style housing units—*danyuan*. The *danyuan* above is communal-style. There are two sets of facilities (kitchen, toilet, and living area), and three families share each set. The *danyuan* below consists of three apartments, each with its own facilities.

Source: Chengshi jianshe zongju guihua shejiju, "Comments on the Plans Selected by the National Planning Standards Selection Conference and Explanations of the *Danyan*," *Journal of Architecture* 2 (1956): 65, 69.

standing of the needs of the people who would use and occupy new buildings.[55] In this spirit, Chinese architects increasingly saw themselves as political activists whose spatial interventions must facilitate the transition to communism (see Figure 6.3).

It was not entirely fortuitous that the push for standardization coincided with the economic austerity drive and the political call for an increase in the speed of collectivization. Nevertheless, standardization in design, particularly in the area of urban housing, played a major role in ensuring that newly constructed urban spaces exhibited an increasingly collectivized character. A new form of social organization—the socialist collective—required an entirely new form of urban environment. Chinese architects of the 1950s were increasingly convinced that physical spatial arrangements could play a crucial role in the transition to socialism. The architectural spaces they designed in the second half of the 1950s echoed some of the ideas that had informed the "social condensers" in the early Soviet Union. The overriding objective was identical: the production of proletarian subjects.

The transformation of the *danyuan* into collectivized living space, however, was only one aspect of a much larger project, for the *danyuan* housing unit was merely one element within a larger collective entity: the *danwei*. If the shift to communism was to be successful, it required not just the collectivization of living space but also the unification of everyday life and productive labor into one collectivized whole. The arena for this radical new social formation was to be the *danwei* compound.

The Emergence of the Danwei Compound

The previous chapter outlined the ways in which numerous aspects of governmental practice contributed to the formation and expansion of the *danwei* system. In particular, strategies for the provision and management of welfare, housing, and employment ensured that the *danwei* quickly became the basic unit of social and economic life for a great majority of urban residents. At the same time, policy developments in urban management and construction resulted in the *danwei* emerging as the basic spatial unit of urban China. This trend was to further bolster the significance of the *danwei* as the key urban site for the production of collective subjectivities.

As explained previously, Chinese planning authorities adopted a "project"-style investment strategy during the FFYP in order to target limited funds as effectively as possible. This ensured that the majority of large-scale *danwei* (factories, power plants, universities, colleges, etc.) were established through direct central investment with little involvement of the city or regional authorities where the *danwei* was located. Investment for each *danwei* project included funds specifically designated for the provision of the basic daily needs of the *danwei* workforce—housing, meals, health care, education, and so on. The Luoyang tractor complex provides a good illustration of this kind of coordination. A key project under the FFYP, it entailed the construction of several factories along with a large residential development to house the new workforce:

In September 1955 work commenced in Jianxi District, Luoyang on a tractor plant, machine factory, bearing factory, and power station. Work was basically completed in July 1957, thus in only twenty-three months a group of modern factories had been constructed. At the same time in Jianxi District a new housing estate had been built consisting of 425 three- and four-story apartment buildings arranged in thirty-six blocks, with a total floor area of 857,600 square meters, providing new homes to 17,152 employees' families. . . . Eight new high schools were built, ten primary schools, eight cinemas, a cultural palace, a concert hall, three general hospitals, two general markets, and two department stores. In Jianxi a new city district of one hundred thousand people had been formed.[56]

As the authors of *Urban Construction in Contemporary China* affirm, "the striking characteristic of socialist urban industrial construction during the FFYP was the coordination of facilities for production with facilities for daily life."[57]

Despite the apparent advantages provided by the project-based development strategy, however, significant problems emerged in regard to the delineation of responsibilities between the *danwei* and the city in which it was located. Numerous disputes emerged over which side should fund particular kinds of infrastructure. By way of response to this problem, in July 1954, the State Planning Commission issued a new regulation that aimed to clearly delimit financial responsibilities in urban construction. This document, "Decision on the Division of Investment for Construction Outside of the Factory," decreed that any infrastructure which was for the sole use of a particular enterprise had to be funded by that enterprise. Items specifically listed in this decision were railway lines and freight stations, infrastructure related to the supply of electricity and heating, telephone lines, municipal works, public utilities, employee housing, welfare service infrastructure, and schools.[58] In addition, the *danwei*/enterprise, rather than the city, was deemed responsible for funding all water pipes, sewerage pipes, and associated facilities, roads, bridges, and culverts that were to be constructed "within the factory area." In the case of large-scale residential estates attached to new industrial zones, the industrial *danwei* whose workers lived in the estate were responsible for funding all necessary facilities; these included (in addition to those items of basic infrastructure mentioned above) shops, cooperatives, and hairdressers.[59]

This decision was critical in reinforcing the "strips and chunks" (*tiao-kuai*) administrative structure—namely, the separation of state-owned *danwei* from the city administration in which they were situated—and transforming this structure into a spatial as well as an organizational phenomenon. Each state-owned *danwei* thus became an island or small kingdom within the city, with almost complete control over its own spatial realm and with a source of funding independent of city authorities.[60] Moreover, because of the priorities established by the FFYP, the vast majority of construction investment went directly into these state-owned *danwei*. By comparison, funds channeled through city authorities for general urban infrastructure construction were relatively insignificant.[61]

The result of this investment policy was that state-owned *danwei* were not only financially and administratively independent of the city but also generally much better funded and thereby able to provide a higher standard of facilities and services for their employees than were available to urban residents in the collective-owned sector or who didn't belong to a *danwei*.[62] The state-owned sector of the economy grew rapidly as a result of these investment policies, and the number of workers employed in that sector (and their families) quickly became the dominant constituent of the urban population. Employees in state-owned *danwei* increased from 41.5 percent of the total urban workforce in 1952 to 61.7 percent by the end of the FFYP in 1957. This percentage continued to increase through the 1960s and early 1970s, reaching a height of 78.2 percent in 1975. These figures demonstrate that state-owned *danwei* rapidly became home to a significant majority of the Chinese urban population (see Table 6.1).

As a spatial unit, then, the *danwei* had its genesis in the project-style investment practices of the central plan. Because of this, the actual process through which the *danwei* compound came into being was rapidly standardized. Once funding was approved for the construction of a *danwei*, the relevant city or regional authorities were required to provide a suitable piece of land to accommodate the new development. As soon as this allocation was made, the land became the sole domain of the new *danwei*.[63] The first task facing the leaders of the new *danwei* was its construction. In the initial phases of construction, *danwei* officials had to negotiate and coordinate with city authorities in order to have the basic services connected to the site. The construction tasks undertaken at this stage were known as the "three connections and one leveling" (*santong yiping*)—namely, the connection of roads, water, and electricity and the leveling of the site in preparation for building.[64] According to standard procedures, the first buildings to be constructed in a new *danwei* were those that were to house *danwei* staff. Initially, however, it was the construction workers who occupied these quarters, living on-site during the building period.

There were several reasons for this practice: it was convenient for workers to be close to the work site, many construction workers had no perma-

TABLE 6.1

The Development of China's Urban Workforce According to Sector

	Total Urban Workforce (millions)	State-Owned Danwei (%)	Urban Collective and Other Danwei (%)	Individual Laborers (%)	Unemployed (%)
1952	28.626	41.5	14.5	30.8	13.2
1957	34.054	61.7	29.3	3.1	5.9
1962	45.37	72.9	22.3	4.8	—
1965	51.36	72.8	23.9	3.3	—
1970	63.12	75.9	22.6	1.5	—
1975	82.22	78.2	21.6	0.2	—
1978	100.44	74.2	20.4	0.1	5.3
1992	159.903	68.1	24.4	5.2	2.3
1999	185.48	46.2	24.7	13.0	3.1

SOURCE: Adapted from Guojia tongjiju shehui tongjisi, ed., *Statistical Material on Chinese Society* (Beijing: China Statistics Press, 1994), 43–46. Figures for "total urban workforce" were calculated by adding the "total urban employees" (p. 45) to "total urban unemployed" (p. 43). The percentage figures by sector were calculated by dividing "total number of employees" in each sector (p. 46) by the "total urban workforce." The figures for 1999 derive from Guojia tongjiju, ed., *China Statistical Yearbook 2000* (Beijing: China Statistics Press, 2000).

nent housing themselves, and, perhaps most significantly in administrative and organizational terms, a construction team was also a *danwei*, so, like the members of any *danwei*, construction workers received a range of benefits through their workplace.[65] The only major difference between construction teams and other *danwei* was that the former periodically changed location, as they moved from one construction project to another.[66] From its very inception, then, a new *danwei* became a living community in which productive labor was closely wedded to everyday collective life.

The Spatial Form of the Danwei

The most prominent architectural feature of the *danwei* is undoubtedly the high enclosing wall that surrounds it. This wall marks out the realm of the *danwei*; within this territory the rules and norms of the *danwei* are supreme. Like the walls of China's past, the *danwei* wall performs a positive function through marking out social space and defining the realms within which particular regimes of government and social interaction hold sway. The *danwei* wall signifies, in clear unambiguous terms, the independence of the *danwei* from the surrounding city, while at the same time it *produces* the space within which a unique form of collectivized social life and socialist government operates.

Some commentators have suggested that the *danwei* compound derives from military practice. Yichun Xie and Frank Costa, for example, in their discussion of urban planning in socialist China, characterize the *danwei* spatial form as embodying a "socialist 'military camp' city pattern."[67] This view has some merit, since the term *danwei* itself was first coined in military usage and, as I have shown, the socialist *danwei* system had its genesis primarily during the Yan'an period, when day-to-day social, economic, and political life was inextricably tied to the military. However, in my view the "military camp" analogy is too simplistic and limiting to encompass the complex nature of the *danwei* and its spatial form. To begin with, this analogy implies that the *danwei* wall is primarily defensive, designed to keep an outside enemy at bay. While the wall could be utilized to exclude outsiders—some military, security, and party *danwei* compounds were guarded and entry strictly monitored—its more significant function, in my view, is to produce a discrete spatial realm. We should focus our attention on what happens within the walls, not on the walls themselves. As I argue in Chapter 2, Chinese walls should be seen primarily as productive rather than negative technologies of sociospatial organization.

Second, the "military camp" analogy implies a degree of discipline, regimentation, and single-minded purpose that simply did not pertain within most *danwei*.[68] While *danwei* were primarily devoted to specific productive, educative, or administrative purposes, the fact that they were also responsible for the provision of welfare and services and were the key locations of everyday life meant that as a social organization the *danwei* was far more complex and varied than the "military camp" analogy would suggest. Finally, it must be pointed out that in political terms the central role of the *danwei* was to promote a collectivized form of socialist life, rather than the rigidly hierarchical mode of organization implied by the "military camp" analogy. This view is borne out by a detailed examination of the specific spatial characteristics of the *danwei*.

I have already outlined the significance of standardization in the construction industry, especially after the antiwaste campaign of 1954–55. In the previous discussion, however, I focused primarily on the standardization of designs for individual buildings, particularly emphasizing developments in relation to the design of housing and industrial plant. It is important to note that the principles of standardization were also applied to the arrangement of building ensembles. Architects and urban planners devoted considerable time and effort to determining the spatial relationships between buildings within *danwei* compounds. Both the design blueprints from that era and the physical architectural evidence that remains from that period point to the conclusion that compound design reached a high level of standardization as early as the FFYP.[69]

At a fairly early stage of planning, two basic forms of *danwei* design emerged. The first form corresponded mainly with large-scale *danwei*, while a second, slightly different design form was adopted for small to medium-sized *danwei*. The largest-scale *danwei* tended to have separate residential compounds adjacent to the compound containing the industrial plants and administrative offices. Indeed, the sheer size of some of these *danwei* gave them the appearance of small cities or industrial towns, as the following description of the Wuhan Steelworks attests: "The mines, power stations, machinery factories, steel furnaces, rolling mills, subsidiary factories, and service centers of Wuhan Steelworks stretch over ten square kilometers. It is more a self-contained city than a factory. The corporation runs its own hospitals, colleges, canteens, cinemas, housing estates, and all kinds of community services for its 140,000 employees and their families."[70] In contrast to these large-scale complexes, small to medium *danwei* tended to combine workplace (factory, office, school, etc.), residential space, and services all within a single compound.[71] For example, an article published in 1956 on standards for the design of institutes of higher education included the following provisions detailing the facilities to be constructed within each campus compound and suggesting that they be grouped in four basic areas:

a. Teaching area: including classrooms, laboratories, factory for work experience, research and experiment facilities, library, meeting hall, and administration buildings.

b. Sports area: including gymnasium (or sheltered exercise area) and a large scale sports ground. Campuses may also locate basketball and volleyball courts in the teaching or dormitory areas.

c. Student dormitory area: including student dormitories, student canteens, bathhouse, and the like. Some campuses may place the unmarried staff dormitories in this area too.

d. Staff dormitory area: including various types of residence and relevant welfare facilities.[72]

Based on a sample campus design included in the article, the "relevant welfare facilities" included a medical clinic, a staff club, a staff canteen, and a kindergarten.[73] Smaller *danwei* could only provide a more rudimentary range of services for their employees—the basics usually included dormitory accommodation, canteen, medical clinic, and bathhouse.[74] Analysis of *danwei* of different sizes shows that, regardless of scale, each aimed to provide for at least the basic needs of its members within the walls of its compound. *Danwei* members would spend most of their time within this discrete space, their daily lives shaped not only by the routines and rhythms of the *danwei* but also by the spatial forms within which they circulated.

Danwei space was designed with two central aims: (1) to symbolize, and reproduce in miniature, the order of the socialist state; and (2) to promote a socialist collectivized lifestyle among its resident members. To understand how these objectives were realized in spatial form, it is necessary to examine the design blueprint of a typical *danwei* in some detail.

The arrangement of architectural elements within the compound adhered to a similar basic principle for both the larger- and smaller-scale *danwei*. As Figures 6.4 and 6.5 show, the basic design principle was to align key architectural elements along a central axis, while lesser subsidiary elements were arranged in groups on either side of the main axis. Large-scale *danwei* often had one or two additional axes situated parallel to the central axis. The purpose of this axial arrangement is clearly symbolic and derives in part from the principles of classical Chinese architecture. Traditional city plans and the designs for temple or palace complexes were always based upon an axial progression of major architectural and spatial elements.[75] Yet the symbolism informing the axiality of the socialist *danwei* is quite different from that of traditional arrangements. Whereas traditional axes were formed by a progression from elements of lesser importance to those of greater importance, symbolizing the strict hierarchical order of Confucian society,[76] the *danwei* reversed the order, placing the principal architectural feature in full view at the forefront of the axis, immediately opposite the entrance to the compound. In this way, a spatial order was established immediately around this central, architecturally dominant focal point.

Reversing the traditional axial principle in designing the socialist *danwei* reflects the influence of the monumental and triumphal architectural style of the Stalinist period in the Soviet Union.[77] It was a style that aimed to provide a clear physical embodiment to the power of socialism and the socialist state. To this end, the location of significant buildings was chosen carefully so as to enhance the symbolic effect to the greatest degree.[78] Under Stalin, the city itself became a text upon which the power of the state was writ large. In China, Stalinist-style monumentalism was utilized at certain key points within most cities. No doubt the best example of this can be found in Tiananmen Square in the heart of Beijing—the vast square flanked by the monumental Great Hall of the People to the west, the Museums of Chinese History and Revolutionary History to the east, and, since 1977, the Mao Mausoleum to the south. However, it was within the minicities of socialist China—the *danwei* compounds—that architectural monumentalism achieved its most significant everyday effect.

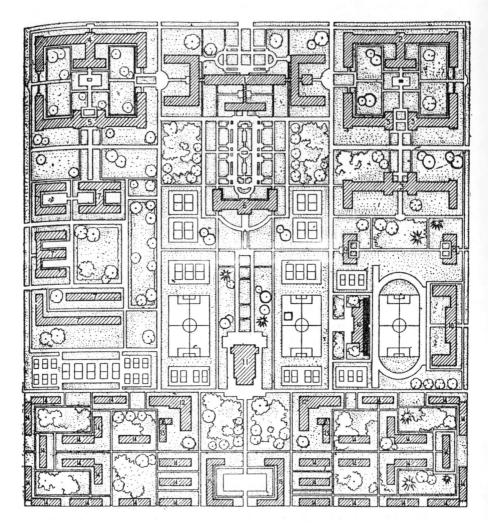

FIGURE 6.4. Plan for Xi'an University of Communications (a university *danwei*). Note the strong axiality of the design—a central vertical axis and two subsidiary side axes. The main entrance to the *danwei* is at top-center, directly in front of the main administrative building (*zhulou*).

Legend: (1) main administrative building (*zhulou*); (2, 3, 4, and 5) teaching and research buildings for various departments; (6) library; (7) work experience factory; (8) medical clinic; (9) trade union club; (10) covered drill ground; (11) the Great Hall; (12) student dining hall; (13) bathhouse; (14) student and unmarried staff dormitories (married staff reside in apartments in an adjacent residential compound); (15) welfare services.

Source: Du Erqi, "The Arrangement of Building Clusters and Individual Building Designs for Colleges of Higher Education," *Journal of Architecture* 5 (1956): 9.

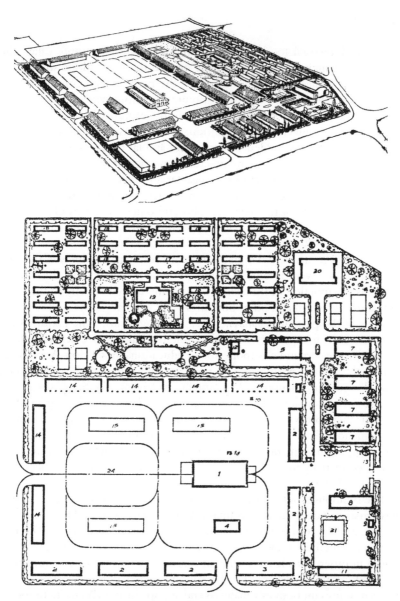

FIGURE 6.5. Aerial view (above) and plan (below) for a motorized tractor repair station in suburban Beijing.

Legend: (1) repair workshop; (2) tractor sheds; (3) combine harvester shed; (4) materials shed; (5) dining hall; (6) guardroom; (7) dormitories; (8) office; (9) toilet; (11) garage; (12) boiler room; (14) tool sheds; (15) open-air repair.

Source: Ma Haoran, "Design for an Agricultural Motorized Tractor Station in Beijing." *Journal of Architecture* 8 (1957): 47, 52.

The architectural focal building of the *danwei*, often simply called the *zhulou*, or "principal building," usually housed the main administrative offices for the *danwei*, including offices for the party branch committee and other senior *danwei* officials. Its positioning therefore symbolized the centrality of the party and its leadership role in the everyday life of *danwei*. The effect of axial arrangements in traditional China was to situate power deep behind layers of walls, hidden, impenetrable, and far removed from the ordinary subject. By contrast, the architectural language of the *danwei* spoke to a more open, populist, and—at times—egalitarian face of state power. In short, while the spatial symbolism of the *danwei* represented the centrality of party and state to the life of the *danwei*, it also embodied the ideals of Mao's famous "mass line"—namely, that leaders must live and work among the masses.

According to standard designs, the other important buildings of the *danwei* compound were arranged along the central axis behind the *zhulou*. Whereas the function of the *zhulou* was usually related directly to the party and central government, other buildings were generally associated with the business of the particular *danwei*. These buildings housed the major workshops or plants for a factory, the offices for an administrative department, or the lecture theaters and classrooms for an educational institution. As with the *zhulou*, the central positioning of these buildings imparted an important symbolic meaning, denoting the centrality of labor in the life of the *danwei* and the socialist nation. The raison d'être of the *danwei* was the organization of labor; therefore, within the *danwei* compound, daily life revolved around the demands of production—whether it be production of material goods, knowledge, or information. It is not strange to find, then, that the *danwei* was organized spatially to reflect the privileged position that socialism accorded productive labor.

The symbolism of the *danwei* compound thus embodied two interrelated ideas: first, it underscored the primacy of the socialist state and the CCP; and second, it reinforced the significance of labor to socialist practice. The former represented the leadership, guidance, and unity of purpose that were required in order to realize the aims of socialism, while the latter represented the practical means through which a socialist society was to be achieved. Labor was important both as a material and as a spiritual prerequisite to socialism. That is to say, socialism was predicated upon *both* an improvement in the material conditions of life, which could be brought about only through productive labor, *and* the production of proletarian consciousness that emerged out of participation in collective labor.[79] *Danwei* design clearly sought to produce a space in which both the productive and the spiritual effects of labor could be nurtured.

In analyzing the spatial formation of the *danwei* compound, however, it would be a mistake to focus only upon the symbolic. After all, compounds were designed to achieve certain practical effects both in the promotion of productive relationships and in the transformation in modes of social interaction. Like their Soviet predecessors, Chinese architects and urban designers believed that spatial forms could play an instrumental role in the production of proletarian consciousness and lifestyles. It is very clear from the literature that architects and designers were particularly concerned with the promotion of collective lifestyles among the residents of *danwei* compounds.[80] For example, in a discussion of the arrangement of housing blocks in a residential compound in Beijing, one architect highlighted the importance of collectivity in the following terms:

> In relation to daily life we must do our utmost to meet the needs of residents for the recreational activities and chores that are undertaken outside of their households. First, the residential style will be collective, and compounds should be arranged according to principles of public usage. Therefore, apart from guaranteeing a basic minimum amount of sunshine, the size of a compound should be calculated on the basis of its suitability for public usage and consideration of making systematic provision of facilities for all kinds of recreation and chores.[81]

To facilitate this kind of collective-oriented lifestyle, the architect suggested grouping two or three housing blocks together to form small compounds (*yuanluo*) within the larger residential compound (*dayuan*). Even though this meant that some buildings would face east instead of south, the architect considered the principle of collectivity to override the issue of sunshine.[82] By establishing a number of smaller compounds (formed by the grouping of buildings) within the *danwei* compound, the plan allowed for certain aspects of social life to be carried out on a smaller, more practical scale of collectivity (see Figure 6.6).

It is apparent from the design materials still available that collective life within the *danwei* was arranged at a number of different levels. At the most basic level of collectivity, every three to five families shared toilets and kitchens within each basic housing unit (*danyuan*). At the next level, each two to three buildings shared facilities like laundries, bicycle sheds, and open space for recreation. Finally, at the *danwei* level, all residents shared facilities like canteens, medical clinics, bathhouses, meeting halls, sports grounds, kindergartens, and primary schools. Clearly everyday collective life within the *danwei* cannot be considered a monolithic whole; rather, the nature of collective interaction changed between the various activities that constituted the daily life of a *danwei* member. While the *danwei* constituted the basic unit of collective identification, *danwei* members undertook many of their daily activities among smaller collective groupings.

The fact that many collective-oriented practices were devolved to smaller

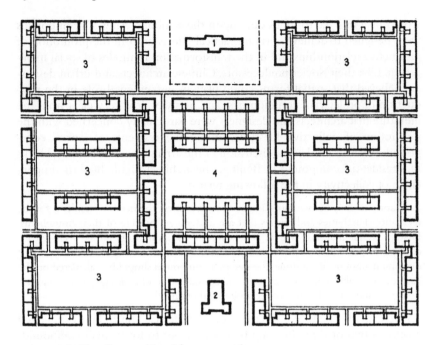

FIGURE 6.6. Plan for a residential compound.
Legend: (1) kindergarten; (2) public bathhouse and laundry; (3) children's play areas, clothes drying, etc.; (4) sports ground.
Source: Ye Zugui and Ye Zhoudu, "On Further Explorations into the Design of Small-Scale Residences," *Journal of Architecture* 2 (1958): 35.

groups within the *danwei*, however, does not undermine the notion of *danwei* collectivism that I have been developing throughout this book. On the contrary, I believe this phenomenon further strengthens the effect of that collectivity. The descriptions above underline the degree to which collectivism was embedded within the micro-level practices of daily life in the *danwei*. The minute planning that went into the production of collective-oriented spaces shows that collectivism was not merely an abstract political ideal promoted by CCP authorities. Rather, it was a principle that informed a whole range of daily practices within the *danwei*. Likewise, it is abundantly apparent that the principle of collectivity was not only reflected in the symbolic form of the *danwei* compound but was also invested to a very practical degree within the everyday spaces around which *danwei* life revolved.

The link between collectivism, social space, and daily life became increasingly central to design practice with the radicalization of the political atmosphere in the latter years of the 1950s. As the movement to increase the pace of collectivization gathered momentum, architects and designers focused more and more intently upon the development of spatial strategies that promoted collective lifestyles. This trend culminated with the launch of the Great Leap Forward and the movement for People's Communes. Between 1958 and 1960, the leading architectural journals published numerous articles on the design of People's Communes. The majority of these were located in rural areas, but since one of the main objectives of the commune movement was to industrialize the countryside and erase the urban/rural divide, the designs for new communes tended to adopt the spatial forms of the urban *danwei* system to foster the integration of labor with daily life.[83]

In urban areas, the People's Commune movement promoted the development of more communal facilities and intensification in the collectivization of social life. At the Second National Work Conference on Urban Design, convened at Guilin in April 1960 by the Ministry of Construction and Engineering, a number of new strategies were promoted for integrating production with daily life inside the commune. These included methods aimed at improving the coordination of resources, like the so-called ten networks (*shiwang*),[84] as well as policy initiatives designed to further the process of communalization. The "five transformations" (*wuhua*), for example, called for "the socialization of housework, the collectivization of daily life, the universalization of education, the normalization of hygiene, and the greening of communes."[85]

The advent of the Great Leap Forward resulted in the push for collectivization extending beyond the *danwei* system, where it was already well established, into the rest of urban society. In the mid-1950s, urban artisans, shopkeepers, hawkers, and tradespeople had undergone a process of collectivization in which they were first encouraged to join cooperatives and then were formed into collective-owned *danwei* under the administration of local city authorities.[86] In economic terms, the aim of collectivization was to increase the efficiency and output of the various small-scale industries involved and also to establish small factories that could play a subsidiary role to the large state-owned industrial sector. In this way, hitherto underutilized urban labor power could be put to more productive use.[87] Politically, collectivization would bring a formerly dispersed and unorganized section of the urban population within the formal organizational structures of the socialist state.

When the People's Commune movement began in 1958, numerous projects were launched to organize members of this newly collectivized small-scale industrial sector, predominantly located in older parts of the cities, into *danwei*-like collective production units. Local architects and planners contributed to this movement by drawing up designs for new urban spaces suited to the demands of highly collectivized life. One such project was the "Great Socialist House" (*shehui zhuyi da jiating*) to be built in Tianjin. Described by the architect as an "early sprout of communism," its purpose is clearly utopian: "The residents are moving from dispersed family life toward a collective-oriented life, where everyone will labor together, live together, study together, and play together. Everyone will have something to do, and there will be someone to look after everything. Each family will be productive and have no idle members. Everyone will be joyful and full of life."[88] The logic espoused in this and many similar projects recalls the language of the Soviet Constructivists. However, the designers emphasized that they did not carry out their work at an abstract level in the design studio, but rather worked among the local people, developing blueprints based upon the ideas, requirements, and suggestions of the local residents.[89]

The result of this mass consultation process was an architectural structure remarkably similar in form to the courtyard homes of traditional China. Of course, the Great Socialist House was many times larger than a traditional home, but like the *siheyuan*, it had four wings that enclosed a large central courtyard—"for collective activities." As well as providing residential space for 176 people, it housed a wide range of on-site services such as a canteen, a child care center, a room for nursing mothers, a medical clinic, a shop, a library, a sewing room, laundries, classrooms, and communal bathrooms. It even included a workshop so that women on maternity leave could continue to participate in production when not actually nursing their children.[90]

The Great Socialist House of Tianjin probably represents the apogee of the movement for the collectivization of urban space. Although it was eventually completed in 1962, many of the promised facilities were never supplied and residents had to cook for themselves in the corridors.[91] Elsewhere, the dire economic results of the Great Leap Forward soon ensured that such utopian spatial projects were removed completely from the drawing boards. Yet economic failures did not signal the end of collectivization or the *danwei*. The more radical aspects of collectivization may have been wound back, but the complex array of governmental strategies that had created the *danwei* as the basic unit of urban life remained largely intact. Indeed, some of the measures introduced after the Great Leap Forward to restabilize the economy resulted in the further consolidation and solidification of the system and increasing dependence of workers on their *danwei*.[92] Moreover, the critical spatial link between production and daily life remained central to the *danwei* system well into the reform period.

One brief example will suffice to demonstrate this point. During the 1960s, the state-owned machine factory studied by You Zhenglin built the following facilities for its workers: a school, a canteen, a medical clinic, a kindergarten, a bathhouse, a water boiler, a cold drink stand, a barbershop, a general store, a dormitory for work/study students, and several residential apartment blocks for married and unmarried staff.[93] These facilities remained under control of the enterprise/*danwei* and were managed within its administrative structure, variously by the "general services department" (*zongwuke*), the "housing department" (*fangguanke*), and the "lifestyle department" (*shenghuoke*).[94] During the Cultural Revolution, no further facilities were added, but in the second half of the 1970s the factory built a guesthouse, expanded the school and kindergarten, and constructed more staff housing. The first decade of the reform period (1979–89) saw an even greater expansion in housing, a further extension of the school, and the construction of a commercial center with outlets selling food, clothing, household electrical goods, and other items of daily necessity. In the mid-1980s, with the growth in the size and scope of services under its control, the factory established a "lifestyle services company" (*shenghuo fuwu gongsi*) to manage this aspect of *danwei* operations.[95] By the end of the decade, the proportion of staff engaged in service provision had increased from 10 to 20 percent of the total *danwei* workforce.[96] This expansion continued into the 1990s and demonstrates the extent to which the *danwei* system that had emerged during the 1950s continued to dominate urban life and urban space in China for almost four decades. In the next chapter, I will examine how this dominance affected economic reform and how it gradually began to decline as city space was rebuilt to reflect a new governmental logic.

Conclusion

In this chapter I charted the emergence of spatial formations and spatial practices specific to the urban Chinese *danwei*. I have shown that an important factor in the emergence of the *danwei* compound was the investment strategy adopted by the central government. Project-style direct investment saw the vast majority of construction funds bypassing city government and instead going directly to individual state-owned *danwei*. Various administrative and planning decisions reinforced the effective separation of *danwei* and city, consolidating the so-called strips and chunks structure through which each *danwei* was able to exercise near absolute power over its spatial realm. In addition, this direct investment strategy provided each centrally administered *danwei* with the resources to support its transformation into a fully serviced production-based residential community.

I also illustrated how developments in architectural and urban design bolstered the formation of the *danwei* system and resulted in a remarkable degree of uniformity in *danwei* spatial forms. The standardization of spatial forms, reflecting both the demands of economic austerity campaigns and the growing political move toward collectivization, further entrenched a distinctive spatial style within the rapidly multiplying *danwei* compounds. The spatial form which emerged was informed by two interrelated design aims: the arrangement of key buildings along a central axis symbolized the primacy of the socialist state as well as the centrality of labor within the *danwei*; the arrangements of living space and common facilities created an environment conducive to the development of socialist collectivity and proletarian consciousness among *danwei* members. In this respect, the architects and urban planners who designed *danwei* spatial forms shared many of the objectives and methods advocated several decades before by the Constructivists of the Soviet Union. Where the architects of the Constructivist movement had found virtually no support for their "social condensers," the designers of the PRC found a much more favorable political environment for spatial innovation, especially as the push for collectivization intensified in the latter half of the 1950s.

Yet it would be a mistake to attribute the *danwei* form solely to radical collectivist trends in 1950s Maoism. As I have shown, many of the policy strategies and practices that influenced the *danwei* formation resulted from administrative and economic considerations rather than from radical political inclinations. But even more significant perhaps is the evident similarity between the socialist *danwei* form and the various compound spaces of traditional and republican China. This is not to say that the reappearance of compound forms throughout Chinese history betokens a seamless cultural continuity. Rather, it can be attributed to a mimetic effect, a kind of cultural memory that reinvokes compound-style spatial formations within vastly different social contexts.[97] In this case, the mimetic effect is underpinned by a collective mode of social practice. The compound form, as the home to the collective unit, has provided a degree of cultural and psychological familiarity within an overall context of dramatic social and political change.

The compound spatial form, once reinvested with an appropriate new set of practices, was clearly well suited to the political, economic, and organizational strategies that characterized the Maoist period of Chinese socialism. However, with the advent of reform, the walled compound seemed to have finally reached its "use-by date." The new socioeconomic paradigm called into play the logic of the market, thus demanding the ever more rapid circulation of goods, capital, and people. The walled compound form that for so long had dominated the urban environment now appeared to be an obstacle to economic development. The fate of the *danwei* under these new circumstances will be the topic of the following chapter.

CHAPTER 7

Reforming the Danwei

In the music shows on the radio you often hear the disc jockey asking listeners who, with enormous difficulty, have phoned in: "What work unit [*danwei*] are you (from)?" The lucky listener, all too often some young kid, quite deliberately attempts, albeit in a very polite way, to twist the answer around a bit: "Would it be okay if I just told you my identity card number?"[1]

By the mid-1990s, so it seems, some "kids" preferred to identify themselves by their individual identity cards rather than revealing their *danwei*.[2] Zhu Huaxin takes this as a sign that conceptions of urban social identity were beginning to shift. In his view, it represented the start of a "gradual transition from the person of the work unit (*danwei ren*) to the social person (*shehui ren*)."[3] In using the term "social person," Zhu invokes the discourse of civil society in which identity is seen as being created through individual agency within the social realm—unmediated by the constraints of any collective groupings. In this respect, he seeks to contrast what he assumes to be modern individualized forms of identity with the old collectivized forms underpinned by the *danwei* system. The passage from *danwei ren* to *shehui ren*, then, marks the rise of the modern individual in urban China—and the death of the *danwei*.

From its emergence in the 1950s, the *danwei* had come to provide identity to its members and legitimacy to their activities. Urban residents were literally "people of the *danwei*," and their ability to enjoy material benefits and to participate in wider society came not from any innate rights of citizenship, but rather from their membership in a *danwei*.[4] In this respect, urban society in China constituted not a collection of individuals, but instead a collection of *danwei*. If Zhu Huaxin is right, this system of identity formation is now well and truly on its way out. But what has led to the decline of the *danwei* and the rise of the individual? Economic reform in recent years, of course, has brought enormous change to urban China, especially with the escalation in economic restructuring since 1992.[5] Changes in the fundamental nature of economic life have been accompanied by dramatic transformations in the physical structure of urban society as a whole. As a result, the *danwei* has apparently lost its previously dominant role as the fundamental social, economic, and spatial unit of urban China. Moreover, within the workplace an entirely new logic of labor management has taken hold, as the following speech suggests:

This week a worker was caught helping another worker by punching her time card in her absence. It was a serious violation and we reserve the right to dismiss her at once. There is no excuse for anybody to clock on for best friends or co-villagers. The helper will be punished more seriously than the one who asked for help. In the factory one should be responsible for oneself only. You may be used to helping each other in the village, but remember that now you are in the factory.[6]

Here a manager in a modern urban factory exhorts rural workers to abandon their "peasant" proclivity for mutual aid and instead to behave as "responsible" individuals. As Pun Ngai points out, efforts to instill labor discipline in this factory turned not just on a regime of training and punishment, but also on a discourse of modernity and "self-improvement" that contrasted "backward" village life with "modern" factory life.[7] What the manager fails to acknowledge, though, is that factory life in the pre-reform (Maoist) factory was also founded on a collectivist rather than individualist logic. In emphasizing the contrast between village and factory, then, this discourse masks the more significant shift from socialist to capitalist labor management practices.

If the "kids" no longer want to identify with their *danwei* and the workers are being exhorted to behave as "responsible individuals," then perhaps the *danwei* and its associated forms of identity and subjectivity really are on the way out. This apparent trend comes as no surprise to social commentators like Cao Jinqing and Chen Zhongya. In their recent study, they see the demise of the *danwei* system as the inevitable result of historical progress and economic development. In China, they assert, "the transition from a planned economy to a market economy implies shifting from a '*danwei*' organizational formation based on abstract collective interests to a contractual organizational formation guided by specific individual interests."[8] In their view, the emergence of "the market" is necessarily associated with the rise of contract and the privileging of individual interest. As the market system is perfected, economic, legal, and social practice will continually bolster the role of the individual. Through this analysis, Cao and Chen seek to provide a theoretical foundation to explain the decline of the *danwei* and the rise of the individual.

Their interpretation is by no means unusual; indeed many attempts to define socioeconomic trends in contemporary China are founded upon a formula that equates the shift from planned economy to market economy with a concomitant shift from collective to individual and from *danwei* to society.[9] What this discourse so often elides, however, is that it is itself the product of another significant shift—the shift from Marx to Weber, which has been driven simultaneously by the rehabilitation of sociology and a loss of faith in the veracity of historical materialism. The problem here is not necessarily the Weberian framework itself, but rather, like the Marxist paradigm it has replaced, it has been applied in a relatively unreflexive way as a predictive model for China's future.[10] It seems that a Marxian teleology of revolution has been replaced by a Weberian teleology of modernity. The future is no longer to be founded upon the egalitarian commune, but instead upon contractual relationships between rational individuals mediated by the market.

Much has, of course, changed in urban China, but in exploring the trends we need to avoid using models that predetermine how we interpret the changes. As in previous chapters, I propose to address the problem of the *danwei* and subjectivity from the perspective of governmentality. The significance and implications of change can best be examined through analyzing the ways in which governmental, managerial, and spatial practices have been transformed in recent years. My analysis will focus, therefore, both on the new managerial practices developed within the *danwei* and on the changing role of the cadre, as well as on some of the broader social, economic, and spatial trends that have emerged from the process of urban restructuring. Of course, I cannot even begin to cover every aspect of change that has affected the *danwei* over the last two decades. Rather, through a selective survey of key developments, I hope to demonstrate that the decline of the *danwei* and transformations in subject formation are far more complex and contingent than many commentators allow.

From the "Mass Line" to the "Bottom Line": Transformations in Workplace Management Practices

There is widespread acknowledgment of the extraordinary transformation that economic reform has brought about in China. Yet the tendency of most commentators to focus on macro developments has meant that many of the consequences of the concomitant shift in micro governing practices have been neglected.[11] Undoubtedly one of the most important outcomes of the reform process has been the re-formation of the rationales and strategies of governmental intervention. In short, the operational logic at all levels has shifted from the ideals of the Maoist "mass line" to the pragmatism of the financial "bottom line." This transformation is clearly discernible in the practices of management in state-owned *danwei*/enterprises.

Attempts to reform the system for the management and remuneration of labor have been central to the economic reform agenda since the early 1980s. For instance, Deng Xiaoping had long considered material incentives to be more effective than ideological incentives in the promotion of labor productivity.[12] His advocacy of this line in the early 1960s was largely responsible for him being labeled a "capitalist roader" by the radical leftists during the Cultural Revolution.[13] It was not surprising, then, that one of the earliest measures adopted to invigorate the economy and promote productivity at the outset of the reform period was the reintroduction of material incentives in the form of a bonus system.[14]

The return to material incentives was the first of many managerial reforms aimed at increasing productivity within the urban workplace. From as early as 1980, advocates of economic reform like economist Xue Muqiao began to call for a major revamp of the entire enterprise (*danwei*) system. Xue argued that more autonomy should be given to enterprise managers both in regard to decisions on investment and resource allocation and in regard to labor management. He believed the latter should include the power to hire, dismiss, promote, and discipline staff. Xue, moreover, was one of the first to call for "smashing the iron rice bowl" (*dapo tiefanwan*), by which he meant winding back the guarantee of lifetime employment and access to welfare benefits enjoyed by the permanent urban workforce.[15] For Xue and other advocates of enterprise reform, the job security and social guarantee provided by the *danwei* system was seen as a major factor in the low productivity of the Chinese economy.[16] In their view, the *danwei* system promoted inefficiency and lack of discipline among workers. The solution to this problem was to create a labor market where workers could be hired and fired according to enterprise needs and rewarded according to their actual productivity. In short, the aim was to bring about the recommodification of labor.[17]

It has taken virtually two decades for the reformers' dreams of a labor market to be realized. The progress of reform has by no means been as smooth or as swift as the promarket reformers would have wished. Rather, their objectives have been reached through a whole series of incremental changes over a long period, culminating in the mass layoffs from state-owned enterprises (SOEs) instituted since 1997. One key change contributing to this gradual transition has been the emergence of a very different style of management within the workplace. The Communist cadres of the Maoist period, who were "both red and expert," have now given way to managers trained in the techniques of "scientific management," who are primarily concerned with market positioning, productivity, and profit.[18]

The emergence of "scientific management" in Chinese industry was the result of a coordinated program of managerial training initiated by the State Economic Commission in the early years of the reform period. A new organization, the Chinese Enterprise Management Association, was set up to oversee the development of management education. It quickly established training courses, produced and disseminated standardized teaching materials, and implemented examination and accreditation systems.[19] The principal aim of this organization was to retrain the estimated 9 million cadres in SOEs who occupied positions at the level of supervisor or above. By the mid-1980s, around half of these cadres had already attended some kind of training course in scientific management.[20]

This retraining encouraged Chinese factory managers to adopt Western-style regimes of industrial efficiency and discipline. Also known as "Taylorism," scientific management methods had emerged in the United States during the early years of the twentieth century with the application of "time and motion" studies to the industrial process.[21] The principle was to break down the labor process into its smallest constituent parts in order to regularize and regulate each worker's movements. The advocates of this method believed that it would achieve the greatest degree of efficiency in industrial production. At its core, "scientific management" was founded upon a separation of the cognitive and physical aspects of labor. The mangers, engineers, and industrial designers were charged with responsibility for designing the labor process and for training, deploying, managing, and monitoring the workers engaged in production. The worker, in contrast, became simply a regulated instrument within the physical process of industrial production.

In Chinese factories the logic of scientific management appeared to mesh well with the shift to individual material incentives; it provided a method to both discipline and measure the output of each individual worker. As early as 1979, according to Lisa Rofel, managers in the Hangzhou silk industry had produced handbooks based upon the principles of scientific management.[22] These handbooks provided workers with exact and detailed instructions on how to perform each productive action associated with their particular role within the production process. Fixing each worker permanently to a given workstation within the workshop further emphasized individual discipline. Known as the "position-wage system" (*gangwei gongzizhi*), this management strategy tied each worker's wage to the particular post the worker occupied within the factory.[23] Each worker, then, became individually responsible for the productivity of his or her workstation at the same time as the worker's labor became subject to a regime of micro discipline.

The rise of scientific management has also been noted by Minghua Zhao and Theo Nichols in their study of three cotton mills in Henan, and by Ching Kwan Lee in a study of SOEs in Guangzhou. These studies suggest that many Chinese factories have adopted a markedly punitive version of "scientific management," primarily utilized to enforce labor discipline and maximize profit through the imposition of numerous restrictions and material disincentives.[24] The principal technique by which managers push workers to ever-higher productivity is through the control of material rewards.

Since 1984, the bonus system has been linked directly to enterprise productivity, and since late 1986, enterprise managers have been given full discretion in the distribution of wages to employees.[25] Under this new wage system, the so-called bonus is in fact a floating component of remuneration, and by the end of the 1980s it constituted up to half a worker's monthly pay.[26] The distribution of "bonuses" at the end of each month is determined by a complex point system, usually calculated on a base of a hundred or a thousand points. Workers can lose points for a whole range of disciplinary infractions within the workplace, including lapses in productivity as well as any lack of attention to personal hygiene and tidiness—so-called spiritual civilization. Workshop managers keep a detailed and secret record of points for each worker throughout the month. At the end of the month, workers are simply informed how many points they earned (or lost) and, therefore, the size of the "bonus" that they will be awarded.[27] This process can lead to quite wide differentials in wages between workers engaged doing the same jobs. It is an important element in the trend toward a more competitive as well as more disciplined labor regime.

Another common strategy used by managers to promote discipline and productivity is the labor emulation campaign. Labor emulation was a staple of the Maoist and the Stalinist factory, but in the reform era the rationale for its employment is very different from that of the past. In the first place, its objective is no longer to increase collective productivity in the service of socialist construction, but rather to increase productivity and profits for the enterprise and to reward a minority of individual workers. For most workers, labor emulation competitions are simply another possible way in which they can lose performance points and bonuses.[28] Perhaps more importantly for management, labor emulation also provides a competitive framework in which workers are forced to vie with, monitor, and police each other.

Mutual policing was an important feature of labor organization during the Maoist period. However, its substance was of an entirely different order from that which is practiced in the reform era. In the past, mutual policing was organized through the work group system—the work group being the smallest collective unit within the workplace. Members of a work group were expected to monitor each other's physical and ideological performance in order to promote fulfillment of production targets and the development of proletarian consciousness. Through this collective process, a strong link was developed between political attitudes and productivity.[29] In the reform period, mutual monitoring by workers during the production process is not directed at the achievement of collective goals, but rather turns upon competition among workers for limited individual rewards. The aim of this practice, therefore, clearly runs counter to the notions of collective spirit and proletarian consciousness fostered in the past. Instead, the result of this management strategy is to individuate and atomize the workforce.[30] Workers are now encouraged to view their workmates as rivals rather than as comrades.[31]

The structural atomization of the workforce has been confirmed through the policy to move employees onto fixed-term employment contracts. In 1983, when authorities first began to promote the use of contracts for new employees, permanent employees made up 96.8 percent of the state sector workforce.[32] In 1986 this policy was confirmed as part of a comprehensive reform of labor regulation, and henceforth all new employees were placed on contracts, which generally ranged in length from two to five years.[33] Contracts, of course, could be renewed after expiration, but for the first time SOE workers faced the realization that long-term security was no longer a feature of employment. In 1992 around one-fifth of the SOE workforce were on (mostly five-year) labor contracts, and by 1997 the figure had increased to 51.6 percent of state employees.[34] The shift from permanent to contract employment is of course not unique to China—it has been a feature of a global push from business and government for more "flexible" labor markets over the last decade or so.[35] However, in China this global trend has merged with the other structural reforms of the *danwei* system to create an even greater impact upon employment conditions.

The contrast between past and present practices in labor management highlights the dramatic shift in the role of the enterprise managers. In the pre-reform era, the workshop manager was a cadre and was expected to be "both red and expert" and to play an active part in the "struggle" to achieve production targets. The cadre was required to set an example for others, as well as to lead and organize production itself. Under the labor practices of the Maoist period, workshop managers were not permitted to remain distant and aloof from the workers. On the contrary, they played an active and integral role in organizing and participating in collective labor. Franz Schurmann describes this distinction well: "The cadre is the Chinese Communist answer to the official. The official commands from his office. The cadre goes out and leads personally."[36] Studies of labor relations in the pre-reform period tend to emphasize the close relationship between shop foremen and their production teams. Andrew Walder, for instance, shows the way in which foremen maintained an intimate connection with workers, in part so as to be able to nurture and recruit suitable workers to take on the crucial role as activists among their fellow team members.[37] As I argue in previous chapters, the cadre's role within this mode of factory organization can best be described as pastoral.

In the current period, however, factory officials have clearly distanced themselves from the workers they directly manage. The cadre (*ganbu*) has become a manager (*jingli*) devoted primarily to the economic profitability of the enterprise. Indeed, the manager's own remuneration is nearly always dependent upon the level of profit achieved.[38] The shift in management techniques employed at the grassroots enterprise level is part of what Maurice Meisner has characterized as "bureaucratic capitalism."[39] Reform of China's labor management system has apparently resulted in the communist cadres of old being metamorphosed into a powerful class of bureaucratic managers who control the resources of state-owned *danwei* and, more importantly, the manner in which these resources are distributed among an increasingly individuated and atomized workforce.[40]

Resisting Labor Discipline

Although the general trends in management described above are well known and widely practiced, this does not mean that they have always been implemented as fully and effectively as authorities may have hoped. In his case study of reform at a state-owned machine factory in Beijing, You Zhenglin, for example, discovered that despite the adoption of very strict provisions relating to labor discipline, managers are generally unwilling to enforce them. The main reason for this aversion to enforcement, according to the author, is simply that workers and managers mostly still live in the same residential compound (*shenghuoqu*)—none of the managers want to risk offending workers whom they are likely to meet on a regular basis outside of working hours.[41] Moreover, their common residence in the *danwei* housing compound facilitates the development of long-term interpersonal relationships, or *guanxi* networks, through which standardized bureaucratic and disciplinary procedures can readily be circumvented. It seems that new "scientific" labor practices are open to subversion where the SOE preserves the spatial link between working and living established under the *danwei* system. This example demonstrates the extent to which sociospatial arrangements inherited from an earlier period and underpinned by a different governmental logic continue to influence the structure of labor relationships.

Rofel also highlights the importance of spatial factors in her study of a state-owned silk factory in Hangzhou.[42] She notes that factory managers' keenness to establish a "scientific" labor regime did not have much effect on labor discipline or levels of productivity. According to Rofel, the major factor that undermines "scientific management" is the spatial arrangement within the factory and the way spaces are appropriated by workers.[43] While it has been possible to introduce a new disciplinary regime into the production process, the spatial arrangements into which these practices have been inserted remain largely unchanged. This point is crucial, as Rofel explains, because like the majority of China's key industrial enterprises, the factory in which her research was undertaken was built in the 1950s according to a very different spatial logic. Attempts to impose "scientific management" practices have had to be superimposed upon an already existing and apparently inhospitable architectural terrain.

Rofel argues that the major point of disjunction between the demands of "scientific management" and existing spatial arrangements is to be found in the rigid spatial separation of managers and workers. Because there is no direct visual communication between the space of the office and the workshop, there is no possibility for enacting a "panoptic," or disciplinary, gaze through which to enforce the regime of "scientific" production. The disciplinary gaze cannot be activated because the Chinese factory embodies a spatial form that was designed according to quite a different logic of management/worker relations. Rofel attributes the separation of office space and workshop space to two factors: first, to the influence of traditional architectural practices such as those exemplified by the Forbidden City in Beijing;[44] and second, to the influence of socialist practices that sought to conceal the fact that workers didn't actually run the factory.[45] Spatial arrangement thus bolstered the practices of managerial power, while at the same time attempting to conceal the very existence of such power.

Rofel's study is insightful because it highlights ways in which existing spatial practices have undermined the implementation of managerial reform within the Chinese factory. However, her analysis of the spatial heritage of the factory is somewhat problematic. For instance, how can the spatial segregation of management and workers within the factory be explained as *both* a visible display of hierarchical power *and* as an attempt to conceal power in order to maintain a proletarian facade? In my view, Rofel too readily conflates the symbolism of the socialist factory layout with that of the traditional compound. While the two share certain features, like the walled compound form and the use of a central axis, they represent quite different symbolic orders. As I argue in Chapter 6, the *danwei* compound reverses the order of the traditional form; whereas in the latter, power is hidden at the deepest most inaccessible point, the former openly exhibits the power of the socialist state and places it in a central position, symbolically among (not hidden from) "the masses." The prominent positioning of the main administrative building aligns the spatial organization of the *danwei*/factory with the symbolic order and the ideals of the Maoist state.

On the other aspect of the spatial question, I think Rofel reads too much into the fact that office space within the workshop environment is hidden from view. No doubt managers have always utilized such spaces to store files and documents that they wish to keep secret from workers. But just because they have an office does not mean they spend all their time secreted there, away from the workshop. Indeed, under the labor practices of the Maoist period, workshop cadre / managers were simply not permitted to remain distant from the workers. On the contrary, they were expected to spend most of their time on the front line of production actively mobilizing their work teams to achieve the latest quotas. Schurmann's work on the role of the cadre, mentioned above, emphasizes this point, as does Walder's famous study of factory labor relations.[46] Labor in the pre-reform period was a collective rather than individual activity and in principle required all workers to participate in management as well as in production. The fact that the foreman's office was out of sight of the workshop did not affect labor discipline because, under the collectivist-oriented practices of the socialist factory, discipline relied upon a constant regime of mutual surveillance among each work team, rather than the singular surveillance of a lone manager or foreman.

The reason the socialist factory fails to provide a spatial environment conducive to the discipline of "scientific management" is not because managers' offices are hidden away out of sight, but rather because Chinese factories were designed to operate according to a collectivist rather than individualist logic. This is supported by You Zhenglin's point that the continued close link between living and working space militates against enforcing new disciplinary regimes. The reform-era shift from collective- to individual-oriented labor practices has given rise to forms of resistance, at least in part, because spaces that were designed to facilitate socialist collectivism within the workplace and that brought together daily life and productive labor are evidently ill suited to the creation of disciplined and individuated worker subjects.

Government reformers have been well aware of the resistance that has emerged at each stage of the restructuring process. In many cases resistance linked to "outdated" spatial practices of the kind mentioned above has been circumvented through the construction of new workshops and factories and the employment of more compliant workers recruited from rural areas. The rapidly expanding private and foreign-owned sectors of the economy have provided the principal impetus for this trend. But as well as creating new workplace environments, such developments have also contributed to the restructuring of city space on a wider scale.

From the Compound to the Street: Reformations of Urban Spatial Practice

Undoubtedly the most obvious outcome of economic reform has been the extraordinary construction boom that has raged through China's cities virtually without a break since the early 1980s. Considerable swaths of new land have been opened up for development, but large sections of existing city districts have, over the course of two decades, been completely rebuilt—in some places more than once. Naturally this process has engendered dramatic transformations within the structure of the urban environment. In combination with other economic and social trends, it has led to the production of entirely new forms of social space. One of the most significant changes has seen the locus of urban life shifting out from the *danwei* compound and onto the street. This movement has been enabled primarily by the emergence of a flourishing new small-scale private enterprise sector geared to serve rapidly expanding consumer demands.

The private sector, which had been all but suppressed during the Maoist period, reemerged soon after the launch of economic reform in 1978. Initially the growth of private business was slow, but after the formulation of a clear set of guidelines in July 1981, the sector began to expand dramatically.[47] According to official statistics, the number of urban residents engaged in private business, referred to as *getihu*,[48] increased from 150,000 in 1978 to around 8 million in 1992 and an incredible 24 million by 1999—representing a 160-fold increase over two decades.[49] As sociologist Shi Xianmin points out in his groundbreaking study of Beijing *getihu*, the dramatic rise of small-scale private business has implications that go far beyond the merely economic. Not only has the *getihu* become a major new social group within the Chinese city; they have also brought about a significant transformation in the operation of the city and in the daily practices of urban residents:[50]

Today Beijing residents have reached the stage where, in their daily lives, they simply can't do without the *getihu*. The housewife can't do without the private vegetable stall when she buys vegetables; young people searching out the latest fashion trends can't do without the private fashion shops; fashionable men and women can't do without the private hairdressers when they want to get their hair styled; hungry travelers can't do without the private restaurants; and people who use the bicycle as their means of transportation can't do without the private bicycle repair stalls. . . . In short, in all locations where services are needed, in all spheres of social life, and everywhere where there is a chance for profit, you can find *getihu* bustling around their stalls and shops.[51]

Through his analysis, Shi Xianmin identifies the key locations in which *getihu* operate. In terms of their effect on the nature and structure of the city, the two most significant concentrations of *getihu* occur along the principal commercial streets and among the lanes and backstreets of urban residential areas.[52] While those who operate around the main commercial centers seek to take advantage of the large number of people, both locals and visitors, who are attracted to the city shopping hubs,[53] those who operate in the back lanes and residential areas seek to meet the mundane needs of urban residents going about their everyday lives. This latter category includes not only those who operate in the lanes of the old city residential districts but also those who do business in and around the *danwei* compounds and residential neighborhoods of the post-1949 socialist city.

The rapid rise of the *getihu* has signified the dramatic emergence of a nonstate sector within the urban economy. In a relatively short space of time, the *getihu* almost completely replaced the state as the primary actor in the retailing, food, and service industries.[54] At the same time, this trend has resulted in the focal point of urban life shifting from the *danwei* compound out onto the newly commodified street. In his discussion of current trends in urban development, theorist Zhu Wenyi notes that one of the principal results of the new commercial activity has been the rapid expansion of street-side shopping strips (*yanjie shangdian*).[55] Zhu suggests that the rise of the shopping street could be understood to signal the return of a feature that had been important to Chinese urban formations since at least the tenth century. At the same time, however, he also suggests that it implies a shift toward a monumental streetscape that is more characteristic of Western cities.[56] The appearance of large modern department stores, shopping malls, and luxury hotels is particularly indicative of this Westernizing trend. Yet, regardless of whether the commercialization of the street can be attributed to a mimetic return to the past or the appropriation of Western urban practice, more significantly it embodies a shift away from what Zhu considers to have been the central tropes of the Chinese city—namely, boundaries (*bianjie*) and enclosures (*yuan*), of which the residential compound is the most common representative.[57] In a general sense, this shift implies that a population that was once contained within enclosed spaces has now been released to "float" along the new corridors of commercial enterprise. In academic discourse at least, the images of the reforming city mesh seamlessly with the rhetoric of the market; the new flows of people correspond directly to the new flows of capital.[58]

The balance of the evidence presented above seems to support the contention, outlined at the beginning of this chapter, that China is shifting from a society dominated by the collective to one centered upon the individual. The introduction of "scientific" management techniques and the move toward contracts and other more "flexible" labor market practices appear to be producing an increasingly individuated worker/subject. The restructuring of urban space apparently augments this transition; both the micro (workplace) and macro (city) environments are undergoing a process of assimilation to the demands of the market. As a result, the *danwei* is displaced from its once dominant position as the city opens up its spaces to the logic of the entrepreneur and the consumer.

The Danwei, *the City, and the Market*

On closer examination, however, we find numerous trends that do not fit this tidy picture of change in China. The reality of urban transition is far more chaotic than the image portrayed, and new subjectivities are far more varied, complex, and hybrid than many commentators are willing to allow for. This is perhaps most clearly highlighted by the phenomenon known—in parody of grander political rhetoric—as "one family, two systems" (*yijia liangzhi*).[59]

As noted above, the rise of the private economy and its chief protagonist the *getihu* has been little short of amazing. Nevertheless, despite the apparent entrepreneurial and independent nature of the *getihu* sector, its emergence and expansion has actually been underpinned by the *danwei* system. Behind the scenes of their venture into the uncertain world of commerce, a large number of *getihu* have adopted the strategy of "one family, two systems" to maintain a link to the security provided by the *danwei*.[60] The basic idea is simple:

> One member of the couple stays in the state-run enterprise to maintain "living in-surance," while the other goes out to become an entrepreneur or join a small col-lective enterprise in order to increase their economic income and enrich their stan-dard of living. As long as they have requirements like capital, skills, and housing, then the original "one family, one system" household can try to become a "one family, two systems" household.[61]

Without the security provided by the *danwei*, many successful *getihu* busi-nesspeople may never have dared to "jump into the sea" (*xiahai*). The sym-biotic relationship between the *danwei* system and the rise of the *getihu* un-dermines the common juxtaposition of a supposedly moribund and inefficient state sector with an apparently flourishing independent private sector. In fact, many *getihu* go out to do business each day in the knowledge that they can come home in the evening to their *danwei*-provided home, that if they become ill they have access to *danwei*-subsidized health care, and that their children can be cared for in *danwei*-supplied child care facilities.[62] In this way, those who practice "one family, two systems" have the best of both worlds; they enjoy the basic material, social, and welfare benefits pro-vided by the *danwei*, while at the same time gaining the financial benefits of the private entrepreneur.[63] Thus, while the streets have become the focus of the rapidly expanding commercial sector, the *danwei* compounds still provide a relatively secure and stable social foundation.[64]

As *danwei* residents adapt their lives to negotiate changed circumstances and take advantage of the opportunities afforded by the "two systems," the *danwei* itself has begun to experiment with new "market-oriented" practices. To the casual observer, the rapid rise in commercial and consumer activity

on the streets of urban China is seen as another sign of the declining importance of the old system. No longer are people dependent upon their *danwei*
to distribute goods or provide services—everything has now become a commodity freely available for sale on the streets. Few realize, however, that in
fact many of the new commercial retail outlets, business ventures, and service providers are either directly run by an "old-fashioned" *danwei* or operated out of premises owned by a *danwei*. Indeed, as the focus of daily life has
shifted from the *danwei* compounds out onto the streets, the *danwei* themselves have begun to turn outward, transforming their enclosing compound
walls into the shopping strips that are now a feature of urban China.

This phenomenon has been documented in the Chinese press, where it is
referred to as "compound wall economics" (*yuanqiang jingji*).[65] A cultural
danwei in Hubei, for example, was reported to have taken advantage of the
fact that its compound walls abutted busy streets by opening and operating
three restaurants and an arts amusement center, as well as leasing out thirty
other shop fronts to *getihu* operators.[66] Perhaps the most famous example of
this phenomenon is the commercial strip (*shangyejie*) built by Beijing University in 1993 along six hundred meters of the south wall of its campus
compound. While many of the new shops were rented out, some were used
as commercial outlets for university-run businesses—most prominently
those in the high-tech sector.[67] The success of this venture attracted other
similar businesses to the area, leading to the formation of a "computer village" in the streets surrounding the university. Moreover, Beijing University's
initiative was nationally publicized and soon copied by colleges, research institutes, and other *danwei* all over China. Not only has this practice provided
much-needed financial benefit for the *danwei* involved; it has also helped to
alleviate the shortage of commercial space, which had become a major problem in many urban centers.[68]

The emergence of "compound wall economics" is an exemplary instance
of the kind of complex negotiations that are taking place between the old
socialist sector, represented by the *danwei* system, and the new private sector,
represented by the *getihu* entrepreneurs. In the same way that individuals
have come to terms with the new marketized and commercialized realities
of the Chinese economy through the practices of "one family, two systems,"
so too the *danwei* has begun to engage with the private sector in order to
promote its own interests. The rapid growth of shopping strips throughout
urban China has masked the equally significant point that behind these
commercial ventures, both physically and economically, lies a *danwei*.

There is no argument with the fact that the old socialist *danwei* system has
undergone dramatic change over the last decade and a half. In many ways its
role has been diminished, yet it has also adapted and persisted within key aspects of urban life. But do these adaptations simply presage a slow process of

decline leading to the eventual extinction of the *danwei*? Perhaps the clearest evidence that the *danwei* system may remain influential long into the future is provided through an examination of recent trends within the growing private enterprise sector (*siying qiye*).

In a study of the high-tech industry in Beijing's Haidian district, Corinna-Barbara Francis suggests that new private enterprises reproduce many features of the *danwei* system.[69] Similarity to the *danwei* manifests in a number of significant ways. To begin with, many private enterprises provide a range of fairly comprehensive material and welfare benefits such as housing, medical care, pensions, and other subsidies to their employees.[70] The problem of housing is a particularly critical issue, since the prohibitive cost of "commodity" housing means that even professionals earning above-average wages find it very difficult to afford.[71] In this context, a company's ability to provide housing to its employees is an important incentive in the recruitment of staff.[72] Conversely, from the company's perspective, provision of housing also operates as a disincentive for employees to leave. By linking housing and other benefits to employment, companies are able not only to attract employees, but also to secure those employees for relatively long periods. Employees, then, may find themselves dependent upon the company to almost the same degree they were once dependent, at least economically and socially, upon the *danwei*.[73] Although employment mobility has in theory been enhanced through the shift toward a labor market and with the rapid rise of the nonstate sector, economic and social conditions may lead simply to the formation of a new kind of private sector *danwei*, reminiscent of the Western-style company town or the Japanese *kaisha* (corporation).[74]

In addition to the provision of housing and welfare, Francis discovered that private enterprise also performed some of the political and social roles that had always been part of the *danwei's* responsibility. In particular, the enterprise was held accountable by local authorities for the behavior of its employees. Thus, in areas such as the maintenance of public security, the enforcement of family planning, and the alleviation of unemployment, private enterprises were required to cooperate extensively with the relevant authorities. Policing urban social order in communist China has always been closely tied to workplace organization, and so far as the police are concerned, whether state-owned or privately owned, the workplace will remain a critical link in the "comprehensive management" of public security.[75] One clear example of this principle is the fact that companies have been subjected to fines when their employees have been charged with criminal offences.[76]

The workplace, then, remains an important site both for the production of identities and for the regulation of behavior. Or, as Francis concludes, newly emerging private enterprises are tending to reproduce "a social structure in which social identity and collective action is shaped by the individual's dependence on and identification with his or her primary social unit."[77] At the more skilled and affluent end of the private sector, such as the high-tech industry surveyed by Francis, this trend no doubt manifests in a relatively benign form of dependency. At the other end of the sector, the infamous sweatshop factories of (predominantly) southern China seem to cultivate a far less benign form of dependency: with their cramped dormitories, locked workshops, and draconian labor regimes, they resemble more prison than *danwei*.[78] Nevertheless, as Pun Ngai argues, these workplaces certainly do effect a transformation in the identity of their workers—from peasant girls to "working girls" (*dagongmei*).[79]

Regardless of the sector, however, the question of workplace dependence is always closely linked to the issue of housing. As I discuss in previous chapters, housing provision was critical to the development of *danwei*-centered identities under the planned economy. In the reform era, while the quality and quantity of housing has dramatically improved, its availability and accessibility have remained problems for significant proportions of the urban population. Faced with such difficulties, the government has attempted to reform the mechanisms for housing provision through the implementation of a range of new policy strategies.

Housing Reform and the Danwei

In many ways, initial reforms to the housing sector served to strengthen the role of the *danwei* in this area.[80] Indeed, despite Deng calling for the commodification of housing as early as 1980,[81] the effect of government policy initiative until the late 1990s was to accentuate rather than lessen the direct role played by the *danwei*.[82] This was primarily due to the increased economic and managerial autonomy granted to the *danwei* as a result of reform.

Under the socialist planned economy, the vast majority of urban housing was constructed through capital investment funds channeled by the state directly to state-owned *danwei*, or to a lesser extent through local government.[83] According to World Bank figures, in 1979 over 90 percent of all urban housing was financed this way.[84] By 1990, however, 86 percent of capital for new public housing was being raised by individual *danwei*.[85] During the eleven years from 1979 to 1990, then, the financial burden of housing construction had clearly shifted from the central government to the *danwei*. This shift in responsibility has been accompanied by a dramatic increase in the rate of housing construction. From 1979 to 1992, the total area of urban housing increased by more than four times, while living space per capita for the urban population more than doubled from 3.6 to 7.3 square meters.[86] From 1950 to 1978, housing accounted for only 5.9 percent of all construction investment. In contrast, during the period from 1979 to 1992, housing averaged 14.6 percent of construction investment.[87]

The significant increase in urban housing during the 1980s was a major positive outcome of reform policy. Nevertheless, the urban population by no means universally enjoyed the results. With responsibility for housing investment devolved to the individual *danwei*/enterprise, the capacity for a *danwei* to provide new housing to its employees depended almost totally upon its own financial situation. As a result, those *danwei* that performed well within the new market-focused economic system were more able to provide their employees with new housing, while those *danwei* that performed badly had a much-reduced capacity to invest in new housing. More than ever before, housing conditions for urban workers rode upon the economic performance of their own *danwei*.[88] Under these circumstances, it is hardly surprising that inequalities in housing provision have increased substantially in recent years.[89]

In response to this problem, during the 1990s the government attempted to instigate major reform within the urban housing system in order to spread the financial burden of provision. The key strategy was to encourage employees to purchase their housing from the *danwei*.[90] This strategy was first attempted in the mid-1980s; however, because employee wages remained low, even heavily subsidized discount prices proved unattractive to residents.[91] Successive rounds of policy development and experimentation have attempted to overcome this disinclination to purchase. However, as Wang and Murie point out, the fact that large numbers of *danwei*-owned houses were sold to their tenants during the 1990s is due primarily to the gradual increase in wage rates rather than to any particular policy breakthrough. Moreover, the vast majority of those who purchased housing did so at dramatically discounted rates that provide the new "owners" with only a limited form of ownership. The circumscribed nature of these new forms of property relationship belies reports in the Western media that have trumpeted the "privatization" of urban housing in China.[92]

Official literature makes the complex nature of housing reform in the 1990s quite clear. For example, the preamble to the 1995 State Council document *Decision on Deepening Reform of the Urban Housing System* sets out the general strategy for reform in the following terms: "To change the system of investment in housing construction from one where the state and the *danwei* are solely responsible to one where the state, the *danwei*, and the individual each take a reasonable part of the burden . . . to establish an economically appropriate, social security style housing supply system for low- to middle-income earners and a commercial housing supply system for high-income earners."[93] Official policy, then, did not seek to promote a simple shift from public to private ownership, but rather to establish a system in which the burden of housing provision was to be shared between the state, the *danwei*, and the individual. Similarly, it was recognized that for low- and middle-income earners (the majority of the urban population) housing provision would continue to be seen as part of the social security network, rather than as a realm wholly dominated by commercialized economic exchange.

These policies have resulted in the formation of a two-tiered housing system consisting of so-called commodity housing (*shangpinfang*), which is sold to those who can afford to pay for new housing at market prices, and subsidized housing, provided to the majority of urban residents primarily through their *danwei*. Commodity housing is constructed by development companies and sold for profit on the open market, while subsidized housing is mostly built by individual *danwei* (local government also construct and manage some housing) and distributed internally to employees within the particular *danwei*.[94]

Despite the great publicity given to the commodity housing market, the majority of urban housing in China is still attached to the urban *danwei*. Since most *danwei* employees cannot afford to pay market prices, housing reformers developed alternative methods for the sale of public housing.[95] Under these policies, *danwei* housing, both new and existing, can be sold either at cost price (*chengbenjia*)—often with heavy discounting for years of service, age of housing, and the like—or at a so-called standard price (*biaozhunjia*), which is usually much less than cost price—the actual standard was set by local government housing authorities based upon local financial conditions.[96] While price discounting encouraged many who would otherwise have not been able to afford it to purchase their housing, such purchases do not provide full ownership rights. According to the new regulations, the purchaser owns only a proportion of the housing equivalent to the proportion they have paid of the full cost price. The residual proportion of the property remains in the hands of the *danwei*.[97]

The ongoing role of the *danwei* in the provision and management of housing is further underlined by the practices surrounding the "housing accumulation fund" system (*zhufang gongjijin zhidu*) that has been instituted in recent years across the country.[98] The main purpose of these funds, which have now been widely established within state-owned *danwei*, is to provide capital specifically for the construction of housing. Regulations concerning these funds stipulate that each employee contribute 5 percent of his or her wage and that the *danwei* contribute another 5 percent.[99] In theory, individual contributions remain the property of the contributor and may be withdrawn by that individual when he or she purchases a home. In practice, however, the fund has generally been used collectively by the *danwei* to fund large-scale housing developments. Moreover, if the housing fund itself is not sufficient for the planned development, the *danwei* contributes the shortfall from retained profits or borrows the extra capital needed from one of the state banks.[100] Housing built in this manner is still substantially subsidized, and although the housing accumulation fund ensures that individuals contribute something to their own housing, it is still a long way short of full privatization.

In capitalist societies, especially since the 1950s, the ideal of home ownership has occupied a particularly symbolic position within both public and popular consciousness.[101] Little wonder, then, that some Western commentators have been quick to characterize housing reform in China as a shift to individual home ownership. Close analysis of the actual policies and practices that have emerged in recent years, however, reveals a far more complex situation. Full privatization has been achieved for only a small proportion of urban housing, principally constituting the elite end of the market. For the majority of urban residents, housing is still linked closely to the *danwei*. Indeed, the reform period saw the role of the *danwei* in the finance and provision of housing actually increase significantly as the state wound back central funding. The much-hyped "sell-off" of state-owned housing in the late 1990s has resulted not in privatization, but rather in the formation of various kinds of joint *danwei*/individual ownership. If the individual takes a larger share of the financial burden involved in the provision and maintenance of housing, it still occurs within a framework in which the *danwei* plays the major role.

Structural limitations to the commodification of housing go beyond the simple question of affordability. Long-term involvement in the provision and maintenance of housing has meant that most basic services—heating, water, electricity, gas, phones, and even cable television—have also been controlled and managed by the *danwei*. As the *danwei* increased its investment in housing during the reform period, it also expanded services to meet the higher expectations of staff. Over time this contributed to a massive increase in the overall welfare and service burden carried by state sector *danwei*.[102] With the shift toward a "modern enterprise system," in recent years authorities have called for the *danwei* to divest itself of responsibility in this area and to "professionalize" all its services. As a result, most *danwei* have now transformed their "housing department" (*fangguanke*) into an "estate management company" (*wuye guanli gongsi*) to take over management of the residential compound. In practice, however, the personnel have not changed and the new "company" generally retains very close connections to the *danwei* and its administrative structures.[103] Moreover, although it levies a monthly fee from each household to cover its costs, many residents still receive some forms of "lifestyle subsidy" (*shenghuo butie*) from the *danwei* to help cover various maintenance expenses.[104]

No doubt the greatest obstacle to the privatization of housing and various associated services has been the spatial structure of the *danwei*. Because *danwei* space was designed primarily as collective space, housing and other communal facilities were all configured within the *danwei* so as to promote the collectivization of everyday social life. In many cases, even the most basic facilities like bathrooms and kitchens were shared among several households within the housing units. Sociospatial arrangements of this type are clearly not conducive to a shift toward the privatization and commodification of housing. Until the entire stock of socialist-era housing compounds has been torn down and rebuilt according to the new market-based principles, some vestiges of socialist *danwei* culture will remain.

From the Danwei *Compound to the Gated Enclave: New Trends in Housing Development*

Given the current rate at which the urban environment is being rebuilt, it may not actually be many years before all the old *danwei* compounds are gone. Regardless of their fate, however, and regardless of what forms of ownership come to predominate within the new developments, the sheer scale of new urban construction has necessarily affected the spatial structure of the city. To understand the changing dynamics of urban life, then, we need to examine the ways in which the new housing estates are refiguring social space.

Perhaps the standout feature of recent housing construction has been the relatively large scale of individual development projects. Moves toward the commercialization of real estate in urban China have certainly not led to a proliferation of small-scale owner-builders.[105] No doubt the scarcity of land and population pressure has influenced planning authorities to promote the kind of high-rise and high-density development that can be undertaken only by large-scale construction firms. At the same time, the decline of central funding for state-sector *danwei* and the financial windfall derived from land sales have both contributed to a resurgence in the power and wealth of the city government.[106] Whereas the operation of the centrally planned economy permitted little scope for urban planning, as discussed in Chapter 6, reform-era policies have revived the possibilities for the coordination of urban development at city and district levels. All these factors have led to the rise of a planning regime that favors large-scale coordinated projects.

The basic spatial unit of the new planning regime is the so-called small district (*xiaoqu*), which in many ways bears an uncanny resemblance to the *danwei* residential compound (*shenghuoqu*).[107] It is a planned neighborhood where housing is integrated with communal facilities like kindergartens, clinics, restaurants, convenience shops, sports facilities, and communications infrastructure all under the control of a professional property management company.[108] The concept of the *xiaoqu* was developed in the late 1980s, as Zou Denong illustrates, through trials sponsored by the Ministry of Construction in the cities of Wuxi, Jinan, and Tianjin. According to Zou's analysis, the *xiaoqu* designers focused particularly on the communal spaces of the compound, striving to promote attributes like social cohesion (*ningjuli*), neighborliness (*linli guanxi*), and feelings of security and belonging.[109] When the trials were deemed successful, the *xiaoqu* compound became the model for residential development throughout China.

While the *xiaoqu* clearly bears some resemblance to the *danwei* of the past, it also differs in important respects. Some *xiaoqu* are attached to large-scale enterprises or institutions (like universities), but the greater majority of them are not connected to any sort of workplace.[110] Not only does this mean that the link between work and daily life has been severed; it also ensures that residents within any given *xiaoqu* will come from a range of backgrounds and workplaces. As a result, residential space will no longer be charged with the intense career-focused social networking that was engendered by the *danwei* system. Instead, relations between neighbors will be centered on the more mundane concerns of day-to-day life. Moreover, as homeowners rather than *danwei* staff members, the residents of the *xiaoqu* are likely to have a more proprietary attitude toward their surroundings and may even join the local "home owners' committee" (*yezhu weiyuanhui*) in order to protect their property interests.[111]

Although a form of communal space, the *xiaoqu* is a privatized realm that residents have bought their way into. Unlike the *danwei*, to which people were assigned, residence in a *xiaoqu* is determined by choice and the ability to pay. As the disparity within urban incomes has continually widened, housing supply has diversified to meet the needs of different social strata. Whereas the socialist cities had generated a fairly ad hoc and largely undifferentiated distribution of social groups throughout urban space, the new city is a place in which social differentiation is becoming increasingly linked to one's location within a stratified spatial order.[112] Money buys a bigger apartment in a better-serviced compound, but it also buys peace of mind and a greater sense of security.[113] Most *xiaoqu* have some kind of barrier—a wall or fence—enclosing them, and many have security guards who monitor and control entry to the compound. The more affluent the *xiaoqu*, the better the security—higher walls, more guards, and more sophisticated electronic surveillance and entry systems.[114] In China, as in many other places throughout the globe, the elite are buying themselves into luxury "gated communities" where they can relax and enjoy the rewards that wealth brings. There they can be among people of their own kind and need not fear any interference from rest of the population who have not fared so well.[115] No doubt it is more than fortuitous that the rise and proliferation of the gated *xiaoqu* has mirrored the decline and contraction of the state sector and the "flood" of rural migrants into the cities. Both these latter trends have important implications for city space that further highlight the degree to which the urban environment is being refigured to reflect new relations of power.[116]

Downsizing the Danwei: Mass Redundancies in the State Sector

The implementation of reform programs in the state sector has entailed ever more draconian policies. For an increasingly large number of urban workers, the problems of growing managerial power and atomization within the workplace, discussed above, now seem relatively trivial when compared to the specter of redundancy (*xiagang*) and unemployment, which has finally arrived with a vengeance in China.

Pressure on job security has been building ever since managers were given power to dismiss workers in 1988. However, this pressure became considerably greater as reform of SOEs gained momentum during the 1990s,[117] culminating with Zhu Rongji's announcement in March 1998 that loss-making enterprises would be "turned around" within three years.[118] Already by 1997, around 15 million workers from SOEs had been made redundant, with forecasts that another 5 million jobs could go.[119] Official statistics released in 2000 show that the total number of SOE employees had dropped by over 26 million, or almost one quarter of the state sector workforce.[120] Redundancy has not been restricted to the productive sector, as Zhu has also announced the intention to reduce personnel in government organizations by 50 percent.[121] These mass redundancies have created far-reaching economic, social, and political effects, and perhaps most critically, have led to a dramatic shift in conceptions of identity for a large proportion of the urban workforce.

Mass redundancies in the state sector are part of a larger program of restructuring, begun in 1994, aimed at lightening the financial burden carried by SOEs. The objective is to create a "modern enterprise system" (*xiandai qiye zhidu*), where the enterprise is responsible only for core business activities. Thus, reforms have been implemented in the areas of welfare, pensions, health care, and housing in order to divest the enterprise from managerial and financial involvement in these aspects of urban life.[122] The implementation of mass redundancies enables SOEs to further reduce overheads through the reduction of the workforce. Overstaffing, which had been a direct result of the full-employment policies of the past, is no longer to be accepted under "market socialism." The result, however, has been to replace the old problem of overstaffing with a new problem of unemployment.

The Chinese government has addressed this new problem in a number of ways, but the most significant in relation to the issue of identity has been a comprehensive program to influence social attitudes. Through the media, campaigns have been launched to transform what has been termed the "traditional employment mentality" (*chuantong jiuye guannian*)—namely, reliance upon the old "iron rice bowl." Workers are now called upon to show initiative and to "create your own rice bowl" (*ziji zao fanwan*).[123] Much publicity has been given to redundant workers who have become self-employed or started up small businesses.[124] Those who have created employment for themselves have become exemplars of the new self-motivated attitudes that are apparently required by the market economy. They are the new "model workers" and provide examples of the opportunities that supposedly await all redundant workers if only they make an effort. Opportunity through self-transformation is the basis of the government's message to this group:

Redundant workers, you should not loose your spirit when you are made redundant; rather you should realize that you have only said good-bye to a particular post and that reform and opening to the outside world have provided you with even more employment opportunities. As long as you conform to the circumstances, transform your mentality, renew your knowledge, and make an effort, then a brand-new world will open up in front of you.[125]

Despite the magnitude of redundancy and the scale of social upheaval, there is little sympathy within government for those who are reluctant to grasp the new "opportunities." In March 1998, Zhu Rongji was reported as commenting that one of the main problems hampering the reemployment of redundant workers was "not that there is no employment available; it's just that there are lots of jobs that redundant workers are not willing to do."[126] In the light of this situation, Zhu reiterated that it was critical to "transform the attitudes of redundant workers to career choices."[127] Under the emerging labor market, the individual worker has been confronted with a new moral imperative: to forget the *danwei* and to remake him- or herself—preferably as an entrepreneur.

Redundancy and the Danwei

Official rhetoric is instructive as an insight into shifting forms of governmental logic, but what actually happens to those who, no longer required by their *danwei*, are declared redundant? Paradoxically, redundancy of itself does not disconnect the relationship between a worker and the *danwei*. As early as 1993, the State Council issued "Provisions on Arrangements for Redundant Employees of State-Owned Enterprises," which required the original enterprise / *danwei* to continue to support any workers made redundant. The "provisions" called on the *danwei* to pay a basic living allowance and to provide redundant workers with some form of retraining.[128] Despite the ongoing push to relieve the *danwei* of its former welfare functions, Zhu Rongji reconfirmed its role in the support of redundant workers in his "Government Work Report" delivered to the NPC in March 1999.[129] According to Zhu, redundant workers would in future be supported by "three lines of guarantee" (*santiao baozhangxian*). For the first three years after being laid off, workers would continue to receive financial support from their original *danwei*. At the end of three years, if they hadn't found alternative employment in the meantime, their relationship with the original *danwei* would be terminated and responsibility for their support would be transferred to the local government social security department. At this stage, the "redundant worker" officially becomes "unemployed" and is entitled to draw unemployment benefit from the government. After a further two years, the former worker who is still unemployed will be removed from unemployment benefits and transferred to the jurisdiction of the Ministry of Civil Affairs, from whom the individual will receive a minimal living allowance.

The fact that the *danwei* is expected to support redundant workers for up to three years is testament to the reality that in urban China there is still very little social infrastructure outside of the *danwei* system. No doubt the government hopes that within the allotted three years the vast majority of displaced state workers will find new sources of employment and, therefore, will not require additional support from the nascent and underfunded national welfare system. One of the problems with this assumption, as Dorothy Solinger has shown, is that the urban job market is very tight and workers made redundant from the state sector have to compete with millions of migrants from rural areas for the few places available.[130] In addition, many *danwei* simply can't support the workers they have made redundant. Of course, the reason for implementing redundancy in the first place is that the *danwei* is already in a difficult financial position. As a result, some sources report that up to half of all redundant workers receive little or no financial support from their *danwei*.[131] Moreover, many SOEs have simply gone bankrupt and closed down operations entirely, leaving the whole workforce out of work and with no source of even rudimentary support.[132] This affects not only current workers but also retired workers, who under the *danwei* system drew their pension, health care, and other benefits from the enterprise.[133] Efforts to establish a universal welfare network have lagged far behind the pace at which the state sector has been restructured.[134] As the *danwei* system falls apart, many urban residents are left with virtually no source of financial or welfare support. It is in this context that the government has moved to promote "community building" (*shequ jianshe*) in an attempt to foster local solutions and local self-help to fill the void left by the demise of the *danwei*.

From the Danwei to the Shequ

The concept of "community" (*shequ*) had reappeared in China with the reemergence of sociology in the early 1980s and was from the start linked to the economic reform agenda.[135] The term was quickly adopted by the Ministry of Civil Affairs (*Minzhengbu*, MCA) and adapted to the development of new policy initiatives in the field of urban welfare provision. The program to expand "community services" (*shequ fuwu*) was supposed to reflect the government's intention to widen both the scope of service provision and the target population. In its "Decision on the Reform of the Economic Structure," the document that launched urban reform in 1984, the government made clear that one of the key objectives of reform was to relieve the *danwei* of its wide-ranging welfare functions. The *danwei* would then be free to pursue its core business while government took over responsibility for the provision of community services to the entire urban population.[136] While this policy shift was seen as vital to the survival of the state sector, it was also presented as a strategy to transform what had hitherto been a fragmented, inconsistent, and incomplete welfare system—since different *danwei* provided different levels and different kinds of support—into one that would be universal, systematic, and comprehensive.[137] In short, its advocates saw the development of community services as an important element in the modernization and rationalization of China's urban society.[138]

Despite these positive beginnings, efforts to establish universal "community services," as already noted, have failed to keep pace with restructuring in the state sector. This realization led, in the early 1990s, to the decision to focus on strengthening basic "community" infrastructure itself; after all, services could not be effectively provided if there was no reliable organizational structure to undertake the work. This is the context in which the concept of community building (*shequ jianshe*) emerged over recent years. With this shift in strategy, the scope of community-based activity is no longer to be confined solely to the realm of service and welfare provision, but is also intended to encompass culture, health, education, morality, policing, and grassroots democracy.[139] The implication of this development is that the community (*shequ*) will take over from the *danwei* as the basic unit of urban life for everything apart from employment. If this change is put into effect, it will signify a major reorganization of urban society.

But what does *community* actually refer to in this context? Official appropriation of the term in China ensured that it was given a very specific definition. Until very recently, MCA discourse defined *community* as the two lowest levels of territorial division within the existing system of urban governance: namely, the territory of the Street Office (*jiedao banshichu*) and the territory of the Residents' Committee (*jumin weiyuanhui*).[140] According to this usage, community was not associated with natural social groupings or those formed by common identity, but rather was seen to correlate to existing grassroots administrative units demarcated by the government. In China, then, the idea of community was quickly confined within a narrow and specific definition underpinned by three key characteristics: first, the nature and functions of community were to be determined by government; second, the community would perform a largely administrative role; and third, each community would have a clearly demarcated territorial space. In order to distinguish this very specific institutionalized version from the broader concept of community, I will refer to the former using the Chinese term *shequ*.

After a period of experimentation throughout the second half of the 1990s,[141] the MCA decided to endorse one basic organizational model of *shequ* for implementation throughout the nation's cities. On 3 November 2000 it issued a document entitled the "Ministry of Civil Affairs' Views on Promoting Urban *Shequ* Building Throughout the Nation."[142] Two weeks later, the Office of the CCP Central Committee and the Office of the State Council issued a joint document to endorse the MCA's views and call upon all governments and party committees throughout urban China to implement the policies outlined therein.[143] The latter document suggests that *shequ* building is a crucial tool in national efforts to promote social development, to raise living standards, to expand grassroots democracy, and to maintain urban stability. While government expectations as to the efficacy of this new project may be somewhat optimistic, it is nevertheless a major program to reorganize and reorder urban China in the light of recent economic, structural, and demographic changes.

According to the latest MCA definition, "*shequ* means a social collective (*gongtongti*) formed by people who reside within a defined and bounded district."[144] Each *shequ*, therefore, has a clearly designated territory, now defined as being "the area under the jurisdiction of the enlarged Residents' Committee."[145] From this explanation, it is apparent that the definition of *shequ* has narrowed even further—it no longer includes the Street Office and is now seen as corresponding to the Residents' Committee (RC) alone. Given this shift in definition, it might seem obvious to interpret the *shequ* as simply an extension of the RC system that was established in the 1950s.[146] Yet, if we look more closely at the literature on *shequ* as well as at the history of the RC, it becomes clear that the two are not so closely connected.

As noted in Chapter 5, the RC was originally established along with the Street Office as a stopgap measure to organize urban residents who did not yet belong to a *danwei*. Throughout the Maoist period, the RC remained on the periphery of urban life. When the reform era was launched in 1978, around 95 percent of urban workers belonged to state- or collective-owned *danwei*.[147] By 1992 this figure had dropped marginally to 92.5 percent.[148] Although the 1992 figure does not take into account the large number of rural migrant laborers who by then had become a significant new component of the urban workforce, it nevertheless demonstrates the continued dominance of the *danwei* within urban life. It was only in the second half of the 1990s that the *danwei* system entered a rapid phase of decline as Zhu Rongji's strategies to restructure the state sector began to take effect. It is no coincidence that this period of dramatic socioeconomic change also saw the emergence of the *shequ* as a potential new unit of urban governance.

The concept of *shequ*, then, arose not as a natural development of the RC and Street Office systems, but rather in response to the collapse of the *danwei* system. This point is emphasized repeatedly in the Chinese literature. In the MCA document "On *Shequ* Building," for example, the historical necessity for *shequ* building is attributed to two principal factors: first, the breakdown of the *danwei* system and hence the transformation of "people of the *danwei*" (*danwei ren*) into "people of society" (*shehui ren*); and second, the "flood" of migrant rural workers into the cities. Moreover, the document explains that these developments demand the establishment of a *new* management system based on the *shequ*.[149] Similarly, in a recent monograph on the subject of *shequ* building, Tang Zhongxin devotes a lengthy section to an explanation of the *danwei* system, charting its decline and demonstrating how this has necessitated the development of a *new* urban management system based on the *shequ*.[150] Conversely, literature on the RC system tends to portray these institutions as historically weak, poorly funded, inadequately staffed, and generally ineffectual—certainly in no fit state to take over the numerous social and political roles performed by the *danwei*.[151] Even the attempts to revitalize the RCs during the 1990s, as described by Benjamin Read, have now clearly been overtaken by the decision to "build *shequ*." Finally, the documentary literature repeatedly links "*shequ* building" with "party building" (*dangjian*) and can be seen in this context as part of the much wider project initiated by Jiang Zemin to strengthen the CCP at the grass roots.[152] In short, it is my view that the *shequ* should be interpreted as a largely new form of urban institution, notwithstanding its superficial resemblance to the RC, and that its origins are directly attributable to the decline of the *danwei* system, the fragmentation of city life, and the search for an alternative strategy of urban governance.

The Shenyang Model

In the second half of the 1990s, Shenyang City in the northeast "rust belt" was one of a number of cities to develop experimental models of *shequ* organization. Shenyang was a major center of heavy industry under the planned economy and has suffered more than most as a result of state sector restructuring. Its high rates of SOE bankruptcy, unemployment, and redundancy no doubt encouraged city officials to explore ways to meet the severe challenges created by the dramatic socioeconomic rupture. When the MCA's 2000 document "On *Shequ* Building" was released, it became obvious that the "Shenyang Model" had been chosen as the MCA's preferred option for national dissemination. At the time of writing, it is still too early to comment on the fate of this model in other locations. However, the simple fact that it has been chosen as the national model for *shequ* building merits a detailed examination.[153]

Perhaps the most fundamental aspect of the Shenyang Model relates to the size of the *shequ*. Authorities in Shenyang came to the conclusion that existing RCs were too small to establish viable "economies of scale." On the other hand, the territory of the Street Office was too large to be conducive to grassroots organization. To overcome this problem, they decided to create new "enlarged" RCs to form the basis of the new *shequ* organization. According to the 1989 "Organic Law," RCs should consist of one hundred to seven hundred households;[154] in Shenyang it was decided that they should be enlarged to encompass a thousand to fifteen hundred households. For example, in the Tiexi district of Shenyang—the heart of the city's old heavy industry sector—the original 445 RCs with an average size of 535 households, or 1,686 people, were reorganized into 190 RCs, averaging 1,255 households, or 3,949 people.[155] The larger scale was also justified as reflecting the shift from low-rise to high-rise as the dominant mode of urban life in recent years. After implementing the enlargement program, the new organizations in Shenyang were no longer referred to as "residents' committees" but were instead called *shequ* management committees (*shequ guanli weiyuanhui*). Strictly speaking, this terminology was illegal, since neither the constitution, which mentions RCs, nor the 1989 "Organic Law" had yet been amended. In their document "On *Shequ* Building," the MCA attempts to redress this problem by combining the two terms, referring to the new organizations as "*shequ* residents' committees" (*shequ jumin weiyuanhui*).[156]

In Shenyang there has been much discussion over the question of how to work out the boundaries for the new *shequ*. On this point, all the documents emphasize the need to create "natural" communities so that people feel a sense of identity and belonging (*rentonggan*) to the *shequ*, thereby fostering a higher level of social cohesion (*ningjuli*).[157] In demarcating *shequ* territories, three basic types have been developed corresponding to different forms of urban space: *danwei* style—based on a single *danwei* compound, including residential areas; residential compound style—based on a single bounded residential compound (*xiaoqu*); and block style—based on urban blocks bounded by roads.[158] The actual decisions on establishing boundaries are made by the district government (*quzhengfu*) in consultation with staff based in its Street Offices but usually involved combining two or three original RCs into one new organization.[159]

The new *shequ* is supposed to inherit all the infrastructure and equipment (office space, furniture, tools, etc.) from the RCs it replaces, but because the shift to *shequ* is primarily about expanding the scope and capabilities of grassroots organization, it also requires considerable new investment in community infrastructure. In Shenyang, the city and district governments allotted specific funding to construct new buildings or renovate old buildings for the use of the *shequ* organizations.[160] The new "*shequ* activity centers" (*shequ huodong zhongxin*) include office space for the management committee, space for inquiry counters, meeting rooms, and other areas for community activities (exercise classes, social events, etc.). Moreover, regulations passed by the city government require developers to provide and integrate *shequ* facilities within all new residential complexes.[161]

The concept of *shequ* building in Shenyang has been interpreted in a remarkably literal sense; it has been as much about constructing new forms of physical space as it has been about building new kinds of organization. The *shequ* activity centers have been erected as close as possible to the center of the *shequ* territory that they serve.[162] This appears to have been a deliberate spatial strategy to symbolize the new urban social order. The message it imparts is that residents should no longer identify with their *danwei*, but rather should recognize the *shequ* as their new collective home.[163] Just as the central positioning of the administrative building and the workshop within the *danwei* symbolized the old workplace-based socialist order, so the prominent placement of the *shequ* activity center speaks to a new social order. This spatial re-formation signals a shift in the foundations of identity; however, the transition is not from the *danwei* to society, as some commentators have claimed,[164] but rather from the *danwei* to the *shequ*. It does not denote progression from an outmoded form of socialist collectivity to a modern form of individuated identity, but rather a transition from one form of collectivity to another. Indeed, despite the embellishment of key MCA *shequ* documents with a discourse of modernization, the language employed in the majority of local Shenyang documents evokes an image of mass mobilization more resonant with the socialist past than the marketized future. This becomes abundantly clear if we look at the specific functions assigned to the *shequ* and the organizational strategies employed by *shequ* cadres.

The Shenyang authorities have devoted considerable attention to the issue of personnel. Whereas volunteers, usually retirees and predominantly elderly women, staffed the former RCs, full-time paid cadres staff the new *shequ*. Most of the new cadres have been recruited from among party and trade union officials made redundant during the recent restructuring.[165] Shenyang Bureau of Civil Affairs documents emphasize that the new staff should meet the following criteria: at least 50 percent should be CCP members; they should be no more than fifty years old, have high levels of political and cultural attainment, have appropriate management experience, have previous experience in mass line work (*qunzhong gongzuo*), have strong organizational instincts, and be committed to the concept of *shequ* building.[166] The shift from RCs to *shequ*, then, has seen the professionalization of community work as younger, better-educated, and politically trained cadres take over from the "grannies" (*lao taitais*) of the past.

This move toward professionalization reflects the increased status and complexity of the new organizations. The *shequ* is charged with a very wide range of responsibilities in policy implementation and community liaison. First, it is expected to provide a range of services to the local population. This work focuses on the various groups within the community who need special care: the elderly, the sick, the disabled, those with financial difficulties, the unemployed, and the laid-off workers.[167] *Shequ* cadres are responsible for administering the state's guarantee to provide a basic living allowance to those who have no other means of support. Given the high rates of unemployment and redundancy in Shenyang, financial aid and employment introduction services make up a significant component of the cadres' day-to-day work.[168] In addition to welfare services, the *shequ* is expected to manage a range of other services for the benefit of the general population—convenience stores, bicycle repair stands, child care, legal advice, and so on. These kinds of undertakings can also offer a source of extra income for the *shequ* (see Figure 7.1).

Second, the *shequ* is charged with responsibility for managing aspects of urban sanitation and health care. Many *shequ* have their own clinics, others arrange consultations with doctors, and most organize periodic information sessions on various health issues. Of course, they are also required to administer the strict family planning policies of the state. In addition, *shequ* cadres manage everyday sanitation work, garbage removal, and general maintenance of the *shequ* environment. Third, the *shequ* organizes a wide range of educational and cultural programs. The educational work mostly centers on the dissemination of CCP government policy and is referred to variously as "socialist education" or "civilized citizen quality education" (*wenming shimin suzhi jiaoyu*).[169] Cultural events are arranged on national holidays and other significant occasions.[170] Fourth, the *shequ* plays an important role in the local coordination of security work. In this area, the cadres work closely with local police and neighboring *danwei* security staff. This work includes arranging security patrols of the entire *shequ* territory, disseminating information on household security, monitoring the behavior of residents who have

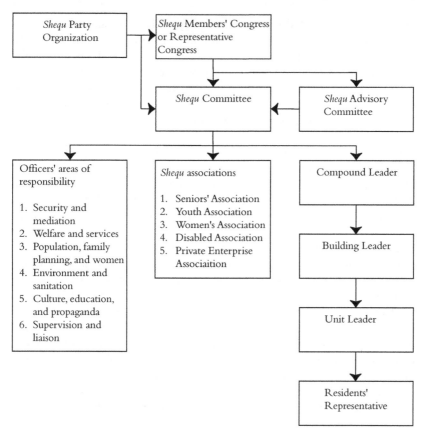

FIGURE 7.1. The "Shenyang Model" *shequ* organization chart.
Source: Translated and redrawn by the author, based on "Shenyangshi shequ zuzhi jigou wangluo shiyitu" ("Diagram of the Shenyang City *Shequ* Organizational Structure and Network"), undated document supplied to the author.

previously been in trouble, ensuring that all residents are registered with the police, solving disputes among residents, and mobilizing volunteers to establish "neighborhood watch" networks (*kanjiawang*).[171]

Finally, the *shequ* is required to coordinate and liaise between various other organizations. Most important, it takes direction from the local Street Office of the District Government and from the local party organization. If the *shequ* contains enough party members, it is required to establish its own CCP branch with the head of the *shequ* committee simultaneously acting as party branch secretary.[172] The *shequ* also liaises closely with any *danwei* and other businesses located within its territory, with the local estate management company (*wuye guanli gongsi*), with the homeowners' committee (*yezhu weiyuanhui*), with local People's Congress delegates, and with any other official organization that wants to make contact with the local population.[173]

From this brief outline it is clear that the duties of the *shequ* cover a wide range of responsibilities, and since each *shequ* is staffed with only three to six full-time cadres (depending on population), managing this heavy workload is an onerous undertaking. But the cadres are not on their own; indeed two of the basic principles underpinning the whole concept of *shequ* building are mass participation and self-help.[174] Like the RC, the *shequ* is officially defined as a "mass organization" (*qunzhong zuzhi*); so one of the cadres' main duties is to mobilize networks of volunteer residents to assist in the work. Regular volunteers are recruited to participate in the various tasks associated with day-to-day management of the *shequ* territory and are organized into a hierarchical system based on the spatial arrangement of the *shequ*. At the top of the volunteer hierarchy is the "compound leader" (*yuanzhang*), who supervises a number of "building leaders" (*louzhang*); each building has several "unit leaders" (*danyuan zuzhang*), and at the bottom of the system are the residents' representatives.[175] Together they provide a comprehensive network for ensuring that all aspects of *shequ* life are kept under close scrutiny and that all the vital daily maintenance and security work is seen to. In theory, at least, it is the volunteer network that links the *shequ* population to the organizational structure and binds its territory into one seamless unit.

Various other techniques have been employed to foster closer relationships between the *shequ* and its residents. One strategy has been to disseminate and popularize "residents' pacts" (*jumin gongyue*) such as the "two-way promise system" (*shuangxiang chengnuozhi*) developed by Tiexi District in Shenyang:

The *shequ* promises to

1. Perform its duties, provide services, be responsive, engage in democratic discussion of business, and accept supervision.

2. Reflect residents' ideas and demands, provide timely feedback, and respond to every matter.

3. Deal promptly with residents' affairs and where possible provide same-day service.

4. Assist retrenched workers to find new employment and manage the basic livelihood allowance for residents in a transparent and fair manner.

5. During holiday periods, visit the families of army personnel and revolutionary martyrs, the disabled, the elderly without families, households with special difficulties, and those with serious illness.

6. Organize volunteers' activity days and arrange cultural entertainment on all major festival days.

The resident promises to

1. Respond to the call of the *shequ* and to enthusiastically participate in *shequ* building.

2. Refrain from illegal criminal activities like viewing pornography, gambling, or taking illegal drugs.

3. Practice family planning, implement birth-control measures, and avoid any births outside of the plan.

4. Take care of the gardens and public facilities.

5. Avoid cluttering the yard and corridors with junk or litter.

6. Speak in a civilized manner, maintain a harmonious family, and avoid disputes with neighbors.

7. Reform habits and customs and refrain from the practice of feudal superstitions.[176]

The "pact" (*gongyue*) has a long history in China. The *baojia* system, for example, set down the duties of ordinary village residents in upholding social and moral order and for mutual aid in times of hardship.[177] In more recent years, the concept of a "pact" has been revived as a technique for promoting civic duty among urban residents.[178] With the "two-way promise system" in Shenyang, the concept has shifted from a one-sided list of duties to a kind of "social contract" in which the duties of the resident are made contingent upon the *shequ* organization meeting its own set of obligations. Put another way, the resident now has the right to expect a range of services from the *shequ* in exchange for compliance with the duties of membership.[179] That a new "contract" is spelled out in such a transparent manner is perhaps a clear measure of the extent to which the old unstated one—the "iron rice bowl"—has fallen by the wayside. Moreover, it may be a sign that authorities are beginning to take the issue of popular legitimacy far more seriously than before.

MCA officials no doubt feel entirely justified in claiming that *shequ* building is a logical modern response to the social problems that have emerged out of economic restructuring. It is certainly not intended as a stopgap measure; on the contrary, it is portrayed as a long-term strategy to modernize, expand, extend, and standardize the provision of social welfare services in urban China. But when we look more closely, beyond the discourse of modernization, we find an organizational structure and operational method that seems to hark back to the "old days" of the mass line rather than look forward to a brave new world of markets and entrepreneurs. In stark contrast to their comrades who work in enterprise, the cadres of the *shequ* have not evolved into "scientific managers" or corporate executives, but have instead immersed themselves among the masses, reviving the pastoral methods of leadership developed in Yan'an as part of a concerted effort to bring the party back to the people. In some respects they are a new generation of "red experts," trained to reestablish social order, collective responsibility, and moral civilization within a fractured urban community. They are the other face of the "socialist market economy," and they force us to realize that transition in China is far more complex than we had ever imagined. Many subjects in urban China are responding to the crises of "late socialism"[180] by "dreaming of better times."[181] If they can't have the *danwei* back, at least they've got the *shequ*.

Conclusion

The *danwei* system has occupied a paradoxical position within the reform agenda. On the one hand, many reformers have viewed it as a major obstacle to market reforms and restructuring and have endeavored to reconfigure and weaken its role.[182] On the other hand, the very existence of the *danwei* and the depth to which it was embedded within a range of economic, social, political, and spatial practices has restricted and circumscribed the possibilities for reform. The *danwei* system, then, has been both an object of the reform agenda and a major factor in determining the kinds of change that have been possible. As the *danwei* continues to influence urban life in China, newly emerging social structures are built upon the complex interplay between continuity and change.

On the one hand, this chapter examines some of the critical ways in which the "traditional" *danwei* has been transformed during the reform period. With the rise of "bureaucratic capitalism,"[183] it is clear that many of the rights and benefits previously enjoyed by workers under the "iron rice bowl" have been stripped away. The move to "scientific management," labor contracts, and "bonus" systems has signaled the shift to a more disciplinary and authoritarian mode of management. In turn, this shift has created a far more pressured workplace and an increasingly atomized workforce. As a result, the collective worker-subject of the socialist past has been transformed into an individualized worker within a highly volatile labor market.

In the long run, this trend, culminating in Zhu Rongji's ambitious program to restructure the state sector, has led to a massive retrenchment of workers. The inexorable policy initiatives to establish a "modern enterprise system" have demanded the production of a new attitude toward employment—"create your own rice bowl" or fall by the wayside. The decline of the state sector has been mirrored by the rise of the private sector, and in particular the explosion in numbers of the ubiquitous small-scale entrepreneur—the *getihu*. As business has mushroomed on the streets of China's cities, the *danwei* has lost its place as the focus of urban life. Whereas formerly workers' day-to-day existence was dominated by collectivized labor and communal consumption within the *danwei* compound, it is now increasingly structured by an ethos of commodification and individual consumption played out in the streets, markets, and shopping malls of the city.

On the other hand, I have shown in this chapter that the *danwei* has retained a significant if diminishing role within the urban scene, even adapting to take advantage of opportunities that have arisen through reform. Established practices can be difficult to transform, especially when they are built into the physical fabric of daily life. Factory spaces designed to reflect a collectivist logic are not readily adaptable to capitalist production methods and have become sites for resistance to workplace reform. Where architectural skeletons of the old *danwei* remain, workers can still exert forms of leverage over their managers. At the same time, the *danwei* system has made a largely unheralded contribution to the rise of private enterprise. In allowing *getihu* entrepreneurs to exploit the possibilities of "one family, two systems," the *danwei* has provided a secure foundation to underpin the inherent risks of small-scale business. For its part, the *danwei* has also followed the *getihu* out into the market, establishing commercial ventures along the streets abutting its compound walls. In this way the wall has become two-sided: the inside of the wall continues to secure the integrity of community space, while the outside of the wall brings the *danwei* into contact with the emerging practices of the market.

In the area of housing, the role of the *danwei* was considerably strengthened during the reform period. With the advent of enterprise profit retention and the devolution of responsibility for infrastructure investment, urban *danwei* funded a massive increase in housing construction that saw living space doubled within a decade. Moreover, despite the much-vaunted commercialization of housing, analysis in this chapter shows that recent practices in housing reform ensure that the *danwei* continues to play the principal role in the funding and provision of housing for many urban residents.

Of course it would be ludicrous to deny that the *danwei* has declined considerably during the reform era. The rapid growth of the private sector and the massive reconstruction of urban space have created new institutional forms to rival and perhaps replace it. Yet, in some ways the new formations bear an uncanny resemblance to those of the past. Many new enterprises have adopted characteristics of the *danwei* system, and while they do not reproduce the socialist labor relations of the past, the corporate practices they pursue tend toward the Japanese model of collective-oriented "enterprise culture" rather than a Western business model. The spatial transformation of the urban environment has seen many of the old *danwei* compounds demolished to make way for new high-rise and high-density development. However the *xiaoqu*, the new basic unit of development, strangely recalls the *danwei* residential compound. Although privatized, it is a form of enclosed communal space combining residence with various services. While the luxury-style *xiaoqu* mirror the global trend toward elitist gated enclaves, the more common forms produce mixed communities of ordinary urban residents. The link between workplace and living space has been largely severed, yet enclosed communal living remains the predominant form of urban life.

Spatial transformations have not only highlighted the economic decline of the *danwei* but also underlined governmental strategies to relieve the *danwei* of its former responsibilities in the provision of services and welfare. But whereas government discourse speaks of a shift from *danwei* to society, implying the universalization of welfare, in fact primary responsibility has been delegated to a new kind of grassroots unit—the *shequ*. Underpinning the current push for *shequ* building is the desire to recoup a stable community-based social order that the *danwei* once represented. The new order, founded on place of residence rather than place of work, seeks to encompass the entire urban population regardless of employment or registration (*hukou*) status. Moreover, through deploying groups of professional cadres to operate the *shequ*, authorities are making a concerted effort to reconnect with the grassroots population. As discussion in this chapter argues, *shequ* building seems in many respects to signal a return to earlier modes of mass mobilization in response to the social fragmentation caused by restructuring. In this vein, the *shequ* cadre resembles the Maoist cadre of old and belies the trend in enterprise toward "scientific" management.

The emergence of the *shequ* points to the complex and perhaps contradictory strategies pursued by government in the current period. Whereas the discourse of "market transition," entrepreneurship, and "small government" underlie much of the restructuring that has occurred in recent years, *shequ* building appears to be an attempt to redeploy a comprehensive "pastoral" style of leadership among the urban population. Only time will tell whether this strategy will lead to a restrengthening of authoritarian control over the grass roots or to some new form of community governance. In the latter case, the *shequ* may come to embody what Nikolas Rose terms "government through community":[184] a governmental strategy that mobilizes the resources of the community in order that it might govern itself within general parameters defined by various agencies. Given the heterogeneous affiliations of the *shequ* and the fairly clear lack of desire on the part of central government to fund local welfare and services, it seems to me that the second option is more likely than the first.

It is of course dangerous to predict the future. Suffice to say, then, that discussions in this chapter demonstrate the complexity and contingency of social change in contemporary urban China. Identities and subject formations are in flux as new modes of labor relations and new forms of urban space and governance emerge to vie with the remnants of the socialist *danwei*. And if the *danwei* has entered its terminal phase, it is still by no means clear that its demise presages a new era built upon individuals and markets. Insofar as there is any coherent "transition" in urban China, it is not a shift from *danwei* to society, but rather from *danwei* to *xiaoqu* and *shequ*. Subjectivities have no doubt diversified in urban China, but the collective and the communal will remain key sources for subject formation in the foreseeable future.

CHAPTER 8

Conclusions

> The essential problem for the intellectual is not to criticize the ideological contents supposedly linked to science, or to ensure that his own scientific practice is accompanied by a correct ideology, but that of ascertaining the possibility of constituting a new politics of truth.
>
> Michel Foucault, 1980[1]

Theorizing the Danwei

It goes without saying that the objective of academic research is the production of knowledge. In writing this book, however, I also wanted to participate in the debates over what Foucault terms the "politics of truth." Or, to put it another way, in producing new knowledge on the *danwei*, I also aimed to challenge the methods and assumptions of what had previously counted as truth so far as the *danwei* was concerned. At the same time, I sought to critically interrogate the very methodologies that I chose to employ, to extend and refine them through application to the specific practices under investigation. In utilizing methodologies like those associated with the concepts of genealogy, governmentality, and spatiality, I hoped both to shed new light on the object of my study, the *danwei* system, and to contribute to the ongoing development of these methodological strategies. Of course, the objectives of knowledge production and the refinement of methodology are closely linked, and throughout this book I have endeavored to maintain that link. However, by way of conclusion I believe it is worthwhile to reflect more specifically upon the methodological implications of this research.

As an object of study, the *danwei* appeared to me to offer great possibilities for the deployment of these methodologies. First, like many aspects of Chinese studies, this was a vastly undertheorized realm of knowledge and had hitherto been addressed only through empirical and functionalist modes of analysis. Since the *danwei* had emerged under unique and specific historical conditions and through the juxtaposition of a wide range of disciplinary, governmental, biotechnical, and spatial practices, it seemed clear that the genealogical method would provide a useful framework for analysis. Second, as the basic unit of social, political, and economic life in urban China, the *danwei* seemed to be an exemplary institution through which to explore the micro physics of power within a Chinese socialist context. Third, I believed the *danwei* to be central to a quite distinctive form of governmental rationality, thus providing new insight into the way the problems of government were conceived and operationalized in China. Finally, and what I found most exciting, was the largely ignored spatiality of the *danwei*—as a spatial form, it was saturated with meanings reflecting the social, political, and economic order to which it belonged.

Of course, I could never hope to produce anything approaching a comprehensive analysis of this complex institution and its long history. Moreover, I had neither the desire nor the training to undertake sophisticated case studies in the field. In opening up space for the kind of interpretive methodological interventions I had in mind, I felt the best approach was to build upon existing scholarship. While I may have adopted a critical attitude toward some studies, I certainly acknowledge a debt of gratitude to the admirable efforts undertaken by the many fine scholars whose work I have consulted. Nevertheless, the ways in which my approach differs from that of others ought to be made explicit. Probably the most obvious point of divergence is that I reject the state-centered analytical framework utilized by most scholars in this field, and specifically the notion of the so-called party/state.[2] In relation to the *danwei*, this approach implies that I do not view it as a seamless extension of the Chinese state. As I conceive it, the *danwei* can best be studied through a broadly interdisciplinary framework that takes into account the complex layering of many influences. Combining this conception with a genealogical method, we can plot the process through which forms of knowledge and governmental rationale come together with a wide range of disciplinary, biotechnical, and spatial practices. Some of these influences, of course, derive from government and CCP policy initiatives and operational methods, but others derive from cultural practices, historical contingencies, local resistance, and other unintended consequences, none of which can be connected directly to the party/state. Indeed, I believe that this study of the *danwei* provides ample evidence to justify my initial skepticism as to the existence of the state in China.[3]

I deal specifically with the various methodological planks of my genealogical approach—power/subjectivity, governmentality, and space—below, but it is also worth noting that the strength of the genealogical approach is precisely in that it encourages the juxtaposition of apparently diverse and disconnected frames of analysis in order to achieve critical new insights. Indeed, I believe one of the central achievements of this work has been to provide a more nuanced and complex picture of the *danwei* than has hitherto been produced. As well as showing that the *danwei* emerged through practices as disparate as economic planning, population registration, and architectural standardization (to name only three), I also demonstrate that the genealogy of certain spatial practices employed within the *danwei* can be variously traced to ancient Chinese works on urban planning, to Haussmann's reconstruction of Paris, and to the almost completely unrealized schemes of Soviet Constructivists.

Power, Subjectivity, and the Danwei

As mentioned above, most previous studies of the *danwei* in China have adopted, either explicitly or implicitly, a state-centered analytic of power. In simple terms, this approach reads the *danwei* as a manifestation of CCP party / state power. The *danwei*, then, is interpreted as the basic social unit through which the CCP has controlled and ruled urban China. Concomitantly, these studies assume a conception of subjectivity founded on the supposed universality of the individual. In this study I reject this standard approach and instead attempt to analyze the *danwei* utilizing a methodology that conceives of power as a complexity of interrelationships between knowledge, institutional disciplinary practice, and biotechnical strategies at the micro level of everyday life. Under this analytical framework, power is seen not as a coercive force of suppression—that is, "power over"—but rather as a complex set of productive relationships. As a realm of micro power relationships, the *danwei* produces a very particular form of collective-oriented subjectivity. The objective of this book is to analyze the various practices that inform the operation of micro power within the *danwei* and thereby work toward a delineation of *danwei* subjectivity.

I begin this study by showing that micro-level practices in China have always been centered on producing collective rather than individual modes of subjectivity. I illustrate this point through analysis of the ways in which family and city were organized, ordered, and policed in traditional times. Shifting then to the Republican period, I demonstrate how many traditional, collective-oriented practices were redeployed within the guilds, gangs, and corporations of the modernizing and industrializing cities. The workplace supplanted the family and clan as the central unit of social organization and thereby became the key site for the production of collective subjectivities. It is in this period also that biotechnics first emerge as, for example, the clerks in the Bank of China become subject to the moral and professional micro disciplines of neo-Confucian corporate practice.

After 1949, production and political participation became the foundations upon which collective subjectivities were built. During the Yan'an period, the CCP developed an organizational practice centered on grassroots mobilization and local-level self-sufficiency, and as the CCP took over the cities, after "liberation," these practices were operationalized through strategies like *baoxialai* and *zuzhiqilai*. The period of socialist construction (beginning with the FFYP in 1953) saw the introduction of policies and practices that ensured that the *danwei* became the mediator for almost all aspects of urban daily life. Labor management, training and education, the distribution of housing and welfare, policing, population registration, the collection and management of personnel information, and political mobilization were all carried out within the *danwei*. Together these practices produced a disciplined, productive, and politically loyal urban population in which commitment to collective effort was exchanged for guarantees of collective welfare.

According to Foucault's analysis of power in various modern institutional settings within Western society, the emergence of detailed fields of knowledge, exacting disciplinary practices, and complex biotechnical strategies resulted in the production of particular forms of individualized subjects. My analysis shows that in socialist China, however, the various micro-level knowledges, disciplinary practices, and biotechnical strategies deployed within the *danwei*, while no less exacting or comprehensive, produced quite a different mode of subjectivity, namely a collective subjectivity focused around production and political participation. It is critical, then, to recognize that different forms of micro-power relationships necessarily produce different modes of subjectivity; moreover, disciplinary forms of power can operate as effectively within collective-oriented societies as within individual-oriented societies. The link between micro-level practice and subjectivity is further illustrated in Chapter 7, where I show how transformations toward more individualized practices (for example, in labor management) have been accompanied by a shift to more individualized discourses of subjectivity.

Governmentality and the Danwei

As Foucault has cogently argued, modern forms of knowledge and institutional practice are founded upon universalist assumptions of the nature of subjectivity and norms of behavior. While practices at the micro level of society aim to produce and police normative behavior through intervention with individual or collective subjects, the rationality upon which these interventions are based is one which views society in a totalized framework.

This form of rationale that allows for the conception of societies as totalities, as populations amenable to transformation through positive intervention, is what Foucault had in mind when he coined the term *governmentality*. In this book I argue that the *danwei* system is inextricably linked to a particular and unique type of governmentality.

Chinese socialist governmentality emerged during the Yan'an period as the CCP, facing a difficult financial and military situation, endeavored to mobilize the population for production and military struggle. While overall strategy was developed under relatively tight central leadership and control, the CCP under Mao also wanted to avoid the dangers of overcentralization and bureaucratization. This scenario led to the development of the famous mass line, a strategy that promoted local self-reliance and initiative under a centralized policy framework. As a rationale of government, the mass line depended upon a vast corps of grassroots CCP cadres to operationalize it. Cadres were required to be both politically loyal and skilled in the techniques of mobilization, production, and leadership—that is, they had to be "both red and expert."

It is with the role of the cadre that Chinese socialist governmentality differs most markedly from forms of governmentality associated with Western liberalism. Under liberal governmentality, the expert has no political allegiance, but rather relies upon a supposed disinterested mastery of knowledge (in any of the various fields) as the basis for intervention in society. The CCP cadre, however, is a political activist as well as a technical expert and in this guise must take on a distinctly pastoral role in the recruitment, guidance, and leadership of a local population, in addition to displaying the requisite technical expertise. Through my analysis of the mass line and the role of the cadre, I show that as a methodological tool the concept of governmentality can be applied usefully to the analysis of Chinese socialism but that this entails modification to some of the central premises that arose out of the study of liberal forms of governmentality.

The "governmentalization" of Chinese society continued apace after 1949. Under the guidance of centralized economic planning, socialist construction saw the development of numerous policies that further bolstered the role of the local-level *danwei* and its cadres. Central to these developments was the project-style investment policy under which funds for almost all aspects of urban economic and social infrastructure were distributed through individual *danwei* rather than through city or regional government. Thus, virtually all governmental intervention in urban society occurred through the *danwei* system and through the agency of local *danwei* cadres. With the advent of reform, however, I show how shifts in governmental rationale (on the one hand devolving greater financial and managerial autonomy to the *danwei*, while on the other hand attempting to establish universal welfare and social security systems) have dramatically affected the role of the *danwei* and its cadres.

But just as the *danwei* appears to enter terminal decline, the *shequ* emerges to take over many of the *danwei's* functions. Where state-sector cadres have mostly evolved into business managers and corporate executives, the *shequ* cadre has reappropriated the mass line and reinvented the pastoral mode of leadership. The rise of the *shequ* and its cadre-force, provides ample warning, if any more were needed, of the dangers inherent in simple assumptions about the nature of China's so-called transition. It seems that within contemporary urban society it is quite possible for "scientific management" and the logic of the market to coexist with a new mass line.

Space and the Danwei

I have left the question of space until last since in many ways it is the spatiality of the *danwei* that holds this study together. Space bears closely upon the issue of genealogy—I have traced aspects of *danwei* spatial practice to traditional China, to the rise of urban planning in Europe, and to the Constructivist architects of the early Soviet Union. Space also plays a critical role in the analysis of micro power—many disciplinary and biotechnical practices turn upon the uses of space within everyday life. Moreover, space is also clearly tied to the problems of governmentality—techniques for ordering and transforming space have been central to governmental planning and intervention since Haussmann's interventions in mid-nineteenth-century Paris. In this way, space bears upon all the major methodological strategies I employ within this study.

To examine the way space has been conceived and the role it has played in everyday social practice is important to the analysis of any society. In the Chinese historical archive, spatial traces appear particularly rich. The spatial order of the traditional compound home (*siheyuan*) mirrored exactly the hierarchical order of the Confucian family, while the configuration of the traditional city similarly provided symbolic representation of the relationships of power that operated within the city. The highly symbolic spatiality of Confucian China is indeed fascinating, but what is of far greater significance to my concerns in this book is the degree to which aspects of symbolic spatial practice reemerge within socialist China. It is to this influence that we can attribute the walled compound spaces constructed under socialism to house the *danwei* of socialist China.

I locate the spatiality of the *danwei* in the intersection of a number of disparate factors. First, the walled compound form and the symbolism of internal spatial arrangements (including the axial alignment of buildings) is the result of a mimetic effect in which familiar forms are reinvoked to secure the boundaries of new modes of social life. Through this process, the ordered space of the family compound is reworked to house the guilds and corporations of Republican China, and then recast to house the collective units of socialist China—the *danwei*. This traditional heritage, however, is only one layer of the *danwei's* complex spatial genealogy. Indeed, I particularly emphasize that *danwei* spatial practice derives to a significant degree from spatial practices that developed far from China. Especially critical in this regard was the emergence of urban planning as a form of governmental intervention and its subsequent wedding to utopian notions of social change.

With Haussmann, space became something that could be subjected to systematic planning and transformation in order to achieve specific economic ends. With later radicals like Robert Owen, Charles Fourier, and Le Corbusier, the planned transformation of space was perceived as a revolutionary technique—new spatial forms could engender revolutionary new kinds of social relationships. Such thinking animated the activities of the radical Constructivist planners and architects in the pre-Stalinist Soviet Union. Yet, while their grander plans for the radically collectivized "social condensers" were not realized, their contributions to the emergence of a systematic and standardized approach to the mass production of socialist urban living spaces played a critically influential role in the development of spatial practice in post-1949 China.

Construction strategies adopted in China during the industrialization drives of the 1950s and 1960s further contributed to the emergence of the *danwei* as a distinctive spatial realm. Project-style investment policy ensured that each *danwei* became a financially independent economic unit with very little structural relationship to the rest of the city space that surrounded it. The wall enclosing the *danwei* simply reinforced, through symbolic representation, the actuality of this independence.

The disparate genealogy of the *danwei* spatial form provides an important insight into the significance of spatial practice within the everyday operation of the *danwei*. The walled compound form reinforces the sense in which the *danwei* is a collectivized social unit, providing both protection and identity to its members. Internal spatial arrangements, particularly the axial alignment of major buildings, are designed to symbolically reproduce the mythical order of the "socialist state," ensuring that the centrality of the party and of productive labor are constantly represented to all who live and work within the *danwei*. Moreover, the standardization of living and working spaces within the *danwei* reinforce the principles of egalitarianism and common identity, as well as suggesting a sense of national unity in the socialist cause.

The reform period has brought significant and unexpected change to the *danwei*, not least through the massive reconstruction that has reshaped much of the urban environment over the last two decades. Yet while the locus of urban life has clearly shifted from the *danwei* compound to the commercial streets and shopping centers of the city, many spatial traces remain to influence the practices of daily life. Indeed, the *danwei* compound continues to provide a secure home to many urban residents who no longer rely upon it as a source of livelihood. Moreover, the new basic unit of urban development—the *xiaoqu*—resembles the *danwei* compound of old in many ways. Though severing the link between work and residence, the *xiaoqu* creates a new form of communal space, bringing together various services and facilities within an enclosed residential compound. Of course, most of the spatial and architectural symbolism associated with the *danwei* as a unit of collectivized socialist production has been totally effaced through redevelopment. Where it remains, it no longer makes sense and hovers specter-like, haunting the present with the once hopeful dreams of socialism.

The history of the *danwei* has been neither neat nor seamless. It has not been a story of inexorable rise and inevitable fall; its genealogy rather charts a course that has been disjointed, complex, and disparate. This story continues, and while the *danwei* as an institution has probably entered a state of terminal decline, many facets of its operation persist in new formations into the present. It seems likely, then, that features of the *danwei* system will affect urban China for many years to come.

Chapter 1

1. Foucault 1980b, 149.

2. For a detailed analysis of the genealogical method, see Dreyfus and Rabinow 1982, 104–25. Other applications of this method to the study of modern China include Dutton 1992b and Anagnost 1997.

3. Zhu Guanglei 1994, 48. (All translations of Chinese texts are mine unless otherwise noted.)

4. Lu Feng 1989, 71.

5. As Zhu Guanglei (1994) suggests in the passage I cite above, the standard translation for *danwei* is "unit." Other translators, as can be seen below, prefer the slightly more specific term "work unit." When I utilize direct quotations, I naturally reproduce the term favored by the translator or commentator concerned. In my own translations and discussions, however, I always use the term *danwei*.

6. He Xinghan 1993, translation in Dutton 1998, 44.

7. Li Hanlin 1993, 23.

8. He Xinghan 1993, translation in Dutton 1998, 43–44. Victor N. Shaw (1996, 6–11) estimates that in 1992 there were between 145 and 180 million people working for approximately 13 million different *danwei* throughout China. This figure only includes actual employees and does not account for dependent spouses and children who also live within and rely upon the *danwei*. Shaw estimates the total *danwei* population to be around 325 million, which is about 28 percent of China's population.

9. Li Hanlin 1993, 23.

10. Yi Zhongtian 1996, 188; translation in Dutton 1998, 58–59.

11. He Xinghan 1993, translation in Dutton 1998, 46–47.

12. Butterfield 1990, 40–41.

13. "Reform" of the *danwei* system began in the mid-1980s but did not really gather much momentum until the mid-1990s. I cover this issue in depth in Chapter 7.

14. The pre-reform socialist *danwei* operated roughly from the mid-1950s to the mid-1980s.

15. The discipline of sociology was officially banned in China from 1952 to around 1979, as it was considered to be antisocialist. It was revived in the early 1980s

in response to Deng's call for "freeing the mind" and for academics to "seek truth from fact." China's most well-known surviving sociologist, Fei Xiaotong, was rehabilitated to direct the revival of sociology, both as a research discipline and as a subject taught in the universities. See Han Mingmo 1990, 55–66.

16. The term "traditional socialism" (*chuantong shehuizhuyi*) is used by commentators, particularly in China, to refer to the type of socialism practiced in the Maoist period and to distinguish it from the new form of socialism, "market socialism," that has emerged in the reform period. Clearly there is also a degree of slippage in the usage of this term in that it can be read to indicate a close connection between "traditional socialism" and traditional Chinese society. Debates around this issue will be addressed later in this book.

17. Walder 1986. Although Walder does not actually use the term *danwei*, his work is widely accepted as being one of the foundational studies on this topic.

18. Walder 1986, 9–10. Despite adopting the term "communist neo-traditionalism" to describe labor relations in Chinese factories, Walder explains that this has nothing to do with China's own traditional past, but rather refers to a standard type established by the Western social sciences, where "the term *tradition* has come to be associated with dependence, deference and particularism, and the term *modern* with independence, contract, and universalism" (p. 10; emphasis in the original).

19. Naughton 1997, 171. Naughton claims that three policy strategies implemented in response to the failure of the Great Leap Forward resulted in the formation of the *danwei* system: the elimination of labor markets and job mobility, the regularization of enterprise financial systems, and the program of administrative simplification.

20. Lu Feng 1993; Lü 1997, 21–41; Womack 1991, 313–32.

21. Perry 1997, 42–59; Yeh 1995, 97–122.

22. Frazier 2002, 234.

23. Lu Feng 1989, 72–73.

24. Ibid., 79.

25. Yang Dongping 1994, 254.

26. Foucault 1979, 31.

27. Ibid., 27.

28. Ibid.

29. Foucault 1978, 143.

30. Dreyfus and Rabinow 1982, 135.

31. Foucault 1991, 100.

32. Gordon 1991.

33. See Soja 1989: 10–42.

34. Foucault 1979, 195–228. The Panopticon was made up of prison cells arranged around a central observation tower such that a single supervisor in the tower was able to see into each cell at any time without in turn being observed by the prisoner.

35. Foucault 1979, 195–228. According to Foucault, the principle applies far beyond the prison—the school, the factory, the hospital, and the asylum are among the other kinds of institutions where these new arrangements of spatio-power have become present. See also Dreyfus and Rabinow, 1982 188–97.

36. Soja 1989, 10–42. This almost pathological neglect of space is repeated even in some of the major surveys of Foucault's own work. For example, in their treatment, Hubert Dreyfus and Paul Rabinow (1982, 188–92) devote only four pages to the question of space. In a well-known collection of critical commentaries on Foucault, Edward Said (1986) is the only critic to make any reference to Foucault's "geographic bent," but even he does not take the issue of space any further.

37. Wheatley 1971.

38. Hsu 1971.

39. F. Bray 1997.

40. Rofel 1992, 93–114.

41. Dutton 1992b and 1998, 192–237.

42. Zhang 2001.

43. I have deliberately excluded the edited collection *Urban Spaces in Contemporary China* (Davis et al. 1995), since, despite the title, it contains very little actual spatial analysis. Instead, this collection focuses primarily on aspects of urban culture, identity, and social organization.

44. For example, Davis et al. 1995.

45. A number of important works deal with these debates in considerable depth; for a discussion of this question from the point of view of an urban sociologist, see Saunders 1986; for a more interdisciplinary approach, see Gottdiener 1994; for an avowedly postmodern critique, see Soja 1989.

46. Soja 1989, 36.

47. See Harvey 1982 and Massey 1984.

48. Lefebvre 1991.

49. See Lefebvre 1976, 14–17.

50. Lefebvre 1991, 229.

51. Ibid., 281.

52. Ibid., 304–5. This reading is applied not only to those who have worked directly for the state, like Haussmann, who redesigned and rebuilt Paris during the third quarter of the nineteenth century, and all the bureaucratic planners who followed him, but is also applied to those who have seen themselves as revolutionaries in opposition to the prevailing order. Indeed, Lefebvre explicitly states that the radical work of the Bauhaus, Le Corbusier, and the Soviet avant-garde architects and planners of the 1920s and 1930s all "turned out to be in the service of the state." I deal in more detail with Haussmann, Le Corbusier, and the Soviet designers in Chapter 4.

53. A good example of this is the vastly divergent approach planners and architects have adopted in addressing the problem of public or welfare housing within the capitalist system.

Chapter 2

1. Yang Dongping 1994, 254.

2. Aldo Rossi (1982) has adopted the term *skeleton* in reference to historical architectural forms in order to suggest their role as both artefacts—recorders of particular periods of human construction—and sites for the continual unfolding of

events. I use the term here especially in order to emphasise the latter as important to understanding the significance of walls in China. The following pages will make this point clear.

3. Chinese Marxist historiography is perhaps the most guilty of simplistic periodization, reading the revolutionary victory of 1949 as the point of transition from a "semi-feudal semi-colonial" period to a modern socialist period. See, for example, Communist Party of China 1981, 1–10. The dominant postwar Western school of Chinese history, exemplified by Fairbank, Reischauer, and Craig (1965), see modernity in China as the direct result of Western influence and hence date the modern in China from the first contacts of China with the West. For a more detailed discussion of Western readings of Chinese history, see Mackerras 1989, 150–71.

4. Sirén, quoted in Needham 1971, 42–43.

5. Jenner 1992, 83–102.

6. Ibid., 83.

7. Barmé and Minford 1989.

8. Ibid., xxviii, 1–62.

9. For example, Jenner (1992, 83–102) argues that practices which exclude foreigners from China, peasants from cities, and outsiders from families can all be attributed to a general Chinese tendency to enclosure.

10. Su Xiaokang and Wang Luxiang 1988.

11. Geremie Barmé and Linda Jaivin (1992, 138–64) provide a useful selection of documents to illustrate the political and cultural significance of the series.

12. Su Xiaokang and Wang Luxiang 1988 (*JPRS Report*, 12).

13. In a recent study of the Great Wall, Arthur Waldron (1990) challenges this assertion by arguing that the building of massive, continuous defensive walls was only one among many strategic approaches adopted at various specific times to deal with the problem of China's security and its relations with its non-Chinese neighbors. According to Waldron, Chinese foreign policy, of which the Great Wall formed a part, should be seen as being the result not of cultural unity, but rather of the clashes between several differing approaches to specific questions of strategy and particular historical challenges. In this light the Great Wall should not be viewed as a symbol of the unity of Chinese culture, for as Waldron puts it, "far from being the product of deep cultural orientations the wall, at least, is the product of particular ideas and circumstances, and that these in no way constitute an exhaustive or even a unique definition of Chineseness" (191). Nicola Di Cosmo (2002, 155–58) similarly debunks the idea that Chinese border walls represent insularity or defensiveness. In his study of early relations between China and its northern neighbors he argues that border walls should be seen as part of an offensive, expansive, and imperial project by early Chinese states to seize and hold as much land as possible.

14. Foucault 1979, 195–228.

15. Yang Dongping 1994, 254.

16. Waldron 1990, 13.

17. Robert Bagley 1999, 165–66.

18. Zhongguo Dabaike Quanshu 1988, 327.

19. Eliade 1976, 18–27.

20. Bourdieu 1979, 133−53.

21. F. Bray 1997, 51−52.

22. Loewe 1968, 129. See also Wheatley 1971, 411−51.

23. Knapp 1990, 3.

24. Similar claims have been made in the Western tradition. Influential fifteenth-century architect Alberti, for example, held that "the city is like a large house, and the house in turn is like a small city." See Rossi 1982, 9.

25. Mote 1977, 138.

26. F. Bray 1997, 93.

27. Although the *Zhou Li* purports to record the ritual practices of the Zhou dynasty (ca. 1100−476 BC), the execution of the Confucians and the destruction of their texts by the Qin emperor, as well as the general chaos which preceded the rise of the Han dynasty, make it more likely that the Zhou Li is in fact a record of Han ritual, attributed to the Zhou in order to gain greater legitimacy (Wright 1977, 46). See also Wheatley 1971, 411; and He Yeju 1985, 21−22.

28. Quoted in Wheatley 1971, 411.

29. See Confucius 1971, 145 (*Analects*, Bk. II, Ch. I).

30. Wheatley 1971, 435.

31. For a detailed elaboration of the design features of each of these capitals, see Yang Kuan 1993.

32. Mote 1977, 107.

33. Zhu Wenyi 1993, 136.

34. According to Yang Kuan (1993, 210−12), the term *li* (2) was a unit of distance and was adopted in the Western Zhou dynasty because each walled neighborhood was supposed to be one *li* square. The term *lü* referred to the gate that led into and out of the *li*, hence the two characters were often used together. He Yeju (1985, 117) explains that the term *fang* (1) was used during the Sui and Tang dynasties. It was apparently adopted because it was a homophone for *fang* (2)—"to guard against." For the sake of brevity, I will use the generic term *li-fang* system to refer to this form of urban neighborhood organization.

35. Yang Kuan 1993, 212 (from *Guanzi*, "Baguan").

36. Ibid. (from *Guanzi*, "Lizheng").

37. Ibid., 261−67; also Mote 1977, 125.

38. On the *baojia* system, see Dutton 1992b, 21−50. *Bao* and *jia* were simply units of household groupings that made up community organizational structures. The names of these units varied throughout the dynastic period. For example, during the Ming dynasty, ten families made up a *pai*, ten *pai* made up a *jia*, and ten *jia* made up a *bao*.

39. He Yeju (1985, 115) cites the chapter "Dasitu" in the *Zhou Li* as the source for this information.

40. The number of families in the *lü*, twenty-five, also corresponded exactly to the number of soldiers who made up one chariot platoon in the Zhou army.

41. He Yeju 1985, 115.

42. Dutton 1992b, 84−89.

43. Alison Dray-Novey (1993, 892−94) shows how vestiges of the *li-fang* system

can be found reappearing in later periods as aids to policing practices. For example, in Qing dynasty Beijing, street gates, or *zhalan*, were used to close off residential lanes at night. Constables let only known residents through the gates.

44. Dutton 1992b, 63–67.

45. Ibid., 67–84, 181. The *baojia* system was revived by the Guomindang regime in 1932.

46. To this day many districts in Chinese cities have the characters *li* or *fang* in their name. Examples from Beijing include Ping'anli and Baizhifang.

47. William Rowe (1984, 336–37), for example, highlights the role played by *baojia* headmen in patrolling and policing order within their local communities in Qing dynasty Hankou.

48. This distinction is central to the philosophical disputes that divided the Confucian and the Legalist schools of thought. For an elaboration of this dispute and the subsequent effects on the legal codes of ancient China, see Ch'ü 1965.

49. Confucius 1979, 63 (Bk. II, Ch. 3).

50. See Tu Wei-ming 1979, 20–21.

51. Ibid., 20.

52. Confucius 1971, 406–7 (*The Doctrine of the Mean*, Ch. XX, Pt. 8).

53. On this point, see also Bodde and Morris 1967, 20.

54. *The Hsiao Ching* 1961, 5. The compiler of this book is not known, but the content is attributed to Confucius and the text is thought to have been written between 350–200 BC. It has been considered an important part of the Confucian canon since the Han dynasty and was designated as one of the "13 Classics" in the Tang dynasty.

55. F. Bray 1997, 55–56.

56. Ibid., 57.

57. Rawson 1999, 391.

58. Von Falkenhausen 1999, 455.

59. Mencius 1970, 268 (Bk. III, Ch. III, Pt. 6).

60. See Boyd 1962, 87–91 and plates 10–14; also Liu Zhiping 1990, 17 and 202.

61. For example, Liu Zhiping 1990 and Liu Dunzhen 1980.

62. Knapp 1990, 1. See also F. Bray 1997, 74.

63. See Knapp 1990, 5–25; and also Liu Dunzhen 1957, 38. Lu Xiang and Wang Qiming (1996, 25–40) provide a detailed analysis of the regional distribution of the different styles of the traditional courtyard house.

64. In one particular illustration, Liu Zhiping (1990, 206) juxtaposes traditional household forms from various parts of (greater) China. This exercise shows that, with the exception of dwellings from the Mongolian, Tibetan, and central Asian tradition, the others all adhere to a common basic courtyard formation.

65. Boyd 1962, 49 (italics in original).

66. F. Bray 1997, 91.

67. Indeed, Wolf and Huang (1980. 58) define the concept of *jia* (family) as consisting of those who eat from the same stove.

68. Duara 1988, 89.

69. Confucius 1971, 315–16 (*Analects*, Bk. XVI, Ch. XIII).

70. Instead of Legge's "passed below the hall," D. C. Lau (Confucius 1979, 141) translates the phrase *guo ting* as "crossed the courtyard." Since "*ting*" can mean "hall" and "courtyard," both readings are correct, though the latter perhaps gives a better sense of the spatial setting of the home.

71. The original text speaks only of there being a "distance" between the gentleman and his son: *you wen junzi zhi yuan qi zi ye.* Legge adds the concept of "reserve" to that of "distance" in his translation. Lau (Confucius 1979, 142) omits "distance" entirely, opting instead for "aloof."

72. See also F. Bray 1997, 124–40.

73. Ma Bingjian 1993, 40. On the distribution of rooms, see also Boyd 1962, 76–82; and Hsu 1971, 316–22.

74. F. Bray 1997, 96–107.

75. Knapp 1990, 52. Francis Hsu (1971, 31) notes that in two-story courtyard homes of West Town (the Yunnan town in which he carried out his research in the early 1940s) the ancestor tablets occupy the central hall of the second story, immediately above the rooms occupied by the head of the family. However, on the most important days of ancestral worship the tablets are brought down to the rooms below.

76. Ma Bingjian 1993, 40.

77. *The Lî Kî* 1885, 470 (Book X, The Nêi Zeh).

78. According to the text (ibid., 471), the *xiangfang* were also designated as the place for childbirth. The patriarch's wife or concubine would be removed from the *zhengfang* to the *xiangfang* before giving birth. Presumably this was in order to forestall any of the possible dangers of childbirth adversely affecting the central axis of ancestral power. If the child survived long enough to be formerly named, child and mother could move back into the *zhengfang*.

79. Boyd 1962, 77. In one of the households examined by Hsu (1971, 320), this wing was rented out to tenants.

80. See, for example, Liu Dunzhen 1957.

81. Knapp 1990, 52–53. This description is also supported by the author's own observations during visits to villages in Shandong.

82. See Foucault 1979, 200–228; and 1990, 146–65.

Chapter 3

1. Perry 1997, 42–59.

2. Much of Michel Foucault's work concerns the implications of the emergence of this particular form of human subjectivity. In *The Order of Things*, he examines the appearance of individualized "man" as an object for study within various disciplines. In *Discipline and Punish*, he discusses how the emergence of this new concept of subjectivity led to significant transformations in disciplinary techniques.

3. For a useful summary of Foucault's arguments related to the processes through which the individual subject becomes a resource for the practices of liberal government, see Dreyfus and Rabinow 1982, 168–83.

4. Mauss 1985. On this issue, also see Hirst and Wooley 1982, 118–39.

5. Zito and Barlow 1994, 9–11.

6. Dutton 1992b; Anagnost 1997, 116.

7. For example, Rowe 1984; Strand 1989, 142–66; Hershatter 1986; Perry 1993; Martin 1996, 168–72; and Goodman 1995, 29–38, 233–36.

8. Perry 1993, 32–33.

9. According to Chen Baoliang, native-place associations are first recorded in the Song dynasty. See Chen Baoliang 1996, 220; see also Golas 1977, 555–60; and Goodman 1995, 4–14.

10. Goodman 1995, 110–17. Bryna Goodman relates a particular case study in which a Guangdong merchants' guild (*huiguan*) went to great efforts in order to overturn a secret marriage entered into by the daughter of a guild member against her father's wishes. Goodman summarizes this case as follows: "In a Confucian context . . . the *huiguan*, as the urban equivalent of lineage elders, was responsible not simply for defending the honor of women from its native place but also for enforcing the authority of men over women" (116–17).

11. Van Der Sprenkel 1977, 616.

12. Perry 1993, 36.

13. For example, the Cantonese carpenters' guild had a monopoly over carpentry work in Shanghai from as early as the mid-nineteenth century (Golas 1977, 570).

14. Perry 1993, 34; see also Rowe 1984, 290–94.

15. Frazier 2002, 31.

16. On this point, see also Hershatter 1986, 139.

17. Mark Frazier notes that the guilds were particularly prominent in the industries connected to machine building and metalworking (Frazier 2002, 31).

18. Perry 1993, 35.

19. Perry is not alone in making this argument. Bryna Goodman and Brian Martin both make similar points on the role of apparently "traditional" forms of organization in the emergence of modern Shanghai; the former in relation to native-place associations, the latter in relation to criminal gangs. See Goodman 1995, 306–12; and Martin 1996, 215–17.

20. Like the process outlined in Berman 1988.

21. See Perry 1993, 50; and Hershatter 1986, 167–75.

22. Martin provides a detailed analysis of the rise of one of the major Shanghai gangs, the Green Gang, charting the expansion of its activities from opium running in the early 1920s to participation in a broad range of criminal, economic, social, and political activities in the 1930s under the leadership of Du Yuesheng. See Martin 1996.

23. Perry 1993, 50; Martin 1996, 83.

24. Perry 1993, 52.

25. Ibid., 53, 56–57.

26. Contractors particularly targeted young rural women for work in the cotton industry, since it was believed that women were more readily intimidated and less likely to cause trouble when they realized the subservient nature of the relationship into which they had placed themselves.

27. The exploitive nature of the labor contract system was one of the key issues pushed by the Communist Party in its attempts to organize workers and stage strikes

in the 1920s. This is one of the reasons why the Green Gang allied itself with Chiang Kaishek and the GMD in the suppression of the communist-led labor movement in 1927. After 1927, trade unions in Shanghai remained firmly under the control of the Green Gang. It is for this reason that I don't discuss the labor movement as a force in urban social organization during this period. I do, however, consider the role of the pre-1949 trade unions and their organizational practices on the transition to socialism in Chapter 5. On the dominance of the Green Gang over Shanghai trade unions, see Martin 1996, 86–93; and Wakeman 1995, 28–29.

28. Perry 1993, 55.

29. Martin 1996, 83.

30. According to Gail Hershatter, for mutual protection, groups of workers would often swear allegiances of "brotherhood" (or "sisterhood" for women workers) under the patronage of a "big brother." Such "brotherhoods" were usually affiliated with one of the gangs active in Tianjin (Hershatter 1986, 169–70).

31. Perry 1993, 55. Martin also reveals that the Green Gang, particularly under Du Yuesheng, played a major role in the mediation of strikes. Through this activity, the Green Gang was able to further cement its control over organized labor as well as assert increased influence over business operations in Shanghai. See Martin 1996, 122–26, 168–72.

32. In this respect, it is interesting to note that the Green Gang's antecedent, the Patriarch Luo sect, was primarily a mutual aid society for boatmen on the Grand Canal. As well as providing a religious organizational structure and facilities for worship, this sect provided members with medical care, accommodation, and burials (Martin 1996, 11).

33. Martin 1996, 18.

34. Ibid., 51.

35. Note, however, that not every industrializing city mirrored exactly the social development of Shanghai. Where Perry highlights the importance of organized groups—artisan guilds and gangs—in ordering life within industrial workplaces in Shanghai, Hershatter emphasizes the weakness of such formal organizations in Tianjin. Nevertheless, Hershatter points out that while their networks may have been less structured and formalized, the workers of Tianjin were indeed dependent on networks of support and protection, many of which originated with their native-place. Thus, whether they were more formalized as in Shanghai, or more ad hoc as in Tianjin, it appears that workers in China's industrializing urban centers relied to a great extent upon forms of social organization that reproduced the kind of collective-oriented relationships that prevailed in traditional rural society.

36. Yeh 1995, 97–122.

37. Ibid., 105–7.

38. Ibid., 108.

39. Ibid., 109–12.

40. Ibid., 121.

41. The name derives from the first syllable of the three provinces, Shaanxi, Gansu, and Ningxia, the borders of which the base area straddled.

42. At its largest, the Jiangxi Soviet encompassed a population of about 3 million;

see Chesneaux, Le Barbier, and Bergère 1977, 232. According to David Apter and Tony Saich (1994, 207), in 1942 the Shaan-Gan-Ning border region, over which the CCP exerted jurisdiction, had a population of around 1.5 million.

43. Mao Zedong 1961–77, 1:129.

44. For example, Schurmann 1968, 416–21.

45. Selden 1971.

46. Mark Selden, in particular, has been criticized for overemphasizing the participatory and egalitarian aspects of the "Yan'an Way." In a recent new edition of the Yan'an study, Selden admits as much, commenting that the period also "harbored seeds of party despotism, ideological fundamentalism and the cult of the leader." See Selden 1995, 243–44.

47. I do not mean to suggest here a synthesis of the totalitarian and egalitarian positions, or even a "third way" between the two. On the contrary, I suggest that the issue be considered in a completely different way. The question to be addressed is not "why did the communists win," but rather how did CCP policies and practices in Yan'an contribute to establishing a form of government that became the basis, eventually, for governing the whole nation.

48. Lü 1997, 21–41.

49. Ibid., 22–24. A full wage system was not introduced until 1955.

50. Mao Zedong, "Economic and Financial Problems," in Watson 1980, 149.

51. Selden 1971, 255–57.

52. Lu Feng 1993, 14.

53. Lü 1997, 24–26.

54. Ibid., 29.

55. Ibid., 29–32.

56. Wang Hui and Leo Ou-fan Lee 1994, 598–605. For example, under the traditional *jingtianzhi*, or "well-field system," land was divided into nine sections (this division resembling the Chinese character for "well"), eight of which were farmed by individual families, while the ninth field was farmed in common and the harvest submitted to the government as tax. The common field was known as *gongtian*.

57. Rowe 1990, 317. By way of distinction, central government property was referred to by the character *guan*.

58. See Duara 1988, 149–52.

59. Rowe 1990, 319. Liang Qichao was the most prominent advocate of this movement.

60. Rowe 1990, 319–25.

61. Of course, the patrilineal family remained the fundamental social unit among the general population who did not become professional revolutionaries. Nevertheless, as Tani Barlow demonstrates, the family (*jiating*) was also mobilized and refigured during the Yan'an period as a site for the inscription of new socialist identities and a metaphor for the socialist state itself (Barlow 1994, 268–78).

62. In his early writings, Lu Feng termed the modern *danwei* a "clan-like" form of organization and argued that many key features of the *danwei* closely resembled features of the traditional clan system. See Lu Feng 1989, 78–82. Lü and Perry (1997, 8) also equate the *danwei* to the traditional family. According to them, "the *danwei*

acts as a patriarch who disciplines and sanctions his children, while at the same time serving as a maternal provider of care and daily necessities."

63. Apter and Saich (1994, 226) emphasize the importance of group interaction for the formation of identity in Yan'an, where, according to their analysis, no room was permitted for individual space.

64. See, for example, the following two volumes of collected essays, both devoted to the problem of governmentality: Burchell, Gordon, and Miller 1991; and Barry, Osborne, and Rose 1996.

65. This can apparently be explained by "something peculiar about the Western passion for government." See Allen 1998, 188–91.

66. To date, only a relatively small number of studies have attempted to utilize the concept in relation to China. These include Sigley 1996 and Li Zhang 2001.

67. See especially Miller and Rose 1990; and Rose and Miller 1992.

68. See Foucault 1991.

69. Rose and Miller 1992, 174.

70. I use *government* in a broad sense to include all party, government, and military organizations engaged in the wide range of activities related to policy making and implementation in the border region.

71. Selden 1971, 150–53.

72. Rose and Miller 1992, 178–89.

73. Ibid., 178–79.

74. Apter and Saich 1994, 224–60.

75. Rose and Miller 1992, 181.

76. Ibid., 182.

77. Mao had long promoted the utility of detailed fieldwork and research to the revolutionary project and had himself undertaken a study of the peasant population in his home province Hunan in 1927. See Mao Zedong 1961–77, 1:23–59.

78. Mao Zedong 1993, 2:360.

79. Ibid., 2:361.

80. Watson 1980, 1–3.

81. Rose and Miller 1992, 183.

82. Ibid., 184.

83. Ibid., 187.

84. Problems of government become amenable to expert intervention through, for example, "translating political concerns about economic productivity, innovation, industrial unrest, social stability, law and order, normality and pathology and so forth into the vocabulary of management, accounting, medicine, social science and psychology" (Rose and Miller 1992, 188).

85. Mao Zedong 1961–77, 1:291. Stalin's original statement can be found in his "Address delivered in the Kremlin Palace to the graduates from the Red Army Academies," May 1935.

86. Although the CCP had been at war with the Japanese since the latter had launched their full-scale invasion in July 1937, this struggle did not begin to put pressure on the finances of the Shaan-Gan-Ning base area until around 1939. Officially the GMD government continued contributing substantial amounts to the finances

of the border region government, under United Front arrangements, until the New Fourth Army incident of January 1941. Nevertheless, GMD forces in position around the base area implemented an economic blockade from 1939. See Watson 1980, 17.

87. Mao Zedong 1961–77, 3:117–22.

88. Ibid., 3:119.

89. Ibid., 3:122.

90. Mao Zedong 1961–77, 1:285.

91. In most cases the "local" cadre was not a native of the area but rather a cadre "sent down" from central party or government organizations.

92. Liu Shaoqi 1984, 1:168. This was a speech made by Liu Shaoqi to the Institute of Marxism-Leninism in Yan'an in 1939 and was one of the documents included in study materials for the Rectification Movement of 1943.

93. Liu Shaoqi 1984, 137–39.

94. Ibid., 140.

95. Apter and Saich 1994, 227.

96. Foucault 1982, 213–15. See also Dean 1999, 74–83.

97. Foucault 1997, 68.

98. Foucault 1982, 214–15.

99. Ibid.

100. Liu Shaoqi 1984, 1:139.

101. For a useful description of the goals and procedures for cadre training in Yan'an, see Apter and Saich 1994, 224–60.

102. Liu Shaoqi 1984, 1:235–36. This was a speech Liu made to a conference of cadres of northwestern Shaanxi in December 1942.

103. Mao Zedong 1961–77, 3:133.

104. Ibid., 3:132–33.

105. Ibid., 3:134.

106. As Selden (1971) points out, it is apparent that the expectation that party and government officials be both "red and expert" emerged first during the Yan'an period rather than during post-1949 political and economic campaigns, as suggested by some commentators. See also Schurmann 1968, 163–67. In his analysis, Franz Schurmann, however, tends to overemphasize the "redness" of the cadre's role, distinguishing the cadre from the "manager" and the "bureaucrat" by way of his commitment to "ideology," rather than "rational organisation" (the "manager") or "routinization" (the "bureaucrat"). As my discussion illustrates, such categories are rather difficult to sustain when considering the complexity and variety of the tasks demanded of the cadre.

Chapter 4

1. Le Corbusier [1929] 1987, 244.

2. Mao Zedong 1961–77, 4:374.

3. Françoise Choay adopts the term "critical planning" to suggest that where once the city had been viewed as "natural," from the late nineteenth century it came to be conceived as an object of critical thought (Choay 1969, 10).

4. For example, see Choay 1969, 8; and Hall 1988, 7.

5. Choay 1969, 9–10; and Hall 1988, 23–44.

6. Miller and Rose 1990, 7; also Hacking 1983.

7. Foucault 1991, 87–104.

8. Gordon 1991, 4.

9. Foucault 1991, 97–101.

10. Miller and Rose 1990, 4.

11. Foucault 1991, 100.

12. Rabinow 1989, 10–11. Rabinow makes few references to "governmentality," preferring the term "welfare" to describe the "bio-technico-political" mode of Foucault's work (8). Nevertheless, it is clear that Rabinow's analysis centers upon that realm of governmental activity that is now widely referred to as governmentality.

13. Foucault 1982, 213.

14. See the various contributions in Burchell, Gordon, and Miller 1991 and Barry, Osborne, and Rose 1996.

15. Foucault 1980b, 148.

16. Choay 1969, 15. Walter Benjamin, for example, states that "the true purpose of Haussmann's work was to secure the city against civil war" (Benjamin 1986, 160).

17. Choay 1969, 16, also Rabinow 1989, 76.

18. Osborne 1996, 116.

19. Of course revolutionary socialist discourse suggested quite a different interventionist practice. This question will be addressed in detail below.

20. Choay 1969, 15.

21. Pinkney 1958, 56.

22. Benevolo 1971, 63.

23. Rabinow 1989, 76–77.

24. With the collaboration of engineer Belgrand, Haussmann was able to increase water supply threefold and almost quadruple the length of the sewer system (Pinkney 1958, 111, 126, 133).

25. Konvitz 1985, 127.

26. Foucault 1980b, 149.

27. Choay 1969, 20–22; and Benevolo 1971, 81–85.

28. Marx and Engels considered it illusory to attempt any plan for future socialist society before the conditions for its realization were made possible—namely, the successful overthrow of the capitalist order.

29. On Owen, see Harrison 1969; on Fourier, see Beecher and Bienvenu 1971.

30. The most comprehensive critique of utopian socialism can be found in Engels [1880] 1972.

31. Harrison 1969.

32. The New Lanark cotton mill was established in 1785 by Scottish merchant David Dale in partnership with English inventor and businessman Richard Arkwright. See Donnachie and Hewitt 1993, 16–23.

33. Other examples from this period include the towns of Stanley, Belper, Milford, and Cromford. See Harrison 1969, 52.

34. Donnachie and Hewitt 1993, 35–74.

35. See Harrison 1969, 43–87. One exception to this general tendency is

Leonardo Benevolo, who devotes a chapter to the ideas and spatial plans of Owen, Fourier, and other utopians in his history of modern architecture. See Benevolo 1971, 148–57.

36. Details in this regard are included in the "Report to the County of Lanark" (Owen 1927, 268).

37. Owen 1927, 268.

38. A design for an Owenite community based upon this formulation was produced by the architect Stedman Whitwell, who accompanied Owen to New Harmony in America. See Harrison 1969, plate 16, opposite 116.

39. Owen 1927, 268.

40. Ibid., 275.

41. Ibid., 276.

42. Owen's views on education and the educational methods he introduced into New Lanark are comprehensively treated within his "Address Delivered to the Inhabitants of New Lanark: On Opening the Institution for the Formation of Character, 1st of January, 1816" (Claeys 1993, 120–42).

43. Harrison 1969, 143.

44. Ibid.

45. On New Harmony, see Harrison 1969, 145. On New Lanark, see Claeys 1993, 125–26.

46. The fate of the various Owenite communities is discussed in Harrison 1969, 181–245.

47. See, in particular, Engels [1880] 1972.

48. Engels specifically addressed the various utopian plans for reform of working-class housing in a series of newspaper articles published in 1872 and later collected and published as a pamphlet under the title "The Housing Question." See Marx and Engels 1975–2004, 23:317–91.

49. See, for example, Lenin 1960–70, 27:253.

50. Numerous works deal with the history of urban reform in the West. See, for example, Hall 1988.

51. French 1995, 29.

52. Lenin 1960–70, 27:259.

53. Ibid.

54. At the time it was in France that the relationship between urban planning and government was perhaps the strongest (Kopp 1970, 37).

55. Banham 1960, 14.

56. Le Corbusier [1931] 1986, 95.

57. Banham discusses the history and contribution of each of these groups in some detail. See Banham 1960, 99–319.

58. French 1995, 32. Visitors included Ernst May, Bruno Taut, and Le Corbusier, who made three visits in the years 1928–30.

59. The problem faced by revolutionary architects in the West is well summarized by Ross King: "It would seem far easier to get one's revolutionary-intentioned painting exhibited or poem published than to have a similarly intended building or part of the city built—neither capital nor the state is likely to knowingly self-destruct, and who else is there to pay for it?" (King 1996, 46).

60. Fishman 1982, 185–86.

61. Le Corbusier [1931] 1986, 271–89.

62. Ibid., 276.

63. Ibid., 289.

64. Fishman 1982, 187.

65. Ironically for Le Corbusier, his utopian modernist urban plans only came anywhere near realization in the Soviet Union, where social revolution had already occurred. His major influence in the West came in the 1950s and 1960s, when governments began to construct great high-rise housing estates to meet the rising need for cheap public housing. Unfortunately, in social terms, the results were generally quite disastrous. The most notorious example being the Pruitt-Igoe estate in St. Louis, declared unlivable and demolished in 1972 only fifteen years after it was opened. See Hall 1988, 235–38.

66. I do not mean to foreclose here on the debate over the relative transformative effect of technology versus politics. Indeed, with hindsight it seems that Le Corbusier was probably more prescient than the Bolsheviks in predicting factors most influential in the course of world development. However, my aim at this point is to establish the theoretical framework upon which the radical Soviet planners and architects based their activities.

67. Kopp 1970, 92.

68. According to one commentator, the influence of his theories, sometimes referred to as Bogdanovism, was second only to those of Lenin, and they met with particular favor from scientists and economists (Sochor 1988, 13; on Bogdanov, also see Jensen 1978).

69. Sochor 1988, 128.

70. Frampton 1992, 168.

71. Sochor 1988, 148–54. Lenin's own views on the cultural question can be found in Lenin 1960–70, 31:316–17.

72. Bogdanov 1923. My treatment of Bogdanov follows that of Dutton 1992b, 200–202, 295–301.

73. Prominent *Proletkult* activists like Lissitzky, Rodchenko, and Tatlin were themselves architects and played active roles in training young architects through institutions such as Inkhuk (the Institute for Artistic Culture) and Vkhutemas (Higher Artistic and Technical Studios). See Frampton 1992, 168–69.

74. On constructivism, see Kopp 1985.

75. Frampton 1992, 174–75.

76. Kopp 1970, 92.

77. Ibid., 130.

78. Ibid. "Stroikom" was the Construction Committee of the RSFSR. The design group was headed by Moses Ginzburg, who was a prominent member of OSA.

79. "Decision of the Plenum of the Construction Committee for the RSFSR," November 26, 1928, SA 1929, no. 1, quoted in Kopp 1985, 64.

80. Kopp 1970, 135.

81. Ginzburg, cited in Kopp 1970, 141 (italics in the original).

82. Kuzmin, cited in Kopp 1970, 112.

83. Ibid., 153.

84. Ibid., 153, 155.

85. Foucault 1979, 200–228. While it may appear dubious to compare a prison to a workplace in this manner, it must be remembered that Bentham saw the Panopticon as an architectural model applicable to all institutional situations where some form of supervision or training was required. Foucault also reads the Panopticon as exemplary of a new form of power that spreads throughout institutional life during the nineteenth century.

86. Kaganovich, *Socialist Reconstruction of Moscow and Other Cities in the USSR*, quoted in French 1995, 42.

87. Frampton 1992, 177.

88. See Tarkhanov and Kavtaradze 1992, 90–114. For a comparison of the Stalinist city with the Fascist and Nazi city, see Hall 1988, 190–202.

89. Bliznakov 1976, 249.

90. These perennial shortages were due to investment priorities dictated by central planning bureaus. Economic resources were ploughed into industrialization and, later, the war effort, at the expense of housing and other facilities for everyday life. See French 1995, 56–57.

91. Bater 1980, 29.

92. Straus 1997, 145–46.

93. Ibid.

94. Ibid., 154–56.

95. Ibid., 148, 155. Indeed, by 1937 failure to make adequate provision of housing or food was used as a reason for the arrest and trial of factory directors.

96. Straus 1997, 153, 161.

97. Kopp 1970, 235.

98. French 1995, 37–38.

Chapter 5

1. Foucault 1991, 99. (This source is a translation of a lecture originally delivered in 1978.)

2. Todorov 1995, 10.

3. Guojia tongjiju shehui tongjisi 1994, 43–46. According to official statistics, 61.7 percent of the workforce belonged to "state-owned" *danwei*, while 29.3 percent belonged to "collective-owned" *danwei*. The remainder of the population were either "individual laborers" (3.1 percent) or unemployed (5.9 percent).

4. Mao Zedong 1961–77, 4:365.

5. "Ba xiaofei chengshi biancheng shengchan chengshi" ("Transform Consumer Cities into Productive Cities"), *People's Daily*, 17 March 1949, reprinted in Zhonggong zhongyang dangxiao dangshi jiaoyanshi 1979, 6:491–92.

6. At that time, Bo occupied a number of senior positions in the CCP's North China Bureau, including second secretary (Liu Shaoqi was first secretary), deputy president, and party secretary of North China People's Government. See Bo Yibo 1991–93, 1:3–4.

7. Bo Yibo 1991–93, 1:11–13. This policy is also outlined by Peng Zhen, the first CCP-sponsored mayor of Beijing (Peng Zhen 1991, 178–85).

8. The basic meaning of the character *bao* is "to wrap up" or "to envelope." From this, *bao* derives the extended meanings of "to guarantee" or "to undertake the whole thing." *Xialai* is a resultative complement, in this case indicating "to bring under." See *A Chinese-English Dictionary* (rev. ed.), Waiyu jiaoyu yu yanjiu chubanshe, Beijing 1995, 30.

9. The difficult financial situation and shortage of resources, however, ensured that the level of support was limited. In the immediate postliberation period, former GMD functionaries who were subject to the *baoxialai* policy had their rations reduced according to a directive that "five people share the food of three." Furthermore, because of shortages of housing, they were required to endure very cramped living conditions (Bo Yibo 1991–93, 1:15).

10. See, for example, Meisner 1986, 92–96.

11. Quoted in Bo Yibo 1991–93, 1:15. Bo provides no reference for the quotation he attributes to Mao.

12. In the next chapter I will show how the provision of food to urban workers through the communal canteen was to become a central and highly symbolic element within the collective life of the socialist *danwei*.

13. Under "New Democracy," CCP industrial policy called for the takeover only of those enterprises which had been operated by the GMD government (central or provincial) or by its major capitalist supporters, a sector referred to as "bureaucratic capital." In 1949 this sector accounted for just over 50 percent of total industrial output, including the vast majority of steel, coal, oil, and machinery output. Smaller-scale industry, operated by the so-called national bourgeoisie, was allowed to operate under its original ownership within certain confines dictated by the CCP, relating to matters such as labor conditions, investment, and taxation. See Wang Haibo 1994, 100–108, 180–81.

14. According to Mark Frazier (2002, 64–90), wartime shortages and hyperinflation (which destroyed the value of wages) had forced many factories in the GMD-controlled cities to provide food and other basic necessities to the workforce in the years leading up to the communist takeover. In this respect, the CCP clearly did not invent factory welfare—they built upon an existing system but imbued it with new political significance.

15. See Yuan Lunqu 1987, 18–20.

16. "Guanyu zhongguo zhigong yundong dangqian renwude jueyi" ("Decision on the current tasks of the Chinese labor movement"), Zhonggong zhongyang dangxiao dangshi jiaoyanshi 1979, 6:462–75.

17. Ibid., 6:472–73.

18. The term *zuzhiqilai* was first popularized by Mao in his "speech to Labor Heroes of the Shaan-Gan-Ning Border Region" in 1943. The injunction to "get organized" was associated with the production campaign that was then in progress. There are clear parallels here with the production push the CCP was promoting in the immediate postliberation period. See Mao Zedong 1961–77, 3:153–61.

19. For a more detailed discussion of the "new world view" promoted in CCP workers' handbooks of the period, see Kaple 1994, 73–80.

20. See "Decision on the Current Role of China's Labor Movement," Zhonggong zhongyang dangxiao dangshi jiaoyanshi 1979, 6:466–67; and Peng Zhen 1991, 180.

21. "Decision on the Current Role of China's Labor Movement," Zhonggong zhongyang dangxiao dangshi jiaoyanshi 1979, 6:467.

22. Ibid.

23. Ibid.

24. As Deborah Kaple (1994, 72–91) demonstrates, China's strategies in this regard were influenced significantly by Soviet labor practices.

25. The proposal to establish Residents' Committees and Street Offices was developed by Peng Zhen and formally legislated in 1954. For a recent overview of their history, see Read 2000, 810.

26. Peng Zhen 1991, 241.

27. Guojia tongjiju shehui tongjisi 1994, 43–46.

28. Andors 1977, 48.

29. Lieberthal focuses especially on the takeover of the transport industry in Tianjin (Lieberthal 1980, 63–71).

30. See Kaple 1994, 45–57.

31. Lenin 1960–70, 3:656–58.

32. See "Decision on the Current Role of China's Labor Movement," Zhonggong zhongyang dangxiao dangshi jiaoyanshi 1979, 6:466–67.

33. Ibid. These functions of the trade union organization were later set down in the Trade Union Law of the People's Republic of China, promulgated by the Central People's Government in June 1950. See Wang Yongxi et al. 1992, 340–41.

34. Lee Tai To 1989, 25. On the experiences gained by CCP authorities through their takeover of urban centers in the Northeast, see Levine 1987.

35. See various contributions concerning the takeover of Beijing factories in Wang Guiling, Dou Kun, and Lü Kenong 1988, 270–320, 546–56.

36. This management strategy was known as the "East China," or "Shanghai," model and was considered an interim measure until fully planned and scientific industrial management based on Soviet techniques could be established. See Andors 1977, 50–53.

37. Mark Frazier's (2002, 97–114) description of the CCP takeover at various factories in Shanghai and Guangzhou shows how difficult and sometimes chaotic the process was. In many cases it clearly took some time to restore production.

38. Lu Yu 1988, 276.

39. Kaple 1994, 98.

40. Several contributors to *Beijing's Dawn* discuss early moves to organize education classes for workers. See Wang Guiling, Dou Kun, and Lü Kenong 1988, 273, 303, 308, 317, 550–51. See also Edgar Snow's 1960 interview with Li Jiebo, vice chairman of the All China Federation of Trade Unions. Li is quoted as describing the trade union as a "ministry of spare-time education," whose main objective is "to prepare men and women who are politically, technically and culturally fitted to manage the national economy" (Snow 1970, 236–43).

41. In June 1950 the Government Administration Council of the Central People's

Government published guidelines on "spare-time" education for workers. These guidelines covered the types of classes to be organized, length of courses, hours per week, and so on. A copy of the guidelines can be found in Shanghai zonggonghui diaocha yanjiushi 1951, 231–36.

42. Lieberthal 1980, 72–73.

43. "Zhonghua renmin gongheguo laodong baoxian tiaoli," passed on 26 February 1951, amended 2 January 1953, by the State Council. A copy of this document is reproduced in Guojia renshiju 1980, 3:549–58.

44. Note that this document initially applied to a limited range of enterprises— namely, state-owned, private, joint state-private, and collective enterprises with over one hundred staff members or workers. The range of industries to which it was applied was also limited; however, by 1956 its application had been extended to include all industrial and commercial sectors of the economy. In addition, the regulations excluded state organs (*guojia jiguan*) and institutional *danwei* (*shiye danwei*—schools, research institutes, hospitals, etc.). This was because most of these kinds of *danwei* had emerged under the supply system during the revolutionary war period and already had welfare systems. Welfare provisions in these sectors were gradually brought into line with the regulations over a number of years. See Liu Chuanji and Sun Guangde 1987, 29–31.

45. Guojia Renshiju 1980, 551–56.

46. Ibid., 550.

47. Ibid., 551–56.

48. For a more detailed history and discussion of welfare provisions delegated to the *danwei*, see Lu Feng 1993, 53–57; and Leung and Nann 1995, 55–62.

49. Details of enterprise-based welfare infrastructure developed at various factories during this period can be found in Frazier 2002, 171–72, 181–83, 186–87, 192–93.

50. See Peng Siming 1988, 549.

51. Tan Liefei 1988, 309–10.

52. Ibid., 307.

53. "Decision on the Current Role of China's Labor Movement," in Zhonggong zhongyang dangxiao dangshi jiaoyanshi 1979, 6:468–69.

54. Ibid., 473.

55. For examples of how this problem affected various factories in Shanghai and Guangzhou, see Frazier 2002, 110–14.

56. See Shanghai zonggonghui diaocha yanjiushi 1951, 80–83.

57. Ibid., 80–81.

58. Li Lisan also held the post of minister for labor and had been responsible for most of the early labor-related policies, including the labor insurance system (Perry 1997, 44–46).

59. Liu's article appeared in print for the first time thirty-four years later in the second volume of his collected works (Wang Yongxi et al. 1992, 342–48; see also Liu Shaoqi 1984, vol. 2).

60. Wang Yongxi et al. 1992, 346.

61. Ibid., 342–46. Deng Zihui wrote a lengthy article in which these views were

set out in detail within the context of the prevailing New Democracy policy frame-work. This article was published in both *Workers' Daily* and *People's Daily* over six consecutive days, 4–9 August 1950.

62. Wang Yongxi et al. 1992, 347–48. Also Liu Shaoqi 1984.

63. Wang Yongxi et al. 1992, 346–47. Gao Gang was secretary of the CCP's Northeast Bureau. His opposition to the Li Lisan/Deng Zihui position was made public in a speech he delivered to a meeting of the executive committee of the Northeast Federation of Trade Unions. Later he enlisted the aid of Chen Boda to oust Li Lisan from leadership of ACFTU.

64. The final decision appears to be have been made by Mao. He is reported to have written a note stating that "serious errors have been committed in trade union work." See entry for 13–22 December 1951 in Ma Qibin et al. 1991, 41–42.

65. Wang Yongxi et al. 1992, 348.

66. The term *economism* was coined by Lenin in his critique of a trend within the Russian social-democratic movement to concentrate on economic rather than po-litical struggles. According to Lenin, this trend was based upon the false assumption that economic development would result in a spontaneous movement toward so-cialism. This assumption contradicted Lenin's view that socialist revolution required the intercession of a highly organized and centralized revolutionary political party. See Lenin 1960–70, 4:255–85; 5:313–20.

67. The term *syndicalism* derives simply from the French term for trade unionism but came to be associated with a belief that capitalism could be overthrown only through the collective struggle of industrial workers operating under their own ini-tiative. Syndicalists, therefore, generally rejected the need for a centralized socialist party to lead the revolution, instead advocating worker self-management and social-ism from below. For Lenin, the principles of syndicalism were closely connected to the trend he had already criticized for "economism." See entry under "syndicalism" in Bottomore et al. 1983, 476–77.

68. See Lee Tai To 1989, 34–35.

69. Li Lisan was permitted to retain his other position as minister for labor but was later targeted in the Cultural Revolution and died in 1967 as a direct result. In 1980 he was posthumously rehabilitated. The decision of 1951 which stripped him of his ACFTU position and condemned his work was also overturned. See Wang Yongxi et al. 1992, 348–49.

70. While Li Lisan's position was by no means as openly oppositional as that of the "workers' opposition" in the Soviet Union, the severity and haste with which it was terminated suggest some close parallels with the suppression of movements for worker self-management within the Soviet Union. On the "workers' opposition," see Carr 1966, 1:203–8, 2:225–29.

71. Although this congress was the first national trade union congress since the foundation of the PRC, it was considered to be in direct line of succession from the preliberation labor congresses, the last of which had been the Sixth National Labor Congress of 1948.

72. Lai Ruoyu 1953. See also Wang Yongxi et al. 1992, 351.

73. Lai Ruoyu 1953.

74. According to Kaple (1994, 7–11), this rationale derives directly from the influence of Stalinism.

75. The first party documents concerning the "three antis" campaign came out on 20 November 1951, just prior to the meeting at which Li Lisan was repudiated. In these early documents, the campaigns against corruption, waste, and bureaucratism were tied to a "movement for increased production and thrift." See Ma Qibin et al. 1991, 40–41.

76. Meisner 1986, 96.

77. Mao Zedong 1961–77, 5:68.

78. Tiewes 1997, 38.

79. Around 80 percent of total funds assigned to capital construction went to industry and related infrastructure. See Li Fuchun 1956, 29.

80. Li Fuchun 1956, 38. Soviet support was the result of a treaty concluded in 1950. Altogether the Soviet Union was involved in 156 major projects.

81. Cao Hongtao and Chu Chuanheng 1990, 52–53. See also Wang and Murie 1996, 973–74.

82. Li Fuchun 1956, 196. According to figures released recently by the Department of Construction, 100 percent of investment in housing during the period of the First Five-Year Plan (1953–57) came out of project-based capital construction investment. Cited in Yang Lu and Wang Yukun 1992, 71.

83. In CCP government discourse, enterprise (qiye) and institution (shiye) were the two main classifications of danwei. The former were production-oriented and included factories, mines, power plants, and the like, while the latter were non-production-oriented and included schools, offices, cultural organizations, newspapers, and so on. For a more complete taxonomy, see Lü and Perry 1997, 8.

84. Wu 1996, 1605–8.

85. City governments were left to provide and manage housing for urban residents who did not belong to a state-funded danwei. To this end, each city did establish a housing bureau, but its funds were generally very limited. In the early 1980s, only around 20 percent of all urban housing was controlled by city housing bureaus, and much of that was pre-1949 housing that had simply come under city management during collectivization in the 1950s. See Yang Lu and Wang Yukun 1992, 89–90.

86. On the establishment of a nationally unified wage system, see Yuan Lunqu 1987, 70–92; Lu Feng 1993, 53; and Frazier 2002, 143–55.

87. This measure was officially introduced in the Central Committee document "Zhonggong guanyu shixing liangshide jihua shougou yu jihua gongyingde jueyi" ("Central Committee Resolution on Implementing the Planned Purchase and Supply of Grain"), 16 October 1953, in Zhonggong zhongyang dangxiao dangshi jiaoyanshi 1979, 8:1–10. Chen Yun's contribution to this decision can be gauged from his speech to the National Grain Congress six days prior to the adoption of the resolution. See Chen Yun, "shixing liangshi tonggou tongxiao" ("Implementing Unified Purchasing and Marketing of Grain"), in Chen Yun 1982, 189–203.

88. For more detailed background on the development of this policy, see Bo Yibo 1991–93, 1:255–83.

89. Lu Feng 1993, 43–44.

90. Yuan Lunqu 1987, 21.

91. Ibid.

92. From "Guanyu laodong jiuye wentide jueding" ("Decision on the Labor and Employment Problem"), quoted in Lu Feng 1993, 31.

93. Yuan Lunqu 1987, 23.

94. Ibid.

95. State Council, "Guanyu laodongli tiaoji gongzuo zhongde jige wentide tongzhi" ("Directives on Several Questions Related to the Redistribution of Labor Power"), quoted in Yuan Lunqu 1987, 26.

96. Ibid. Previously the policy of *baoxialai* had been applied to the workforce in the so-called bureaucratic capital sector, which had been appropriated immediately by the new socialist state, and to former functionaries of the GMD state and army. See above.

97. Lee 1987, 33.

98. Brødsgaard 2002, 363.

99. Lee 1987, 35–37.

100. See, for example, Oi 1989, 30–31; Lu Feng 1993, 46–47; and Cheng and Selden 1997, 23–50.

101. Dutton 1992b, 195–214.

102. Ibid., 220.

103. Lu Feng 1993, 48. See also Oi 1989, 30.

104. Dutton 1992b, 212.

105. Ibid., 224. Also see Lee 1991, 332–35.

106. Shaw 1996, 75–76.

107. Wang Min and Liu Yipeng 1994, 345.

108. Li Lulu, Li Hanlin, and Wang Fenyu 1994, 10. According to interviews undertaken by Victor Shaw (1996, 83), many collective *danwei*, joint ventures, and private enterprises are now willing to recruit staff regardless of the release of the person's file.

109. The *Shehuibu* was the precursor to the Public Security Bureau.

110. This decision was contained within a document entitled "Jinhou gongzuo fang'an" ("Work Program for the Present and the Future"), reproduced in *Public Security Historical Materials*, vol. 2 (28), p. 207. I am indebted to Michael Dutton for this reference.

111. For example, in August 1952 the Department of Public Security promulgated a document entitled "Provisional Regulations Regarding the Organization of Committees for the Protection of Public Order." It stipulated that Public Order Committees be established in all *danwei* and residential neighborhoods in both urban and rural areas. The task of these committees was to assist Public Security police in maintaining order and in detecting counterrevolutionaries and other criminals. See Lu Feng 1993, 29.

112. *Ke* and *chu* both translate as "section" or "department." In PRC administrative usage, a *chu* is ranked above a *ke* and usually has more personnel. Thus, in larger *danwei* the security section would have the status of a *chu*; in smaller *danwei* it would be ranked as a *ke*.

113. Vogel 1971,85.

114. On the relationship between Public Security police and *danwei* security personnel, as well as on the relationship between the *danwei* and the police, see Li Jianhe et al. 1990, 13, 229.

115. Schurmann 1968, 283–84.

116. Ibid., 282.

117. Frazier (2002, 195) concludes from his case studies that there was a "consensus among workers and managers to resist the mandates of the Soviet model."

118. See Andors 1977, 58.

119. These remarks were made during a speech to the Congress by Li Xuefeng, director of the Party's Industrial Bureau. The quotes appear in Schurmann 1968, 285.

120. Foucault 1991, 87–104.

121. On the role of the factory cadre, see Walder 1986; on the school cadre, see Bakken 2000.

122. See Chapter 3 for more detailed discussion on the concept of bio-power.

123. Not all cadres would necessarily have direct links to the masses. In larger units there would be some cadres in senior leadership positions with relatively little day-to-day contact with the masses. My principal concern, however, is with the lower-level cadres who constituted the link between the leadership and the population.

124. See Shue 1988, 12–22.

125. Andrew Walder's *Communist Neo-Traditionalism* (1986) has been the most influential in establishing this view of the cadre. For a clientalist view of rural China, see Oi 1989.

126. On activists and model workers, see Walder 1986, 162–89; on *guanxi* within the urban setting, see Yang 1994, 75–108.

127. For example, see Lu Feng 1993; and Womack 1991.

128. For example, see leading reform economist Xue Muqiao's comments in *Beijing Review* 23, no. 12 (24 March 1980): 21–26.

129. Verdery 1996, 19–30.

Chapter 6

1. Lefebvre 1991, 54.

2. Ibid., 421.

3. Ibid.

4. The most prominent public buildings to be constructed during this period were the "10 Great Buildings," vast monumental developments undertaken in Beijing to celebrate the tenth anniversary of "New China" in 1959. The ten projects were (1) the Great Hall of the People, (2) the Museums of the Revolution and Chinese History, (3) the National Agricultural Exhibition Hall, (4) the Cultural Palace of the Nationalities, (5) the Beijing Railway Station, (6) the Beijing Workers' Stadium, (7) the Nationalities Hotel, (8) the Museum of Revolutionary Military History, (9) the Welcome Guesthouse (now known as the Diaoyutai State Guesthouse), and (10) the Overseas Chinese Hotel.

5. Yang Dongping 1994, 249–58. See also Xie and Costa 1993, 103–14; and Gaubatz 1995, 29–33.

6. See Chapter 2 for a discussion of this issue.

7. Bliznakov 1993, 85. In Moscow half a million workers were housed through this method between 1918 and 1924.

8. The problems of accommodation are mentioned in a number of memoirs dealing with the takeover of the cities. For example, see Li Xin 1988.

9. Sit 1995, 92.

10. Beijing jianshe shishu bianji weiyuanhui 1986, 29.

11. Ibid.

12. Liang Sicheng was the son of political reformer Liang Qichao. He graduated from Beijing's Qinghua University in 1923 before pursuing study in the United States at Pennsylvania and Harvard universities. After returning to China, he spent the 1930s and 1940s teaching architecture and undertaking major studies of China's traditional architecture. In 1946 he established a department of architecture at Qinghua University, where he remained professor and head of department until his death in 1972. Liang Sicheng's stand on the preservation of ancient Beijing and its various monuments finally resulted in his being declared a "rightist" and undergoing considerable political persecution. See Lin Zhu 1996.

13. Yang Dongping 1994, 188–201. Liang Sicheng (1951) argued for the preservation of Old Beijing because he saw it as both one of the world's best-conserved examples of an ancient capital and also a sublime realization of classical Chinese spatial form.

14. To promote this idea, the Liang group sponsored a design competition that resulted in the submission of various plans for the proposed administrative and government center. See Beijing jianshe shishu bianji weiyuanhui 1986, 23–36; and a briefer but more critical commentary in Wu Liangyong 1994, 17–24.

15. Sit 1995, 93. The location favored by this group was the area immediately to the west and south of the Forbidden City, namely Zhongnanhai and the area surrounding Tiananmen. These places had been home to government offices under both imperial and nationalist regimes.

16. According to Yang Dongping (1994, 196), this decision was confirmed in a speech made by Mao in August 1953 at the National Conference on Financial and Economic Work, "Combat Bourgeois Ideas in the Party." While the principal target of this speech was Bo Yibo, for his "bourgeois error" in proposing a tax policy based on equality between public and private enterprises, Mao also criticized what he saw as dispersal and weakening of decision-making power that had occurred since the takeover of the cities. In calling for a return to decisive centralized decision making, he used the debate over the fate of the Beijing city wall as an example of where the Central Committee ought to step in and make a decision. See Mao 1961–77, 5:109.

17. Yang Dongping, for example, portrays Liang Sicheng as a heroic lone figure in the defense of Beijing's city wall and ornamental gates. See also Lin Zhu 1993. Jianying Zha provides a more balanced account, discussing the arguments from both sides. See Zha 1995, 63–64.

18. According to Wu Liangyong (1994, 22), the clear separation between the old and the new called for by Liang was also founded upon a belief in the close rela-

tionship of form to function. Liang was convinced the ancient city form could not meet all the technical needs of a modern capital, hence the need for a new administrative district. Yet, at the same time, he was convinced that the old walled city could remain the residential and cultural heart of the city. Liang (1986, 46–50) even suggested that the city wall itself could become a key feature of the cultural life of the city. The top of the wall could be used as a public promenade, while the old gate towers could be transformed into teahouses, art galleries, and exhibition halls.

19. In October 1949 the Government Administration Council (*zhengwuyuan*) established the Basic Construction Department (*jiben jianshechu*) under its Planning Bureau (*jihuaju*) that was responsible for the central planning and coordination of urban development. Following this, each city set up a city planning committee (*chengshi jihua weiyuanhui*) with responsibility for urban development. In August 1952 the duties of the Basic Construction Department were taken over by the newly established Ministry of Building and Engineering (*jianzhugongchengbu*). See Cao Hongtao and Chu Chuanheng 1990, 34–35.

20. Ibid., 36.

21. Ibid., 147.

22. Ibid., 149.

23. Yang Dongping 1994, 253.

24. I am aware that this term has previously been translated as "branches and areas," but I feel that "strips and chunks" more accurately reflects the colloquial feel of the Chinese phrase. For a general survey of this system during the Maoist period and beyond, see Unger 1987. For further commentary on the connection between the strips and chunks structure and the *danwei* system, see Lu Feng 1989, 77–78.

25. For example, a steel factory would come under the jurisdiction of the Ministry for Iron and Steel, a university under the Ministry of Higher Education, and so on.

26. This was part of a "Report on Government Work" (*Zhengfu gongzuo baogao*) delivered by Zhou to the First Session of the First NPC, 23 September 1954. For a discussion of this speech and its effect on the architecture and planning world, see Gong Deshun, Zou Denong, and Dou Yide 1989, 67–70.

27. Gong Deshun, Zou Denong, and Dou Yide 1989, 41–67. The main object of criticism was the so-called national style (*minzu xingshi*), which had seen many new office buildings, schools, and factories adorned with traditional Chinese-style roofs. In fact, the idea of a "national style" in architecture had originated in the Soviet Union under Stalin as the officially approved, patriotic representation of "socialism in one country." Although no Stalinist, Liang Sicheng was the major victim of the campaign because of his support for the use of traditional Chinese elements in modern architecture. See also Liu Dunzhen 1955 and Niu Ming 1955.

28. The various debates, critiques, and "self-criticisms" associated with this campaign can be found in the pages of the *Jianzhu xuebao* (*Journal of Architecture*) in the issues for 1957 and 1958.

29. See Cao Hongtao and Chu Chuanheng 1990, 148.

30. Ibid., 91.

31. Gong Deshun, Zou Denong, and Dou Yide 1989, 128–31.

32. See Chapter 4 and Rabinow 1989.

33. Parkins 1953, 60.

34. For a detailed discussion of the scope and influence of Soviet advisers in the area of architecture and design, including a substantial number of photographs of buildings from the period, see Gong Deshun, Zou Denong, and Dou Yide 1989, 41–67.

35. Gong Deshun, Zou Denong, and Dou Yide 1989, 204. According to the authors, the newly centralized organization was constituted through the amalgamation of a number of disparate units, including an architecture company set up by the General Office of the North China Highway Transportation Company in 1949 and the Engineering Office of the CCP's Supply Department.

36. Cao Hongtao and Chu Chuanheng 1990, 36. In August 1952 thirty-nine "key cities" were called upon to establish construction committees to lead and oversee the coming large-scale construction projects. Under these committees were to be two standing committees, one responsible for urban planning and architectural design, the other responsible for the supervision and inspection of all construction work.

37. The exact date for this change in name is unclear; however, by 1955 the new name was being used in articles and documents. For example, see Li Chunling 1955, 95–100.

38. Gong Deshun, Zou Denong, and Dou Yide 1989, 43–44.

39. Ibid. There were several machinery ministries each responsible for different sectors.

40. For discussion of the issues related to design principles and standards to be followed in university and college design, see Du Erqi 1956.

41. Climate of course was a relevant variable in housing design, although in most instances the only difference between housing in cold and warm climates was the provision or nonprovision of central heating.

42. Cao Hongtao and Chu Chuanheng 1990, 60.

43. For standard examples of both forms of housing, see Chengshi jianshe zongju guihua shejiju 1956, 57–72.

44. Gong Deshun, Zou Denong, and Dou Yide 1989, 67.

45. Ibid., 68.

46. The first public elaboration of this campaign was made in a *People's Daily* editorial in March. See "Fandui jianzhuzhongde langfei xianxiang" ("Oppose Waste in Architecture"), *The People's Daily*, 28 March 1955.

47. According to Chinese socialist usage, "productive" *danwei* referred to those whose primary function was the production of material goods, while "nonproductive" *danwei* where those which did not directly produce material goods—for example, schools, universities, research institutes, entertainment troupes, and so on.

48. Gong Deshun, Zou Denong, and Dou Yide 1989, 69.

49. The problem of rent was later to become virtually a nonissue as government and *danwei* progressively increased housing subsidies and reduced rentals to minimal levels.

50. For a summary of these shortcomings, see Li Yongguang 1956, 99.

51. Cao Hongtao and Chu Chuanheng 1990, 197.

52. Li Chunling 1955, 95.

53. Gong Deshun, Zou Denong, and Dou Yide 1989, 69–70, see also photographs on 70–71.

54. See Zhao Guanqian 1988, 222–23.

55. For example, Tu Tianfeng 1958, 34.

56. Cao Hongtao and Chu Chuanheng 1990, 54.

57. Ibid., 52.

58. Ibid. The Chinese title for this document is "Guanyu changwai gongcheng touzi huafende jueding." Beyond the *danwei* system, where these facilities and infrastructure were in general public use throughout the city or region, responsibility for funding fell to the relevant ministry (e.g., ministries for rail, electricity, fuel, posts and communications, and education) or to the city authorities in the case of municipal works such as water pipes, sewerage, roads, bridges, and culverts.

59. Cao Hongtao and Chu Chuanheng 1990, 52–53.

60. Note that not all *danwei* were state-owned. So-called "collective" *danwei* accounted for a little over 20 percent of the urban workforce for most of the period under consideration. Collective *danwei* came in several varieties. Some were attached to state-owned *danwei* and therefore enjoyed many of the benefits provided through direct central funding. Others came under city, regional, or district administration and therefore had far more limited financial resources upon which to draw.

61. Cao Hongtao and Chu Chuanheng 1990, 80. According to figures quoted by the authors, investment funds provided to cities for urban construction as a percentage of total national construction investment were as follows: 1952, 3.76 percent; FFYP (1953–57), 2.6 percent; 1958, 2.19 percent; 1961, 0.7 percent.

62. Many commentators have noted the much superior benefits and living conditions enjoyed by workers in the state-owned sector over those in the collective (city-operated) sector. See, for example, Yang Dongping 1994, 249–58; and Perry 1997, 42–59.

63. Cheng Xuan 1990, 73; and Sit 1985, 86. In 1954 a regulation was passed to forbid the buying and selling of land; henceforth all land was allocated administratively.

64. Cao Hongtao and Chu Chuanheng 1990, 53.

65. The construction industry was the first for which coordinated recruitment and job assignment were carried out. See Chapter 5 for details.

66. Once the national demand for construction workers eased after the high tide of construction had passed, many construction workers remained on-site to join the workforce of the new *danwei*.

67. Xie and Costa 1993, 106.

68. Of course, there were also military *danwei* where such factors were undoubtedly more prevalent.

69. For documentary materials on compound design, I have relied mainly on works published in *Jianzhu xuebao* (*Journal of Architecture*).

70. Leung Wing-yue 1988, 45. The description quoted here is from the mid-eighties. However, although it has undergone some more recent development, the major part of the Wuhan Steelworks was constructed during the First Five-Year Plan, at which time it was a key development project.

71. I refer here primarily to urban *danwei* compounds, but it is interesting to note

that some rural collective production units adopted very similar spatial forms. See, for example, Yan Yizhi 1955, 86–89.

72. Du Erqi 1956, 5.

73. Ibid., 9.

74. See, for example, Pang Shuzi and Xu Hongbo 1956, 28–35; and Liang Wenhan 1957, 43–48.

75. In his study of Chinese architectural and urban planning history, Andrew Boyd (1962, 49) suggests that the basic principles of design "appeared early in the tradition and were applied very widely, whether to the plan of a little homestead, the layout of a temple, a palace or a city ensemble." These basic principles were: "(a) *walled enclosure*; (b) *axiality*; (c) *north-south orientation*; and (d) *the courtyard*."

76. See, for example, Wheatley 1971, 425.

77. The origins of this style in the modern era derived primarily from the monumental urbanism developed by Haussmann in Paris under the patronage of Louis Napoleon. One of the central features of Haussmann's plan was the placement of monumental architectural structures at key symbolic points throughout the city. As well as finding favor in Stalin's Soviet Union, this state-sponsored monumental style gained prominence in Mussolini's Italy and Hitler's Germany. See Frampton 1992, 210–23.

78. See Tarkhanov and Kavtaradze 1992.

79. See the section on Bogdanov and proletarian culture in Chapter 4. Michael Dutton (1992a) makes a similar point on the relationship between labor and proletarian consciousness within the Chinese context.

80. Here I include the larger-style *danwei* with their separate residential compound as well as the small to medium all-in-one *danwei* compound.

81. Hua Lanhong 1957, 24.

82. Ibid.

83. For example, see Jin Oubu 1960, 34–38; Wu Luoshan 1959, 1–3; and Pei Xuan, Liu Jumao, and Shen Lanqian 1958, 9–14.

84. This called for establishing networks for production, canteens, kindergartens, services, education, hygiene and health, commerce, recreation and sports, conservation, and garages (Cao Hongtao and Chu Chuanheng 1990, 76).

85. Ibid.

86. As noted above, these locally run "collective" *danwei* enjoyed very few of the benefits of the state-owned *danwei* owing to state investment policies which naturally favored the state-owned system.

87. A collection of major documents and commentaries on the collectivization of handicraft and other small-scale industry can be found in Ji Long and Zheng Hui 1992.

88. Tu Tianfeng 1958, p.34.

89. Ibid.

90. Ibid., 35.

91. Zou 2001, 230.

92. Naughton 1997. While I obviously disagree with Barry Naughton's contention that the *danwei* system only emerged during the 1960s, his work on eco-

nomic policy during this period does show some of the ways in which it was consolidated.

93. You Zhenglin 2000, 16, 140.

94. Ibid., 25.

95. Ibid., 26–27. An important secondary reason for establishing the service company was to provide more employment opportunities for the spouses and children of factory staff. While the company took over management of existing services provided and funded by the *danwei*, it was also expected to expand services and set up small businesses to create more jobs and generate some income of its own.

96. You Zhenglin 2000, 54.

97. Walter Benjamin, "On the Mimetic Faculty," in Benjamin 1986, 333–36.

Chapter 7

1. Zhu Huaxin 1993.

2. The Resident Identity Card (*jumin shenfen zheng*) was introduced in 1985 in order to provide a universal and standardized form of identification for all PRC citizens. I will address the broader implications of the ID card later in this chapter.

3. Zhu Huaxin 1993.

4. This point was reinforced in the early 1990s when Chinese authorities argued that the right to work was the fundamental basis for all human rights in China. See Information Office of the State Council of the People's Republic of China 1991, 43–49.

5. This escalation was initiated by Deng Xiaoping during his famous "Southern Tour" to Shenzhen, Zhuhai, and Shanghai in January and February and then confirmed at the Fourteenth Party Congress held in October 1992. For description and analysis, see Fewsmith 2001, 44–71.

6. From a speech by a personnel officer to staff at the Meteor Electronics Company, Shenzhen. Recorded by Pun (1999, 5).

7. Pun 1999, 3–6.

8. Cao Jinqing and Chen Zhongya 1997, 2. Also see Cao Jinqing 1993.

9. For example, Lu Feng 1989; Li Lulu, Li Hanlin, and Wang Fenyu 1994; and Shaw 1996. This discourse also permeates CCP-government rhetoric on reform, albeit without making explicit reference to the underlying logic. For example, see Renmin Ribao 1993; and Zheng Gongcheng 1996.

10. Wang Hui (2001) provides an insightful analysis on the origins of this kind of "scientistic" thinking within Chinese scholarship.

11. You Zhenglin (2000, 2), for example, suggests that the main focus of interest in SOE reform has been on the relationship between enterprise directors and the state rather than on the micro reorganization of the enterprise's internal relationships.

12. Barry Naughton (1993, 494) suggests that a belief in material incentives was one of the few consistent and defining features of Deng's economic thinking.

13. The key evidence for Deng's support of material incentives in the early 1960s can be found in the document "Regulations for Work in State-Owned Industrial Enterprises" ("Guoying gongye qiye gongzuo tiaoli"), otherwise know as the "Sev-

enty Articles on Industry" ("Gongye qishitiao"). In the wake of the disastrous Great Leap Forward, this document, drafted by Bo Yibo under the guidance of Deng, advocated reducing the role of the party in industry, strengthening managerial authority and responsibility, and returning to material incentives under the principle of "distribution according to labor" (*anlao fenpei*), thereby replacing the egalitarian distribution of the radical period. In 1967 this document came under attack from Zhang Chunqiao and Yao Wenyuan, who declared it to be a "black program for demolishing socialism and restoring capitalism." See Bo Yibo 1991–93, 2:951–83; and Wang Haibo 1995, 168–85.

14. The bonus system was revived in 1979 (Naughton 1996, 103–5).

15. Baum 1994, 95. Xue Muqiao's views can be found in *Beijing Review* V23, no. 12 (24 March 1980): 21–26.

16. For example, see Huang Xiaojing and Yang Xiao 1987, 147–60.

17. Meisner 1996, 259.

18. For a broader historical view of this shift and its relationship to reform policies and the party, see Lee 1991.

19. Warner 1992, 26–31.

20. Ibid., 128.

21. F. W. Taylor's *The Principles of Scientific Management* (1911) was the founding text for this approach to management.

22. Rofel 1992, 99.

23. Rofel 1999, 110–15.

24. Zhao and Nichols 1996, 20; Lee 1999, 61–64.

25. Naughton 1996, 207–10.

26. Tang and Parish 2000, 133. For a detailed outline of the various stages of wage reform and its implications, see also Ji 1998, 111–33.

27. Zhao and Nichols 1996, 12–18.

28. Ibid., 8–9.

29. Walder 1986, 102–13.

30. As discussed above, Pun Ngai (1999, 3–6) has shown how the process of atomization, carried out in a Shenzhen factory among women workers from rural backgrounds, involves not only regimes of discipline and punishment but also a discourse of modernity that links "self-improvement" with notions of individual responsibility.

31. Ji 1998, 156–59.

32. White 1987, 366.

33. Naughton 1996, 210–11.

34. Guojia tongjiju 1998, 34. In Shanghai and Jiangsu, over 65 percent of the state-sector workforce had shifted to labor contracts by 1997.

35. Transformations in the nature of work in the West have been documented and analyzed by numerous social theorists. See, for example, Castells 2000, 216–354; and Bauman 2000, 130–67.

36. Schurmann 1968, 234.

37. Walder 1986.

38. Lee 1999, 57.

39. Meisner defines "bureaucratic capitalism" as "the use of political power and

official influence for private pecuniary gain through capitalist or quasi-capitalist methods of economic activity." See Meisner 1996, 300.

40. This concentration of managerial power is also the source for the dramatic increase in corruption in recent years. Even in loss-making *danwei*, managers can usually still find ways to embezzle large sums of money. In colloquial dialogue, this phenomenon is referred to as having "a rich abbot in a poor monastery" (*miao qiong fangzhang fu*; Lee 1999, 57).

41. You Zhenglin 2000, 269.

42. Rofel 1992, 1999. The study is based on research the author undertook during visits in the mid-1980s and early 1990s.

43. Rofel 1992, 101–3. These subversions include the ability of workers to find places to rest and chat during their shifts, either at a table they had claimed as their own "territory" or in among the machinery, hidden from supervisory gaze.

44. As I discuss in Chapter 2, buildings within traditional compounds were arranged according to rules of social hierarchy—the largest and most centrally located buildings were occupied by those with highest status, while the smaller periphery buildings were occupied by those of lower status. This applied to all types of traditional compounds, whether they were ordinary homes, temples, government offices, or palaces.

45. Rofel 1992, 105.

46. Walder 1986.

47. Young 1995, 15–17.

48. *Getihu* is an abbreviation of *geti gongshanghu*, which translates literally as "individual industrial and commercial households." In official statistics, those engaged in this sector are also referred to as *geti laodongzhe*, or "individual laborers." The *getihu* is officially defined as a small business with fewer than eight employees. Larger private businesses, namely those with eight or more employees, were officially recognized from June 1988 and designated *siying qiye*, or "privately operated enterprises." See Young 1995, 5, 107.

49. Guojia tongjiju 2000, 118.

50. Shi Xianmin 1993, 4.

51. Ibid., 1–2.

52. Ibid., 189–367. Apart from these locations, the other main sites of *getihu* activity are in department stores, where they operate from rented counters, and in specially designated marketplaces.

53. Piper Rae Gaubatz (1995, 47), too, notes that the reinvigoration of life in the "downtown" shopping and commercial districts has been a major feature of recent urban development.

54. By 1989, private business accounted for over 80 percent of all retail, food, and service outlets. See Young 1994, 107.

55. Zhu Wenyi 1993, 183.

56. Ibid.

57. Ibid., 119–22, 124–28.

58. On the historical link between urban planning and liberal economic theory, see the discussion on Haussmann in Chapter 4.

59. "One family, two systems" is a pun on the Deng slogan "one country, two sys-

tems," which refers to the CCP policy allowing Hong Kong, Macao, and potentially Taiwan to maintain their own economic and political systems under PRC sovereignty.

60. This point has been overlooked by most commentators, who have been intent on emphasizing the supposed independence of the *getihu* sector. Shi Xianmin (1993, 180–88) is particularly remiss in this regard through his characterization of the *getihu* as a new and completely independent social force. In contrasting the lifestyle, attitudes, and status of the *getihu* with the *danwei* member, he makes no mention of the fact that many *getihu* are able to depend upon a *danwei* for certain benefits, either through their own *danwei* (many people run a business in their spare time while remaining in a *danwei*), their partner's, or their parent's *danwei*.

61. Leng Mou 1992.

62. Zhu Huaxin 1993.

63. As Michael Dutton's (1998, 220–21) interview with a legal professional shows, the *danwei* can also provide the entrepreneur access to a very useful *guanxi* network.

64. Ching Kwan Lee (1999, 51–55) points out that it is invariably the male partner who "jumps into the sea" of private business while the female partner remains in the *danwei*. In this respect, "one family, two systems" tends to reinforce gender inequalities even while improving a family's income potential.

65. Ye Jundong and Zhou Jialu 1994, p. 37.

66. Ibid.

67. Yuan Zujun (2001) reviews the history of Beijing University's venture in the context of a decision by local authorities to demolish the commercial strip. District planners had decided that it no longer accorded with the local environmental plan. After demolition, the university simply rebuilt the original wall.

68. Young 1995, 78–79.

69. Francis 1996, 839–59.

70. Ibid., 845–49. Stephen Frost (1999) has found a similar situation in his research into one of the newly emerging Chinese industrial conglomerates, the Hai'er Group, based in Qingdao, Shandong.

71. "Commodity" housing (*shangpinfang*) refers to the new private sector of the housing industry. I examine this issue in more detail below.

72. Francis 1996, 849.

73. Note that the method of housing provision in new private enterprises may differ substantially from methods used under the socialist *danwei* system. Although some larger companies (like Hai'er in Qingdao; see Frost 1999) provide *danwei*-style housing compounds for their employees, other companies simply purchase individual apartments within large commercial housing developments. In the latter case, the spatial link between workplace and living space is severed. The full implications of these trends for the relationship between employee and workplace remain to be documented.

74. Anita Chan (1997, 105–6) argues that labor practices in China appear to be shifting toward a Japanese model based on notions of corporate community rather than toward the full labor market conditions hoped for by some commentators.

75. In the face of dramatic increases in crime rates and the growing mobility of urban populations, the Public Security Bureau has continually reiterated the importance of expanding the scope of "comprehensive policing" to encompass all the new sites of potential security problems. For example, see Dutton 1998, 107–11, 224–27.

76. Francis 1996, 855.

77. Ibid., 859.

78. Chan (2001) provides a comprehensive range of case studies exposing the draconian (and often criminal) work practices in this sector.

79. Pun 1999.

80. For example, see Wu 1996, 1609–11; Bian et al. 1997, 223–48; and Wang and Murie 1996, 981.

81. Liu Zhifeng 1994, i.

82. Bian et al. 1997, 224.

83. Notable exceptions to this general investment strategy were the cities of Shanghai and Tianjin, where a fairly high proportion (66 percent and 46 percent, respectively) of urban housing was constructed and managed by the city housing bureau. In other major cities, an average of around 60 percent of housing was controlled by *danwei*, 25 percent by the city housing bureau, and 15 percent was under private ownership. These percentages are calculated from figures recorded in Yang Lu and Wang Yukun 1992, 89–90.

84. Wu 1996, 1610. See also World Bank 1992.

85. Bian et al. 1997, 229.

86. Guojia tongjiju shehui tongjisi 1994, 93–97.

87. Ibid., 96.

88. See Li Lulu, Li Hanlin, and Wang Fenyu 1994, 5–16; Dittmer and Lu Xiaobo 1996, 250–55; and Lee 1988, 397–99.

89. Wu 1996, 1619–23. Another major area of inequality in housing relates to the large "floating" population, predominantly rural residents who have migrated to the cities in recent years in search of employment. Although some are provided accommodation by their employers, most are forced to rent on the "unofficial" housing market. The endemic shortage of housing combined with the often dubious legal status of the rural migrant of course means that rental prices are highly inflated while the housing is often of a very poor standard. For an illuminating study of strategies adopted by migrants from Zhejiang to cope with this problem in Beijing, see Zhang 2001.

90. These aims have been established and reiterated through major resolutions passed by the State Council in 1988, 1991, and again in 1994. For a discussion of the former two resolutions, see Wang and Murie 1996, 977–82. For a copy of the 1994 resolution, related speeches, and a detailed guide to its implementation, see Liu Zhifeng 1994.

91. Wang and Murie 1996, 976.

92. For example, "Private Chinese Buyers Cut State Ownership of Housing," *Australian Financial Review*, 15 May 1997.

93. Liu Zhifeng 1994, 1–2.

94. Alternatively, as Min Zhou and John Logan (2002, 148–49) reveal, some *danwei* purchase commodity housing and then sell it to *danwei* staff at subsidized rates.

95. In 1998, according to Li Rongxia (1998, 14), an average market-price apartment cost three to four hundred thousand yuan, with the most luxurious sold for as much as eight hundred thousand yuan. Since the average price was about thirty to forty times the average urban salary of around ten thousand yuan per year, full-cost commercial housing was simply not an option for the majority of the urban working population.

96. Liu Zhifeng 1994, 124.

97. Randolph and Lou 2000, 180–85.

98. Wang and Murie 1996, 979–80. It was first trialed in Shanghai in 1991.

99. Liu Zhifeng 1994, 73–86.

100. Interview with an official in the Property Section, Construction Bank of China, Gangcheng branch, Wuhan, China 19 June 1997.

101. Saunders 1990.

102. For example, see Li Peilin and Zhang Yi 2000, 217–29.

103. Reform of the telephone system is one area in which the role of the *danwei* has been diminished. In the past, all telephone lines within a *danwei*, both office and home connections, were extension numbers that could be reached only through the central switchboard of the *danwei*. In recent years a massive program of telecommunication reform has converted most extensions into direct lines.

104. Reported by various informants.

105. Apart from anything else, as Zhou and Logan point out (2002, 144), it is very difficult for individuals to obtain bank loans for housing construction.

106. Wang and Murie 1999, 1478.

107. The term *xiaoqu* is not new, but its usage since the late 1980s is taken to imply a new form of *xiaoqu*—*xinxiaoqu*.

108. Based on observation and survey of real estate advertisements. See also Read 2003, 40.

109. Zou Denong 2001, 459–65.

110. Wu 2002, 163.

111. Read 2003.

112. Wu 2002, 161–66.

113. Fraser 2000, 27.

114. One luxury development I visited in Beijing had two sets of staffed boomgates, closed-circuit television, electronic-coded access to lobbies and lifts, as well as security guards patrolling the compound twenty-four hours a day.

115. On Beijing's elite enclaves, see Giroir 2002. Teresa Caldeira (1999) examines gated enclaves in Saõ Paulo, Brazil, and Don Luymes (2002) surveys the phenomenon in the Unites States.

116. Li Zhang's study (2001) of the rise and fall of Zhejiangcun in Beijing provides a very insightful analysis of how one group of migrant workers attempted to appropriate urban space and the way in which local and Beijing authorities responded. Below I focus on the spatial impact of restructuring on the established urban population.

117. Lee 1999, 55–56.

118. *Renmin ribao (People's Daily) (RMRB)*, 20 March 1998.

119. Li Ning 1997, 14. Between 1990 and 1996 in Shanghai alone, 1.09 million workers from state-owned enterprises were made redundant. The extent of cutbacks can be gauged from the Shanghai textile industry, which reduced total employees from a high of 551,600 in 1988 to around 250,000 by 1998.

120. The total number of SOE employees fell from a high of 109.55 million in 1995 to 83.36 million in 1999. This represents a reduction of 24 percent in SOE employment (Guojia tongjiju 2000, 126).

121. Zhu Rongji 1999.

122. Zheng Gongcheng 1996.

123. Song Xuechun, "Chongxin shanggang kan Qingdao" ("Getting Back to Work—Have a Look at Qingdao"), *RMRB*, 4 May 1999.

124. In one example, *RMRB* profiled three former redundant state workers who had each "made it" in private business; one has established a successful dog-breeding venture, the second was selling vegetables in a market, and the third was part of a group of thirty redundant women workers who jointly started up a steamed bread factory. See "Xiagang zhigong: zouchu yipian xin tiandi" ("Redundant Workers: Coming Out into a New World"), *RMRB*, 16 January 1998.

125. Ibid.

126. "Zhu Rongji zai Dongbei sishengqu dangzheng fuzeren zuotanhuishang qiangdiao shishi zaijiuye gongcheng shiguan daju, liangshi liutong tizhi fei gaige buke" ("At a meeting of leading party and government cadres of the four Northeast provinces, Zhu Rongji emphasized that implementation of the reemployment project concerned the overall situation and that the grain circulation system must be reformed"), *RMRB*, 28 March 1998.

127. Ibid.

128. Li Ning 1997 p. 10.

129. Zhu Rongji 1999.

130. Solinger 2002, 307–15.

131. Chan 2001, 13.

132. For a general overview of the situation, see Weston 2000.

133. Hurst and O'Brien 2002. According to the authors, pensioners have been prominent activists and participants within the ad hoc protest movement demanding better treatment for redundant workers.

134. Solinger 2002, 319–25.

135. The Chinese term *shequ* was adopted by the first generation of Chinese sociologists in the 1930s and 1940s as a translation for the English word "community." It disappeared from use when the PRC government had banned sociology in the early 1950s.

136. Chan 1993, 22.

137. One of the key objectives was to expand the provision of services for children and the elderly, the two groups most affected by demographic changes in family structure. This strategy emerged from the first national conference on community services held at Wuhan in 1987 (Guo Chongde 1993, 2, 295–309).

138. Ibid., 18–23.

139. Cui Naifu (Minister of Civil Affairs), "Yao zhua shequ jianshe" ("We Must Grasp Community Building"), speech delivered 31 May 1991, in Ma Xueli and Zhang Xiulan 2001, 9.

140. Ibid., and Guo Chongde 1993, 35.

141. Through the 1990s, the MCA promoted the concept and encouraged city and district governments to undertake experiments and trials to develop practical methods for the implementation of "community building." Cities such as Qingdao, Shijiazhuang, Hangzhou, Wuhan, Shanghai, Chongqing, and Shenyang have been particularly prominent in these developments. The collection edited by Ma Xueli and Zhang Xiulan (2001) includes both primary documents as well as analysis of most of these regional experiments.

142. Minzhengbu 2000. Henceforth referred to as "On *Shequ* Building."

143. Copies of these two documents appear in Ma Xueli and Zhang Xiulan 2001, 1–8.

144. Minzhengbu 2000, 3.

145. Ibid. I will discuss the rationale for enlarging the RC territory below.

146. RCs were established by law in 1954. For a recent overview of the history and role of RCs, see Read 2000.

147. This is not to suggest that RCs covered only 5 percent of the population. Many employees in the collective sector and even some in the state-owned sector did not enjoy *danwei* housing and would have come under the jurisdiction of an RC. I know of no attempts to estimate the proportion of the urban population in this category.

148. Guojia tongjiju shehui tongjisi 1994, 43–46.

149. Minzhengbu 2000, 4.

150. Tang Zhongxin 2000, 103–25.

151. See Chan 1993, 167–76; and Read 2000, 806–20.

152. For example, see Minzhengbu 2000.

153. The analysis below is based on field trips in September 2001 to Beijing and Shenyang, where I was able to interview both central and local MCA officials, as well as collect relevant documents issued by various levels of government. In Shenyang I also visited a number of *shequ*, where I was able to interview some *shequ* staff and collect further documentary materials.

154. This law was an attempt to standardize grassroots governance throughout urban China and led to RC-type organizations, often known as "staff and family committees" (*zhigong jiashu weiyuanhui*), being established within every *danwei*. Although they were in theory self-governing "mass organizations," in fact they remained closely under the control of the *danwei* within which they were located. See Bai Yihua and Ma Xueli 1990.

155. Shenyangshi minzhengju 1999, 60–61.

156. Minzhengbu 2000, 10.

157. Shenyangshi minzhengju 1999, 32, 101–2.

158. Ibid., 61, 149.

159. Ibid., 11, 51.

160. Ibid., 17, 26.

161. In the course of my field trip, I was able to visit several purpose-built "*shequ* activity centers*," including one that was integrated into a brand-new residential development.

162. Based on the author's own observations.

163. While all the documents emphasize the shift away from the *danwei* system, they nevertheless recognize that in many cases the *danwei* still controls considerable social resources. To deal with this issue, Shenyang government officials have called on every *danwei* to make its social infrastructure available for the use of all residents of the *shequ* within which the *danwei* is located, regardless of their employment status. This is seen as an important measure to facilitate the transition from *danwei* to *shequ* as the basis of social identity (Shenyangshi minzhengju 1999, 4–5; also Minzhengbu 2000, 6–7).

164. See the discussion at the beginning of this chapter.

165. Strictly speaking, *shequ* staff are not state cadres because they are not paid cadre wages and their posts are not listed on the state's official organizational charts. Nevertheless, they are habitually referred to as "cadres" (or grassroots cadres, *jiceng ganbu*) both by local government officials and by local *shequ* residents. I will adopt this usage.

166. Shenyangshi minzhengju 1999, 15, 61; see also Minzhengbu 2000, 11.

167. Shenyangshi minzhengju 1999, 27.

168. Interview with *shequ* cadre Tiexi District, Shenyang, 11 September 2001.

169. Shenyangshi tiexiqu 2000, 7.

170. Shenyangshi minzhengju 1999, 27–28; Minzhengbu 2000, 9.

171. Shenyangshi minzhengju 1999, 30–31.

172. Ibid., 14. All CCP members must register with the party branch of the *shequ* within which they reside, even if their primary party affiliation is with the party branch at their workplace. Several informants suggested to me that this policy has been implemented in order to strengthen party discipline—party members are now under party jurisdiction at home as well as at work. Indeed, at one *shequ* center, I observed a large notice board on public display that listed the names and residential locations of all party members who lived within that *shequ*.

173. Shenyangshi minzhengju 1999, 21–23. Some of this information also derives from "Shenyangshi shequ zuzhi jigou wangluo shiyitu" ("Diagram of the Shenyang City *Shequ* Organizational Structure and Network"), undated document supplied to the author.

174. Some of the documents summarize this principle as "the four selfs"—self-management, self-education, self-service, and self-supervision, for example see Minzhengbu 2000, 7.

175. "Shenyangshi shequ zuzhi jigou wangluo shiyitu."

176. Shenyangshi tiexiqu 2000, 21.

177. Dutton 1992b, 70–78.

178. Bai Yihua, and Ma Xueli 1990, 108–9.

179. The rights of the resident are also embodied in the fact that *shequ* cadres are subject to periodic election and can be voted out of office. No doubt the electoral

aspect of *shequ* building is worth further study, but it is not in my view central to the concept. Moreover, in this study I wish to present a broader institutional analysis and avoid the usual "fetishization of the ballot box" that informs much scholarly output in contemporary Chinese studies.

180. The term "late socialism" is borrowed from Zhang 2001.

181. Dutton (1995) uses this phrase to refer to the way in which the Chinese police have attempted to adapt the "campaign" methods of the past to cope with the unfamiliar policing problems of the present.

182. For example, see Lu Feng 1989, 71–88; and Zhu Guanglei 1994, 48–52.

183. Meisner 1996, 300.

184. Rose (1999, 175–76) argues that this has resulted from a process through which the growth of professional and technical knowledge on the nature of communities has been linked to the administrative and managerial practices of government agencies.

Chapter 8

1. Foucault 1980a, 133.

2. As an alternative to the totalizing concept of the party/state, throughout this study I have deliberately used the more neutral phrase "the CCP-led government" where I wished to emphasize the connection between party and government.

3. I should clarify that this skepticism extends to all "states," not just the one alleged to exist in China.

PINYIN	CHARACTER	TRANSLATION
an	暗	dark
anlao fenpei	按劳分配	distribution according to labor
Baizhifang	白纸坊	name of district in Beijing
baojia	保甲	household registration system
baoweichu	保卫处	security department
baoweike	保卫科	security department
baoxialai	包下来	bring under a guarantee
bi	比	unit made up of five families
bianjie	边界	boundaries
bianzhi	编制	staff quota system
biaoxian	表现	attitude (especially political)
biaozhunjia	标准价	standard price
bumen	部门	department
chengbenjia	成本价	cost price
chengshi guihuachu	城市规划处	Department of Urban Planning
chengshi jihua weiyuanhui	城市计划委员会	City Planning Committee
chuantong jiuye guannian	传统就业观念	traditional employment mentality
chuantong shehuizhuyi	传统社会主义	traditional socialism

PINYIN	CHARACTER	TRANSLATION
dagongjia	大公家	"big public family" (government sector, Yan'an)
dagongmei	打工妹	working girls
dangjian	党建	party building
danwei	单位	unit, work unit
danwei ren	单位人	person of the *danwei*
danyuan	单元	housing unit
danyuan zuzhang	单元组长	housing unit leader
daozuofang	倒座房	south wing of courtyard house
dapo tiefanwan	打破铁饭碗	smash the iron rice bowl
dayuan	大院	Compound
duifang	对方	the other side, the opposition
fang (1)	坊	walled residential district
fang (2)	防	guard against
fangguanke	房管科	housing department
ganbu	干部	Cadre
gangwei gongzizhi	岗位工资制	position-wage system
gaotang	高堂	northern and most important wing of the courtyard house
geti gongshanghu	个体工商户	individual industrial and commercial households
geti laodongzhe	个体劳动者	individual laborers
getihu	个体户	small-scale entrepreneur
gong	公	"public," "common," "just," "fair," or "impartial"
gonghui (1)	公会	public associations
gonghui (2)	工会	trade union
gongjizhi	供给制	supply system (implemented in Yan'an)
gongmin	公民	citizen
gongtian	公田	communal field
gongtongti	共同体	social collective (community)

PINYIN	CHARACTER	TRANSLATION
gongyue	公约	pact
guan	官	government (owned)
guanxi	关系	connections
guo ting	过庭	"pass below the hall" (phrase from *The Analects,* Bk. XVI, Ch. 13)
guojia jiguan	国家机关	state organs
hangyuan shouce	行员手册	employee's handbook
hukou	户口	household registration system
jia	家	family
jian	间	side room
jianshe danwei	建设单位	construction units
jianzhu gongchengbu	建筑工程部	Ministry of Building and Engineering
jianzhu gongchengbu shejiyuan	建筑工程部设计院	Design Institute of the Ministry of Construction and Engineering
jiating	家庭	family
jiawu	家物	family assets
jiazhang	家长	head of family, parent
jiben jianshechu	基本建设处	Basic Construction Department
jiceng ganbu	基层干部	grassroots cadre
jiedao banshichu	街道办事处	street office
jihuaju	计划局	Planning Bureau
jingli	经理	manager
jingtianzhi	井田制	well-field system
jumin gongyue	居民公约	residents' pact
jumin shenfen zheng	居民身份证	resident's identity card
jumin weiyuanhui	居民委员会	residents' committee
junzi	君子	gentleman, "superior man"
kanjiawang	看家网	"neighborhood watch" network
lao taitai	老太太	granny
li (1)	礼	rules of propriety, ritual, etc.

PINYIN	CHARACTER	TRANSLATION
li (2)	里	walled residential district
ling qi luzao	另起炉灶	build another stove (establish an alternative power base)
linli guanxi	邻里关系	neighborliness
liwei	里尉	head of walled residential district
louzhang	楼长	building leader
lü	闾	unit made up of five *bi* or twenty-five families
lüli	闾里	walled residential district
lüyousi	闾有司	gatekeeper of walled residential district
mianzi	面子	face (prestige, reputation)
miao qiong fangzhang fu	庙穷方丈富	"a rich abbot in a poor monastery"
ming	明	bright
minju	民居	vernacular dwellings
minzhengbu	民政部	Ministry of Civil Affairs
minzu xingshi	民族形式	national style
ningjuli	凝聚力	cohesion
paichusuo	派出所	police station
Ping'anli	平安里	name of district in Beijing
qiye danwei	企业单位	enterprise *danwei* (e.g., factory)
qunzhong gongzuo	群众工作	mass-line work
qunzhong zuzhi	群众组织	mass organization
quzhengfu	区政府	district government
renshi dang'an	人事档案	personnel dossier or file
renshichu	人事处	personnel department
rentonggan	认同感	sense of identity and belonging
sanfan	三反	three antis (campaign)
santiao baozhangxian	三条保障线	three lines of guarantee
santong yiping	三通一平	"three connections and one leveling"
shangpinfang	商品房	commodity housing

PINYIN	CHARACTER	TRANSLATION
shangyejie	商业街	commercial street (or strip)
shehui ren	社会人	social person (or person of society)
shehui zhuyi da jiating	社会主义大家庭	"great socialist house"
shehuibu	社会部	Social Department (precursor to the Public Security Bureau)
sheji zongju	设计总局	General Design Office
shenghuo butie	生活补贴	lifestyle subsidy
shenghuo fuwu gongsi	生活服务公司	lifestyle services company
shenghuoke	生活科	lifestyle department
shenghuoqu	生活区	residential compound (of a *danwei*)
shequ	社区	community
shequ fuwu	社区服务	community services
shequ guanli weiyuanhui	社区管理委员会	*shequ* management committee
shequ jianshe	社区建设	community building
shequ jumin weiyuanhui	社区居民委员会	*shequ* residents' committee
shiwang	十网	the "ten networks"
shiye danwei	事业单位	institutional *danwei*
shuangxiang chengnuozhi	双向承诺制	"the two-way promise system"
si	私	private
siheyuan	四合院	courtyard house
siying qiye	私营企业	private enterprise
tangwu	堂屋	central room of *zhengfang*
tianjing	天井	"well of heaven," small courtyard
tiao-kuai jiegou	条块结构	"strips and chunks" (or "branches and regions") structure
tiefanwan	铁饭碗	iron rice bowl
ting	庭	central room of *zhengfang*
tonggou tongxiao	统购统销	unified purchasing and marketing system

PINYIN	CHARACTER	TRANSLATION
tongpei	统配	unified job assignment system
tongyi jieshao	统一介绍	unified job introduction system
wenming shimin suzhi jiaoyu	文明市民素质教育	"civilized citizen quality education"
wufan	五反	five antis (campaign)
wuhua	五化	the "five transformations"
wuye guanli gongsi	物业管理公司	estate management company
xiafang	下放	"sent down" (cadres)
xiagang	下岗	redundancy
xiahai	下海	jump into the sea—leave a state sector job to go into private business
xian shengchan, hou shenghuo	先生产，后生活	"production first, life later"
xiandai qiye zhidu	现代企业制度	modern enterprise system
xiangfang	厢房	east and west wings of courtyard house
xiao	孝	filial duty
xiaogongjia	小公家	"little public family" (the collective sector, Yan'an)
xiaoqu	小区	small district (residential compound)
yanjie shangdian	沿街商店	street-side shopping strips
yezhu weiyuanhui	业主委员会	home owners' committee
yijia liangzhi	一家两制	one family, two systems
you wen junzi zhi yuan qi zi ye	又闻君子之远其子也	"I have also heard that the superior man maintains a distant [reserve] towards his son." (Legge)
yuan	院	enclosures
yuanluo	院落	enclosed compound
yuanqiang jingji	院墙经济	compound wall economics
yuanzhang	院长	compound leader
zhalan	栅栏	street-gates
zhengfang	正房	northern and most important wing of the courtyard house

PINYIN	CHARACTER	TRANSLATION
zhengwuyuan	政务院	Government Administration Council
zhi neng jin, bu neng chu	只能进，不能出	"you can only get in, you can't get out"
zhigong jiashu weiyuanhui	职工家属委员会	staff and family committees
zhongyang sheji gongsi	中央设计公司	Central Design Company
zhufang gongjijin zhidu	住房公积金制度	housing accumulation fund system
zhulou	主楼	principal building
ziji zao fanwan	自己造饭碗	create your own rice bowl
zongwuke	总务科	general services department
zutang	祖堂	north and most important wing of the courtyard house
zuzhi qilai	组织起来	get organized

Bibliography

Allen, Barry. 1998. "Foucault and Modern Political Philosophy." In *The Later Foucault: Politics and Philosophy*, ed. Jeremy Moss. London: Sage.

Anagnost, Ann. 1997. *National Past-Times: Narrative, Representation, and Power in Modern China*. Durham, NC: Duke University Press.

Andors, Stephen. 1977. *China's Industrial Revolution: Politics, Planning, and Management, 1949 to the Present*. New York: Pantheon.

Apter, David E., and Tony Saich. 1994. *Revolutionary Discourse in Mao's Republic*. Cambridge. MA: Harvard University Press.

Bagley, Robert. 1999. "Shang Archaeology." In *The Cambridge History of Ancient China: From the Origins of Civilization to 221 BC*, ed. Michael Loewe and Edward L. Shaughnessy, 124–231. Cambridge: Cambridge University Press.

Bai Yihua and Ma Xueli, eds. 1990. (白益华) (马学理)《居民委员会工作手册》(*A Handbook for Residents Committee Work*). Beijing: 中国社会出版社 (China Social Press).

Bakken, Borge. 2000. *The Exemplary Society: Human Improvement, Social Control, and the Dangers of Modernity in China*. Oxford: Oxford University Press.

Banham, Reyner. 1960. *Theory and Design in the First Machine Age*. Cambridge, MA: MIT Press.

Barlow, Tani. 1993. "Colonialism's Career in Post-War China Studies." *Positions* 1 (1): 224–67.

———. 1994. "Theorizing Woman: Funü, Guojia, Jiating (Chinese Woman, Chinese State, Chinese Family)." In *Body, Subject, and Power in China*, ed. Angela Zito and Tani Barlow. Chicago: Chicago University Press.

Barmé, Geremie, and Linda Jaivin, eds. 1992. *New Ghosts, Old Dreams*. New York: Times Books.

Barmé, Geremie, and John Minford, eds. 1989. *Seeds of Fire: Chinese Voices of Conscience*. Newcastle upon Tyne, UK: Bloodaxe Books.

Barry, Andrew, Thomas Osborne, and Nikolas Rose, eds. 1996. *Foucault and Political Reason: Liberalism, Neo-Liberalism, and Rationalities of Government*. Chicago: University of Chicago Press.

Bater, James H. 1980. *The Soviet City: Ideal and Reality*. London: Edward Arnold.

Baum, Richard. 1994. *Burying Mao: Chinese Politics in the Age of Deng Xiaoping*.

Princeton, NJ: Princeton University Press.

Bauman, Zygmunt. 2000. *Liquid Modernity*. Cambridge: Polity.

Beecher, Jonathon, and Richard Bienvenu, eds. 1971. *The Utopian Vision of Charles Fourier: Selected Texts on Work, Love, and Passionate Attraction*. Boston: Beacon Press.

Beijing jianshe shishu bianji weiyuanhui. 1986. (北京建设史书编辑委员会) 《建国以来的北京城市建设》 (*Urban Construction in Beijing Since 1949*). Beijing.

Benevolo, Leonardo. 1971. *History of Modern Architecture*. Vol. 1, *The Tradition of Modern Architecture*. Trans. H. J. Landry. Cambridge, MA: MIT Press.

Benjamin, Walter. 1986. *Reflections: Essays, Aphorisms, Autobiographical Writings*. Ed. Peter Demetz. New York: Schocken Books.

Berman, Marshall. 1988. *All That Is Solid Melts into Air: The Experience of Modernity*. New York: Penguin Books.

Bian, Yanjie, John R. Logan, Lu Hanlong, Pan Yunkang, and Ying Guan. 1997. "Work Units and Housing Reform in Two Chinese Cities." In *Danwei: The Changing Chinese Workplace in Historical and Comparative Perspective*, ed. Xiaobo Lü and Elizabeth J. Perry, 223–48. New York: M. E. Sharpe.

Blecher, Marc J., and Gordon White. 1979. *Micropolitics in Contemporary China: A Technical Unit During and After the Cultural Revolution*. New York: M. E. Sharpe.

Bliznakov, Milka. 1976. "Urban Planning in the USSR: Integrative Theories." In *The City in Russian History*, ed. Michael F. Hamm, 243–56. Lexington: University Press of Kentucky.

———. 1993. "Soviet Housing During the Experimental Years, 1918 to 1933." In *Russian Housing in the Modern Age: Design and Social History*, ed. William Craft Brumfield and Blair A. Ruble, 85–148. Cambridge: Cambridge University Press.

Bo Yibo. 1991–93. (薄一波) 《若干重大决策与事件的回顾》 (*Recollections of Some Major Policy Decisions and Events*. Vols. 1 and 2). Beijing: 中共中央党校出版社 (Central Party School Press).

Bodde, Derk, and Clarence Morris. 1967. *Law in Imperial China*. Cambridge, MA: Harvard University Press.

Bogdanov, A. A. 1923. *A Short Course of Economic Science*. Trans. J. Fineburg. London: Labor Publishing Company.

Bottomore, T., L. Harris, V. G. Kiernan, and R. Miliband, eds. 1983. *A Dictionary of Marxist Thought*. Oxford: Blackwell.

Bourdieu, Pierre. 1979. *Algeria 1960*. Trans. Richard Nice. Cambridge: Cambridge University Press.

Boyd, Andrew. 1962. *Chinese Architecture and Town Planning: 1500 BC–AD 1911*. London: Alec Tiranti.

Bray, David, 1997. "Space, Politics, and Labor: Towards a Spatial Genealogy of the Chinese Work-Unit." *Asian Studies Review* 20 (3): 35–42.

Bray, Francesca. 1997. *Technology and Gender: Fabrics of Power in Late Imperial China*. Berkeley: University of California Press.

Brødsgaard, Kjeld Erik. 2002. "Institutional Reform and the Bianzhi System in China." *China Quarterly* 170: 361–86.

Burchell, Graham, Colin Gordon, and Peter Miller, eds. 1991. *The Foucault Effect: Studies in Governmentality*. London: Harvester Wheatsheaf.

Butterfield, Fox. 1990. *China: Alive in the Bitter Sea*. 2nd ed. New York: Random House.

Caldeira, Teresa P. R. 1999. "Fortified Enclaves: The New Urban Segregation." In *Cities and Citizenship,* ed. James Holston, 114–38. Durham, NC: Duke University Press.

Cao Hongtao and Chu Chuanheng, eds. 1990. (曹洪涛) (储传亨)《当代中国的城市建设》 (*Urban Construction in Contemporary China*). Beijing: 中国社会科学出版社 (China Social Science Press).

Cao Jinqing. 1993. (曹锦清) "从单位建制到个人主体：市场经济与人的社会化" ("From the *Danwei* System to the Individual Subject: The Market Economy and Human Socialization"). 《探索与争鸣》 (*Probing and Contending*) 5: 32–36.

Cao Jinqing and Chen Zhongya. 1997. (曹锦清) (陈中亚)《走出理想城堡：中国单位现象研究》 (*Leaving the Ideal Castle: Research on China's Danwei Phenomenon*). Shenzhen: 海天出版社 (Haitian Press).

Carr, E. H. 1966. *The Bolshevik Revolution: 1917–1923*. Vols. 1 and 2. Harmondsworth, UK: Penguin Books.

Castells, Manuel. 2000. *The Rise of the Network Society*. 2nd ed. Oxford: Blackwell.

Chakrabarty, Dipesh. 1992. "Postcoloniality and the Artifice of History: Who Speaks for 'Indian' Pasts?" *Representations* 37: 1–26.

Ch'ü, T'ung-tsu. 1965. *Law and Society in Traditional China*. Taiwan: Rainbow Bridge Book Company.

Chan, Anita. 1997. "Chinese *Danwei* Reforms: Convergence with the Japanese Model?" In *Danwei: The Changing Chinese Workplace in Historical and Comparative Perspective,* ed. Xiaobo Lü and Elizabeth J. Perry, 91–113. New York: M. E. Sharpe.

———. 2001. *China's Workers Under Assault: The Exploitation of Labor in a Globalizing Economy*. Armonk, NY: M. E. Sharpe.

Chan, Cecilia L. W. 1993. *The Myth of Neighborhood Mutual Help: The Contemporary Chinese Community-Based Welfare System in Guangzhou*. Hong Kong: Hong Kong University Press.

Chen Baoliang. 1996. (陈宝良)《中国的社与会》 (*China's Societies and Associations*). Hangzhou: 浙江人民出版社 (Zhejiang People's Press).

Chen Yun. 1982. (陈云)《陈云文稿选编（1949–61）》 (*Selected Speeches of Chen Yun 1949–61*). Beijing: 人民出版社 (The People's Press).

Cheng, Tiejun, and Mark Selden. 1997. "The Construction of Spatial Hierarchies: China's Hukou and *Danwei* Systems." In *New Perspectives on State Socialism in China,* ed. Timothy Cheek and Tony Saich, 23–50. New York: M. E. Sharpe.

Chengshi jianshe zongju guihua shejiju. 1956. (城市建设总局规划设计局) "全国标准设计评选会议对选出方案的意见和单元介绍" ("Comments on the Plans

Selected by the National Planning Standards Selection Conference and Explanations of the *Danyuan*"). 《建筑学报》 (*Journal of Architecture*) 2: 57–72.

Cheng Xuan. 1990. "Problems of Urbanisation Under China's Traditional Economic System." In *Chinese Urban Reform: What Model Now?* ed. Kwok et al., 65–77. New York: M. E. Sharpe.

Chesneaux, Jean, Françoise Le Barbier, and Marie-Claire Bergère. 1977. *China from the 1911 Revolution to Liberation*. New York: Pantheon.

Choay, Françoise. 1969. *The Modern City: Planning in the 19th Century*. New York: George Braziller.

Claeys, Gregory, ed. 1993. *Selected Works of Robert Owen*. Vol. 1. London: William Pickering.

Communist Party of China. 1981. *Resolution on CPC History—1949–81*. Beijing: Foreign Languages Press.

Confucius. [1893] 1971. *Confucian Analects: The Great Learning and The Doctrine of the Mean*. Trans. James Legge. Reprint, New York: Dover Publications.

———. 1979. *The Analects*. Trans. D. C. Lau. Harmondsworth: Penguin Classics.

Dai Nianci. 1957. (戴念慈) "一个社会科学学院的规划和设计" ("The Planning and Design of an Academy of Social Sciences"). 《建筑学报》 (*Journal of Architecture*) 1: 14–25.

Davis, Deborah S., Richard Kraus, Barry Naughton, and Elizabeth Perry, eds. 1995. *Urban Spaces in Contemporary China*. Cambridge: Cambridge University Press.

Dean, Mitchell, 1999. *Governmentality: Power and Rule in Modern Society*. London: Sage.

Di Cosmo, Nicola. 2002. *Ancient China and Its Enemies: The Rise of Nomadic Power in East Asian History*. Cambridge: Cambridge University Press.

Dittmer, Lowell, and Lu Xiaobo. 1996. "Personal Politics in the Chinese *Danwei* Under Reform." *Asian Survey* 36 (3): 246–67.

Donnachie, Ian, and George Hewitt. 1993. *Historic New Lanark: The Dale and Owen Industrial Community Since 1785*. Edinburgh: Edinburgh University Press.

Dray-Novey, Alison. 1993. "Spatial Order and Police in Imperial Beijing." *Journal of Asian Studies* 52 (4): 885–922.

Dreyfus, Hubert, and Paul Rabinow. 1982. *Michel Foucault: Beyond Structuralism and Hermeneutics*. New York: Harvester Wheatsheaf.

Du Erqi. 1956. (杜尔圻) "高等学校建筑群的布局和单体设计" ("The Arrangement of Building Clusters and Individual Building Designs for Colleges of Higher Education"). 《建筑学报》 (*Journal of Architecture*) 5: 1–27.

Duara, Prasenjit. 1988. *Culture, Power, and the State: Rural North China, 1900–1942*. Stanford, CA: Stanford University Press.

Dutton, Michael. 1988. "Policing the Chinese Household: A Comparison of Modern and Ancient Forms." *Economy and Society* 17 (2): 195–223.

———. 1992a. "Disciplinary Projects and Carceral Spread: Foucauldian Theory and Chinese Practice." *Economy and Society* 21 (3): 276–94.

———. 1992b. *Policing and Punishment in China: From Patriarchy to the People*.

Cambridge: Cambridge University Press.

————. 1995. "Dreaming of Better Times: 'Repetition with a Difference' and Community Policing in China." *Positions* 3 (2): 415–47.

————. 1998. *Streetlife China*. Cambridge: Cambridge University Press.

Eliade, Mircea. 1976. *Occultism, Witchcraft, and Cultural Fashions*. Chicago: University of Chicago Press.

Elvin, Mark, and G. William Skinner, eds. 1974. *The Chinese City Between Two Worlds*. Stanford, CA: Stanford University Press.

Engels, Fredrick. [1880] 1972. *Socialism: Utopian and Scientific*. Moscow: International Publishers.

Fairbank, John King, Edwin O. Reischauer, and Albert M. Craig. 1965. *East Asia: The Modern Transformation*. Boston: Houghton Mifflin.

Fan Jin, Zhang Dazhong, and Xu Weicheng, eds. 1989. (范瑾) (张大中) (徐惟诚)《当代中国的北京》 (*Contemporary China's Beijing*). 2 vols. Beijing: (China Social Science Press).

Fewsmith, Joseph. 2001. *China Since Tiananmen: The Politics of Transition*. Cambridge: Cambridge University Press.

Fishman, Robert. 1982. *Urban Utopias in the Twentieth Century: Ebenezer Howard, Frank Lloyd Wright, and Le Corbusier*. Cambridge, MA: MIT Press.

Foucault, Michel. 1978. *The History of Sexuality*. Vol. 1, *An Introduction*. Trans. Robert Hurley. New York: Random House.

————. 1979. *Discipline and Punish: The Birth of the Prison*. Trans. Alan Sheridan. Harmondsworth, UK: Penguin.

————. 1980a. "Truth and Power." In *Power/Knowledge*, ed. Colin Gordon, 109–33. New York: Pantheon.

————. 1980b. "The Eye of Power." In *Power/Knowledge*, ed. Colin Gordon, 146–65. New York: Pantheon.

————. 1982. "The Subject and Power." In *Michel Foucault: Beyond Structuralism and Hermeneutics*, ed. Hubert L. Dreyfus and Paul Rabinow, 208–26. New York: Harvester Press.

————. 1991. "Governmentality." In *The Foucault Effect: Studies in Governmentality*, ed. Graham Burchell, Colin Gordon, and Peter Miller, 87–104. London: Harvester Wheatsheaf.

————. 1997. "Security, Territory, and Population." In *Michel Foucault: Ethics, Subjectivity, and Truth*, ed. Paul Rabinow, 67–71. London: Allen Lane, The Penguin Press.

Frampton, Kenneth, 1992. *Modern Architecture: A Critical History*, 3rd ed. London: Thames and Hudson.

Francis, Corinna-Barbara. 1996. "Reproduction of *Danwei* Institutional Features in the Context of China's Market Economy: The Case of Haidian District's High-Tech Sector." *China Quarterly* 147 (September): 839–59.

Fraser, David. 2000. "Inventing Oasis: Luxury Housing Advertisements and Reconfiguring Domestic Space in Shanghai." In *The Consumer Revolution in Urban China*, ed. Deborah Davis, 25–53. Berkeley: University of California Press.

Frazier, Mark W. 2002. *The Making of the Chinese Industrial Workplace: State, Revolution, and Labor Management*. Cambridge: Cambridge University Press.

French, R. Antony. 1995. *Plans, Pragmatism, and People: The Legacy of Soviet Planning for Today's Cities*. London: UCL Press.

Frost, Stephen. 1999. "From State-Owned Enterprise to Multi-National: The Case of the Hai'er Group." Paper presented to the Sixth Biennial Conference of the Chinese Studies Association of Australia, 8–10 July, at Murdoch University, Perth, Western Australia.

Gaubatz, Piper Rae. 1995. "Urban Transformation in Post-Mao China: Impacts of the Reform Era on China's Urban Form." In *Urban Spaces in Contemporary China: The Potential for Autonomy and Community in Post-Mao China,* ed. Deborah S. Davis, Richard Kraus, Barry Naughton, and Elizabeth J. Perry, 28–60. Cambridge: Cambridge University Press.

Giroir, Guillaume. 2002. "The Phenomenon of the Gated Communities in Beijing or the New Forbidden Cities." *Bulletin de l'Association des Géographes Français* 4: 423–36.

Golas, Peter J. 1977. "Early Ch'ing Guilds." In *The City in Late Imperial China,* ed. G. William Skinner. Stanford, CA: Stanford University Press.

Gong Deshun, Zou Denong, and Dou Yide. 1989. (龚德顺) (邹德侬) (窦以德) 《中国当代建筑史纲要》 (*An Outline of Modern Chinese Architectural History*). Tianjin: 天津科学技术出版社 (Tianjin Science and Technology Press).

Goodman, Bryna. 1995. *Native Place, City, and Nation: Regional Networks and Identities in Shanghai, 1853–1937*. Berkeley: University of California Press.

Gordon, Colin. 1991. "Government Rationality: An Introduction." In *The Foucault Effect: Studies in Governmentality,* ed. Graham Burchell, Colin Gordon, and Peter Miller, 1–51. London: Harvester Wheatsheaf.

Gore, Lance L. P. 1999. "The Communist Legacy in Post-Mao Economic Growth." *China Journal* 41 (January): 25–54.

Gottdiener, Mark. 1994. *The Social Production of Urban Space*, 2nd ed. Austin: University of Texas Press.

Gu Mengchao, ed. 1989. (顾孟潮) 《中国建筑评析与展望》 (*Chinese Architecture: Analysis and Prospects*). Tianjin: 天津科学技术出版社 (Tianjin Science and Technology Press).

Guo Chongde, ed. 1993. (郭崇德) 《中国城市社区服务发展道路》 (*The Path of Development for Community Services in China's Cities*). Beijing: 中国社会出版社 (China Social Press).

Guojia renshiju, ed. 1980. (国家人事局) 《人事工作文件选编》 (*Selected Documents on Personnel Work*). 3 vols. Beijing.

Guojia tongjiju shehui tongjisi, ed. 1994. (国家统计局社会统计司) 《中国社会统计资料》 (*Statistical Material on Chinese Society*). Beijing: 中国统计出版社 (China Statistics Press).

Guojia tongjiju, ed. 1998. (国家统计局) 《中国劳动统计年鉴 1998》 (*China Labor Statistics Yearbook 1998*). Beijing: 中国统计出版社 (China Statistics Press).

———. 2000. (国家统计局) 《中国统计年鉴 2000》 (*China Statistical Yearbook 2000*). Beijing: 中国统计出版社 (China Statistics Press).

Hacking, Ian. 1983. *Representing and Intervening*. London: Cambridge University Press.

Hall, Peter. 1988. *Cities of Tomorrow: An Intellectual History of Urban Planning and Design in the Twentieth Century*. Oxford: Basil Blackwell.

Han Mingmo. 1990. (韩明谟) "社会学的重建、探索和突破" ("Explorations and Breakthroughs in the Rebuilding of Sociology"). 《中国社会科学》 (*China Social Science*) 1: 55–66.

Harvey, David. 1982. *The Limits to Capital*. Oxford: Blackwell.

Harrison, J. F. C. 1969. *Robert Owen and the Owenites in Britain and America: Quest for the New Moral World*. New York: Routledge and Kegan Paul.

He Xinghan. 1993. (贺星寒) "人在单位中" ("People in the Work Unit"). In 《散文与人》 (*People and Prose*), ed. Shao Yanxiang (邵燕祥) and Lin Xianzhi (林贤治), 157–66. Guangzhou: Huachen Press. (Translation in Michael Dutton, *Streetlife China*, 42–53. Cambridge: Cambridge University Press.)

He Yeju. 1985. (贺业钜) 《考工记营国制度研究》 (*Research on the System of City Design in the Kaogongji*). Beijing: 中国建筑工业出版社 (China Architecture Industry Press).

Hershatter, Gail. 1986. *The Workers of Tianjin, 1900–1949*. Stanford, CA: Stanford University Press.

Hershkovitz, Linda. 1993. "Tiananmen Square and the Politics of Space." *Political Geography* 12 (5): 395–420.

Hirst, P., and P. Wooley. 1982. *Social Relations and Human Attributes*. London: Tavistock.

The Hsiao Ching. 1961. Trans. Mary Lelia Makra. New York: St. John's University Press.

Hsu, Francis L. K. 1971. *Under the Ancestors' Shadow: Kinship, Personality, and Social Mobility in China*. Stanford, CA: Stanford University Press.

Hua Lanhong. 1957. (华揽洪) "北京幸福村街坊设计" ("The Design of Beijing's Xingfu Village Neighborhood"). 《建筑学报》 (*Journal of Architecture*) 3:16–33.

Huadong shejiyuan. 1955. (华东设计院) "东北某厂住宅区详细规划设计内容介绍" ("A Summary of the Detailed Planning and Design of a Factory Residential District in the North East"). 《建筑学报》 (*Journal of Architecture*) 2: 24–40.

Huang Xiaojing and Yang Xiao. 1987. "From Iron Rice Bowls to Labor Markets: Reforming the Social Security System." In *Reform in China: Challenges and Choices,* ed. Bruce L. Reynolds, 147–60. New York: M. E. Sharpe.

Hurst, William, and Kevin J. O'Brien. 2002. "China's Contentious Pensioners." *China Quarterly* 170: 345–60.

Information Office of the State Council of the People's Republic of China. 1991. *Human Rights in China*. Beijing: Foreign Press.

Jenner, W. J. F. 1992. *The Tyranny of History: The Roots of China's Crisis*. London: Allen Lane, The Penguin Press.

Jensen, K. M. 1978. *Beyond Marx and Mach: Aleksandr Bogdanov's Philosophy of Living Experience*. Dordrecht: Reidel.

Ji Long, and Zheng Hui, eds. 1992. (季龙) (郑惠) 《中国手工业合作化和城镇集体

工业的发展》 (*The Collectivization of China's Handicraft Industry and the Development of Urban Collective Industry*). Beijing: 中共党史出版社 (Chinese Communist Party History Press).

Ji Xiaolan. 1995. "China's Housing Strategy." *Beijing Review* (April 3–16): 8–11.

Ji, You. 1998. *China's Enterprise Reform: Changing State/Society Relations After Mao.* London: Routledge.

Jin Oubu. 1960. (金瓯卜) "建筑设计必须体现大办城市人民公社的新形势" ("Architectural Design Must Embody the New Push to Build Urban People's Communes"). 《建筑学报》 (*Journal of Architecture*) 5: 34–38.

Kaple, Deborah A. 1994. *Dream of a Red Factory: The Legacy of High Stalinism in China.* New York: Oxford University Press.

King, Ross. 1996. *Emancipating Space: Geography, Architecture, and Urban Design.* New York: Guilford Press.

Knapp, Ronald. 1990. *The Chinese House: Craft, Symbol, and the Folk Tradition.* Hong Kong: Oxford University Press.

Konvitz, Josef W. 1985. *The Urban Millennium: The City-Building Process from the Early Middle Ages to the Present.* Carbondale: Southern Illinois University Press.

Kopp, Anatole. 1970. *Town and Revolution: Soviet Architecture and City Planning, 1917–1935.* Trans. Thomas E. Burton. New York: George Braziller.

———. 1985. *Constructivist Architecture in the USSR.* London: Academy Editions.

Kwok, R. Yin-Wang, William L. Parish, Anthony Gar-On Yeh, and Xu Xueqiang, eds. 1990. *Chinese Urban Reform: What Model Now?* New York: M. E. Sharpe.

Lai Ruoyu. 1953. (赖若愚) "关于中国工会工作的报告——为完成国家工业建设的任务而奋斗" ("A Report on China's Trade Union Work—Struggle to Fulfill the Task of State Industrial Construction"). In 《中国工会第七次全国代表大会主要文件》 (*Key Documents from the Seventh National Trade Union Congress of China*). Beijing.

Le Corbusier. [1929] 1987. *The City of Tomorrow and Its Planning.* Trans. Frederick Etchells. Reprint, New York: Dover Publications.

———. [1931] 1986. *Towards a New Architecture.* Trans. Frederick Etchells. Reprint, New York: Dover Publications.

Lee, Ching Kwan. 1999. "From Organized Dependence to Disorganized Despotism: Changing Labor Regimes in Chinese Factories." *China Quarterly* 157: 44–71.

Lee, Hung Yung. 1991. *From Revolutionary Cadres to Party Technocrats in Socialist China.* Berkeley: University of California Press.

Lee, Peter N. S. 1987. *Industrial Management and Economic Reform in China, 1949–1984.* Hong Kong: Oxford University Press.

Lee Tai To. 1989. *Trade Unions in China, 1949 to the Present: The Organization and Leadership of the All China Federation of Trade Unions.* Singapore: Singapore University Press.

Lee, Yok-shiu F. 1988. "The Urban Housing Problem in China." *China Quarterly* 115: 387–407.

Lefebvre, Henri. 1976. *The Survival of Capitalism.* London: Allison and Busby.

————. 1991. *The Production of Space*. Trans. Donald Nicholson-Smith. Oxford: Blackwell.

Leng Mou. 1992. (冷眸), "北京居民'一家两制'" ("Beijing Residents 'One Family, Two Systems'").《人民日报》(海外版) (*People's Daily*, overseas edition), 6 August.

Lenin, V. I. 1960–70. *Collected Works*. 45 vols. Moscow: Progress Publishers.

Leung, Wing-yue. 1988. *Smashing the Iron Rice Pot: Workers and Unions in China's Market Socialism*. Hong Kong: Asia Monitor Resource Center.

Leung, Joe C. B., and Richard C. Nann. 1995. *Authority and Benevolence: Social Welfare in China*. Hong Kong: Chinese University Press.

Levine, Steven I. 1987. *Anvil of Victory: The Communist Revolution in Manchuria, 1945–1948*. New York: Columbia University Press.

Li Chunling. 1955. (李椿龄) "降低标准后的二区住宅定型设计介绍" ("Discussion on Finalizing the Design for Two Residential Districts After the Reduction of Standards").《建筑学报》(*Journal of Architecture*) 1: 95–100.

Li Fuchun. 1956. *First Five-Year Plan for Development of the National Economy of the People's Republic of China in 1953–1957*. Beijing: Foreign Languages Press.

Li Hanlin. 1993. (李汉林) "中国单位现象与城市社区的整合机制" ("China's *Danwei* Phenomenon and the Mechanisms of Conformity in Urban Communities").《社会学研究》(*Sociology Research*) 5: 23–32.

Li Han-lin, Wang Fen-yu, and Li Lu-lu. 1996. *Work Unit—The Basic Structure of Chinese Society—Data Material*. Beijing: Beijing Publishing House.

Li Jianhe, Wang Taiyuan, Wang Hongjun, and Yang Fenglian. 1990. (李健和) (王太远) (王宏君) (杨凤莲)《公民如何与公安机关打交道》(*Procedures for Citizens in Dealing with Public Security Organs*). Beijing: 法律出版社 (Legal Press).

The Li̍ Kî (I–X). 1885. Trans. James Legge. Vol. 27 of *The Sacred Books of the East*, ed. F. Max Müller. Oxford: Clarendon Press.

Li Lulu, Li Hanlin, and Wang Fenyu. 1994. (李路路) (李汉林) (王奋宇) "中国的单位现象与体制改革" ("China's *Danwei* Phenomenon and Structural Reform").《中国社会科学季刊》(*Chinese Social Sciences Quarterly*) 2: 5–16.

Li Ning. 1997. "Promising Reemployment Project." *Beijing Review* 18–24 (August): 9–14.

Li Peilin and Zhang Yi. 2000. (李培林) (张翼)《国有企业社会成本分析》(*An Analysis of the Social Costs of SOEs*). Beijing: 社会科学文献出版社 (Social Science Document Press).

Li Rongxia. 1998. "Residential Houses Go to the Market." *Beijing Review* 18–24 (May): 12–14.

Li Xin. 1988. (李信) "接管千年古都的房地产" ("Taking Control of Real Estate in the Thousand-Year-Old Ancient Capital"). In《北京的黎明》(*Beijing's Dawn*), ed. Wang Guiling (王桂玲), Dou Kun (窦坤), and Lü Kenong (吕克农), 458–60. Beijing: 北京出版社 (Beijing Press).

Li Yongguang. 1956. (李邕光) "目前住宅标准设计所存在的一些问题及讨论" ("Some Questions and Debates on Current Housing Design Standards").《建筑学报》(*Journal of Architecture*) 2: 99–103.

Liang Sicheng. 1951. (梁思成) "北京—都市规划的无比佳作" ("Beijing—An

Incomparable Masterpiece of City Planning"). 《新观察》 (*New Survey*) 2 (7/8 April).

———. 1954. "中国建筑的特征" ("The Special Characteristics of Chinese Architecture"). 《建筑学报》 (*Journal of Architecture*) 1: 36–39.

———. 1986. "关于北京城墙废存问题的讨论" ("Discussion on the Question of Whether or Not to Demolish Beijing's City Wall"). In 《梁思成文集》 (*Collected Works of Liang Sicheng*), 4: 46–50. Beijing: 中国建筑出版社 (China Architecture Press).

Liang Wenhan. 1957. (梁文翰) "新建的南海糖厂" ("The Newly Built Nanhai Sugar Factory"). 《建筑学报》 (*Journal of Architecture*) 10: 43–48.

Lieberthal, Kenneth G. 1980. *Revolution and Tradition in Tientsin, 1949–1952*. Stanford, CA: Stanford University Press.

Lin Zhu. 1993. (林洙) "建筑大师梁思成遗恨北京古城墙" ("Great Architect Liang Sicheng's Regrets Over Beijing's Ancient City Wall"). 《书摘》 (*Extracts*) 2: 43–45.

———. 1996. 《建筑师梁思成》 (*Liang Sicheng: Architect*). Tianjin: 天津科学技术出版社 (Tianjin Science and Technology Press).

Liu Chuanji and Sun Guangde. 1987. (刘传济) (孙光德) 《社会保险与职工福利》 (*Social Security and Worker Welfare*). Beijing: 劳动出版社 (Labor Press).

Liu Dunzhen. 1955. (刘敦桢) "批判梁思成先生的唯心主义建筑思想" ("A Critique of Mr Liang Sicheng's Idealistic Architectural Thinking"). 《建筑学报》 (*Journal of Architecture*) 1: 69–79.

———. 1957. 《中国住宅概说》 (*An Outline of Chinese Residences*). Beijing: 中国建筑工业出版社 (Chinese Architecture Industry Press).

———. 1980. 《中国古代建筑史》 (*A History of Classical Chinese Architecture*). Beijing: 中国建筑工业出版社 (Chinese Architecture Industry Press).

Liu Hongru, ed. 1993. (刘鸿儒) 《中国住房制度改革咨询手册》 (*An Information Handbook to the Reform of China's Housing System*). Shenyang: 辽宁人民出版社 (Liaoning People's Press).

Liu Shaoqi. 1984. *Selected Works of Liu Shaoqi*. 2 vols. Beijing: Foreign Languages Press.

Liu Yiji. 1957. (刘义基) "北京钢筋混凝土予制构件厂简介" ("A Brief Summary of the Beijing Reinforced Concrete Component Provision Factory"). 《建筑学报》 (*Journal of Architecture*) 10: 54–60.

Liu Yipeng. 1994. (刘义鹏) 《最新劳动人事管理政策法律实务》 (*The Latest Policies, Laws, and Practices Relating to Labor and Personnel Management*). Hebei: 中国文化出版社 (China Culture Press).

Liu Zhifeng, ed. 1994. (刘志峰) 《城镇住房制度改革》 (*Urban Housing Reform*). Beijing: 改革出版社 (Reform Press).

Liu Zhiping. 1990. (刘致平) 《中国住宅建筑简史》 (*A Brief History of Chinese Residential Architecture*). Beijing: 中国建筑工业出版社 (China Architecture Industry Press).

Liu Chuanze. 1987. (刘传泽) 《社会保险与职工福利》 (*Social Insurance and Worker Welfare*). Beijing: 中国劳动出版社 (China Labor Press).

Lo, C. P. 1994. "Economic Reforms and Socialist City Structure: A Case Study of Guangzhou, China." *Urban Geography* 15 (2): 128–49.

Loewe, Michael. 1968. *Everyday Life in Early Imperial China During the Han Period, 202 BC–AD 220*. London: B. T. Batsford.

Lu Feng. 1989. (路风) "单位：一种特殊的社会组织形式" ("The Danwei: A Unique Form of Social Organization"). 《中国社会科学》 (*Chinese Social Science*) 1: 71–88.

———. 1993. "The Origins and Formation of the Unit (*Danwei*) System." *Chinese Sociology and Anthropology* 25 (3).

Lu Xiang and Wang Qiming. 1996. (陆翔) (王其明) 《北京四合院》 (*Beijing Courtyard Houses*). Beijing: 中国建筑工业出版社 (China Architecture Industry Press).

Lü, Xiaobo. 1997. "Minor Public Economy: The Revolutionary Origins of the *Danwei*." In *Danwei: The Changing Chinese Workplace in Historical and Comparative Perspective*, ed. Xiaobo Lü and Elizabeth J. Perry, 21–41. Armonk, NY: M. E. Sharpe.

Lü, Xiaobo, and Elizabeth J. Perry, eds. 1997. *Danwei: The Changing Chinese Workplace in Historical and Comparative Perspective*. Armonk, NY: M. E. Sharpe.

Lu Yu. 1988. (陆禹) "北平工矿企业的新生" ("The Rebirth of Beiping's Industrial and Mining Enterprises"). In 《北京的黎明》 (*Beijing's Dawn*), ed. Wang Guiling (王桂玲), Dou Kun (窦坤), and Lü Kenong (吕克农), 270–77. Beijing: 北京出版社 (Beijing Press).

Luymes, Don. 2002. "The Fortification of Suburbia: Investigating the Rise of Enclave Communities." In *The City: Critical Concepts in the Social Sciences*, ed. Michael Pacione, 278–301. London: Routledge.

Ma Bingjian. 1993. (马炳坚) 《北京四合院》(*Quadrangles of Beijing*). Beijing: 北京美术摄影出版社 (Beijing Arts and Photography Press).

Ma Haoran. 1957. (马浩然) "北京农业机器拖拉机站的设计" ("Design for an Agricultural Motorized Tractor Station in Beijing"). 《建筑学报》 (*Journal of Architecture*) 8: 47–53.

Ma Qibin, Chen Wenbin, Lin Yunhui, Cong Jin, Wang Nianyi, Zhang Tianrong, and Bu Weihua, eds. 1991. (马齐彬) (陈文斌) (林蕴晖) (丛进) (王年一) (张天荣) (卜伟华) 《中国共产党执政四十年，1949–89》 (*The Chinese Communist Party: 40 Years of Government, 1949–1989*). Enlarged edition. Beijing: 中共党史出版社 (Chinese Communist Party History Press).

Ma Xueli and Zhang Xiulan, eds. 2001. (马学理) (张秀兰) 《中国社区建设发展之路》 (*The Development of Community Building in China*). Beijing: 红旗出版社 (Red Flag Press).

Mackerras, Colin. 1989. *Western Images of China*. Oxford: Oxford University Press.

Mao Zedong. 1961–77. *Selected Works of Mao Zedong*. 5 vols. Beijing: Foreign Languages Press.

———. 1993. (毛泽东) 《毛泽东文集》 (*Collected Works of Mao Zedong*). Vol. 2. Beijing: 人民出版社 (The People's Press).

Martin, Brian G. 1996. *The Shanghai Green Gang: Politics and Organized Crime, 1919–1937*. Berkeley: University of California Press.

Marx, Karl, and Frederick Engels. 1975–2004. *Collected Works*. 50 vols. Moscow: Progress Publishers.

Massey, Doreen. 1984. *Spatial Divisions of Labour: Social Structures and the Geography of Production*. Hampshire, UK: Macmillan.

Mauss, Marcel. 1985. "A Category of the Human Mind: The Notions of Person; the Notion of Self." Trans. W. D. Halls, in *The Category of the Person*, ed. M. Carrithers, S. Collins, and S. Lukes, 1–25. Cambridge: Cambridge University Press.

Meisner, Maurice. 1986. *Mao's China and After: A History of the People's Republic*. New York: The Free Press.

———. 1996. *The Deng Xiaoping Era: An Inquiry into the Fate of Chinese Socialism, 1978–1994*. New York: Hill and Wang.

Mencius. [1895] 1970. *The Works of Mencius*. Trans. James Legge. Reprint, New York: Dover Publications.

Miller, Peter, and Nikolas Rose. 1990. "Governing Economic Life." *Economy and Society* 19 (1): 1–31.

Minzhengbu. 2000. (民政部) 《民政部关于在全国推进城市社区建设的意见》 (*The Ministry of Civil Affairs' Views on Promoting Urban Shequ Building Throughout the Nation*). Beijing.

Mote, F. W. 1977. "The Transformation of Nanking." In *The City in Late Imperial China*, ed. G. William Skinner, 101–54. Stanford, CA: Stanford University Press.

Naughton, Barry. 1993. "Deng Xiaoping: The Economist." *China Quarterly* 135: 491–514.

———. 1996. *Growing Out of the Plan: Chinese Economic Reform, 1978–1993*. Cambridge: Cambridge University Press.

———. 1997. "*Danwei*: The Economic Foundations of a Unique Institution." In *Danwei: The Changing Chinese Workplace in Historical and Comparative Perspective*, ed. Xiaobo Lü and Elizabeth J. Perry, 169–94. Armonk, NY: M. E. Sharpe.

Needham, Joseph, with Wang Ling and Lu Gwei-Djen. 1971. *Civil Engineering and Nautics*. Vol. 4, part 3 of *Science and Civilization in China*, ed. Joseph Needham. Cambridge: Cambridge University Press.

Niu Ming, 1955. (牛明) "梁思成先生是如何歪曲建筑艺术和民族形式的" ("How Mr. Liang Sicheng Has Distorted Architectural Art and the National Form"). 《建筑学报》 (*Journal of Architecture*) 2: 1–8.

Oi, Jean C. 1989. *State and Peasant in Contemporary China: The Political Economy of Village Government*. Berkeley: University of California Press.

Osborne, Thomas. 1996. "Security and Vitality: Drains, Liberalism, and Power in the Nineteenth Century." In *Foucault and Political Reason: Liberalism, Neo-Liberalism, and Rationalities of Government*, ed. Andrew Barry, Thomas Osborne, and Nikolas Rose, 99–121. Chicago: University of Chicago Press.

Ouyang Can. 1957. (欧阳骖) "郑州肉类联合加工厂的设计" ("Design of the Zhengzhou Meat Processing Factory"). 《建筑学报》 (*Journal of Architecture*) 10: 49–53.

Owen, Robert. 1927. *A New View of Society and Other Writings*. London: J. M. Dent and Sons.

Pang Shuzi and Xu Hongbo. 1956. (庞树滋) (徐宏波) "新建的中国青年出版社印刷厂" ("The Newly Built China Youth Press Printing Factory"). 《建筑学报》 (*Journal of Architecture*) 8: 28–35.

Parkins, Maurice Frank. 1953. *City Planning in Soviet Russia*. Chicago: University of Chicago Press.

Pei Xuan, Liu Jumao, and Shen Lanqian. 1958. (沛旋) (刘据茂) (沈兰茜) "人民公社的规划问题" ("Problems in Designing People's Communes"). 《建筑学报》 (*Journal of Architecture*) 9: 9–14.

Peng Siming. 1988. (彭思明) "解放初期的工会工作" ("Trade Union Work in the Early Period After Liberation"). In 《北京的黎明》 (*Beijing's Dawn*), ed. Wang Guiling (王桂玲), Dou Kun (窦坤), and Lü Kenong (吕克农), 546–51. Beijing: 北京出版社 (Beijing Press).

Peng Zhen. 1991. (彭真) 《彭真文选：1941–90》 (*Selected Works of Peng Zhen, 1941–90*). Beijing: 人民出版社 (The People's Press).

Perry, Elizabeth J. 1993. *Shanghai on Strike: The Politics of Chinese Labor*. Stanford, CA: Stanford University Press.

———. 1997. "From Native Place to Workplace: Labor Origins and Outcomes of China's Danwei System." In *Danwei: The Changing Chinese Workplace in Historical and Comparative Perspective*, ed. Xiaobo Lü and Elizabeth J. Perry, 42–59. Armonk, NY: M. E. Sharpe.

Pinkney, David H. 1958. *Napoleon III and the Rebuilding of Paris*. Princeton, NJ: Princeton University Press.

Pun Ngai. 1999. "Becoming *Dagongmei* (Working Girls): The Politics of Identity and Difference in Reform China." *China Journal* 42: 1–20.

Rabinow, Paul. 1989. *French Modern: Norms and Forms of the Social Environment*. Cambridge, MA: MIT Press.

Randolph, Patrick A., and Lou Jianbo. 2000. *Chinese Real Estate Law*. The Hague: Kluwer Law International.

Rawson, Jessica. 1999. "Western Zhou Archaeology." In *The Cambridge History of Ancient China: From the Origins of Civilization to 221 BC*, 352–449. Cambridge: Cambridge University Press.

Read, Benjamin L. 2000. "Revitalizing the State's 'Nerve Tips.'" *China Quarterly* 163: 806–20.

———. 2003. "Democratizing the Neighborhood? New Private Housing and Home-Owner Self-Organization in Urban China." *China Journal* 49: 31–59.

Renmin Ribao, ed. 1993. (人民日报) 《党政机关和事业单位机构改革指导》 (*A Guide to the Reform of Party, Government, and Institutional Danwei Organs*). Beijing: 人民日报出版社 (People's Daily Press).

Reynolds, Bruce L., ed. 1987. *Reform in China: Challenges and Choices*. Armonk, NY: M. E. Sharpe.

Rofel, Lisa. 1992. "Rethinking Modernity: Space and Factory Discipline in China." *Cultural Anthropology* 7 (1): 93–114.

———. 1999. *Other Modernities: Gendered Yearnings in China After Socialism*.

Berkeley: University of California Press.

Rose, Nikolas. 1999. *Powers of Freedom: Reframing Political Thought.* Cambridge: Cambridge University Press.

Rose, Nikolas, and Peter Miller. 1992. "Political Power Beyond the State: Problematics of Government." *British Journal of Sociology* 43 (2): 173–205.

Rossi, Aldo. 1982. *The Architecture of the City.* Cambridge, MA: Opposition Books, MIT Press.

Rowe, William T. 1984. *Hankow: Commerce and Society in a Chinese City, 1796–1889.* Stanford, CA: Stanford University Press.

———. 1990. "The Public Sphere in Modern China." *Modern China* 16 (3): 309–29.

Said, Edward. 1986. "Foucault and the Imagination of Power." In *Foucault: A Critical Reader,* ed. David Couzens Hoy, 149–55. Oxford: Blackwell.

Saunders, Peter. 1986. *Social Theory and the Urban Question.* 2nd ed. London: Routledge.

———. 1990. *A Nation of Home Owners.* London: Unwin Hyman.

Schurmann, Franz. 1968. *Ideology and Organisation in Communist China.* 2nd ed. Berkeley: University of California Press.

Selden, Mark. 1971. *The Yenan Way in Revolutionary China.* Cambridge, MA: Harvard University Press.

———. 1995. *China in Revolution: The Yan'an Way Revisited.* Armonk, NY: M. E. Sharpe.

Shanghai zonggonghui diaocha yanjiushi, ed. 1951. (上海总工会调查研究室) 《工会工作手册》 (*Handbook on Trade Union Work*). Shanghai: 劳动出版社 (Labor Press).

Shaw, Victor N. 1996. *Social Control in China: A Study of Chinese Work Units.* Westport, CT: Praeger.

Shenyangshi minzhengju, ed. 1999. (沈阳市民政局) 《沈阳市社区建设资料汇编》 (*Collected Materials on Shequ Building in Shenyang City*). Shenyang.

Shenyangshi tiexiqu, ed. 2000. (沈阳市铁西区) 《沈阳市铁西区社区规章制度汇编》 (*A Collection of Regulations for the Shequ of Tiexi District, Shenyang City*). Shenyang.

Shi Xianmin. 1993. (时宪民) 《体制的突破》 (*Breaking Out of the System*). Beijing: 中国社会科学出版社 (China Social Science Press).

Shue, Vivienne. 1988. *The Reach of the State: Sketches of the Chinese Body Politic.* Stanford, CA: Stanford University Press.

Si Ping. 1956. (祀平) "关于居住建筑布置方案的讨论" ("Discussion on the Arrangement of Residential Architecture"). 《建筑学报》 (*Journal of Architecture*) 2: 103–7.

Sigley, Gary. 1996. "Governing Chinese Bodies: The Significance of Studies in the Concept of Governmentality for the Analysis of Government in China." *Economy and Society* 25 (4): 457–82.

Sit, Victor F. S. 1985. *Chinese Cities: The Growth of the Metropolis Since 1949.* Oxford: Oxford University Press.

———. 1995. *Beijing: The Nature and Planning of a Chinese Capital.* Chichester,

UK: Wiley.

Skinner, G. William, ed. 1977. *The City in Late Imperial China*. Stanford, CA: Stanford University Press.

Snow, Edgar. 1970. *Red China Today: The Other Side of the River*. Harmondsworth, UK: Penguin Books.

Sochor, Zenovia A. 1988. *Revolution and Culture: The Bogdanov-Lenin Controversy*. Ithaca, NY: Cornell University Press.

Soja, Edward W. 1989. *Post Modern Geographies: The Reassertion of Space in Critical Social Theory*. London: Verso.

Solinger, Dorothy. 2002. "Labor Market Reform and the Plight of the Laid-off Proletariat." *China Quarterly* 170: 304–26.

Strand, David. 1989. *Rickshaw Beijing: City People and Politics in the 1920s*. Berkeley: University of California Press.

Straus, Kenneth M. 1997. "The Soviet Factory as Community Organizer." In *Danwei: The Changing Chinese Workplace in Historical and Comparative Perspective*, ed. Xiaobo Lü and Elizabeth J. Perry, 142–66. Armonk, NY: M. E. Sharpe.

Su Xiaokang and Wang Luxiang. 1988. (苏晓康) (王鲁湘) 《河殇》(*River Elegy*). Beijing: 现代出版社 (The Modern Press). (Trans. Foreign Broadcast Information Service. 1988. *JPRS Report*. JPRS-CAR-88-002-L, 6 December: 5–37.)

Tan Liefei. 1988. (谭列飞) "门头沟煤矿的新生" ("The Rebirth of the Mentougou Coal Mine"). In 《北京的黎明》 (*Beijing's Dawn*), ed. Wang Guiling (王桂玲), Dou Kun (窦坤), and Lü Kenong (吕克农), 305–10. Beijing: 北京出版社 (Beijing Press).

Tan Shen. 1991. (谭深) "城市'单位保障'的形成及特点" ("The Formation and Characteristics of the Urban '*Danwei* Guarantee'"). 《社会学研究》 (*Sociological Research*) 5: 82–87.

Tang, Wenfang, and William L. Parish. 2000. *Chinese Urban Life Under Reform: The Changing Social Contract*. Cambridge: Cambridge University Press.

Tang Zhongxin. 2000. (唐忠新) 《中国城市社区建设概论》 (*An Outline of Urban Community Building in China*). Beijing: 红旗出版社 (Tianjiin People's Press).

Tarkhanov, Alexei, and Sergei Kavtaradze. 1992. *Stalinist Architecture*. Trans. Robin Whitby, Julia Whitby, and James Paver. London: Laurence King.

Tiewes, Frederick C. 1997. "The Establishment and Consolidation of the New Regime, 1949–57." In *The Politics of China*, 2nd ed., ed. Roderick MacFarquhar, 5–86. Cambridge: Cambridge University Press.

Todorov, Vladislav. 1995. *Red Square, Black Square: Organon for Revolutionary Imagination*. Albany: State University of New York Press.

Tu Tianfeng. 1958. (涂添凤) "天津市鸿顺里社会主义大家庭建筑设计介绍" ("Introduction to the Architectural Design for a Great Socialist House in Hongshunli, Tianjin City"). 《建筑学报》 (*Journal of Architecture*) 10: 34–35.

Tu Wei-ming. 1979. *Humanity and Self-Cultivation: Essays in Confucian Thought*. Berkeley, CA: Asian Humanities Press.

Unger, Jonathan. 1987. "The Struggle to Dictate China's Administration: The

Conflict of Branches vs Areas vs Reform." *Australian Journal of Chinese Affairs* 18: 15–45.

Van Der Sprenkel, Sybille. 1977. "Urban Social Control." In *The City in Late Imperial China,* ed. G. William Skinner, 609–32. Stanford, CA: Stanford University Press.

Verdery, Katherine. 1996. *What Was Socialism, and What Comes Next?* Princeton, NJ: Princeton University Press.

Vogel, Ezra F. 1971. "Preserving Order in the Cities." In *The City in Communist China,* ed. John Wilson Lewis, 75–93. Stanford, CA: Stanford University Press.

Von Falkenhausen, Lothar. 1999. "The Waning of the Bronze Age." In *The Cambridge History of Ancient China: From the Origins of Civilization to 221 BC,* ed. Michael Loewe and Edward L. Shaughnessy, 450–544. Cambridge: Cambridge University Press.

Wakeman, Frederic. 1995. *Policing Shanghai, 1927–1937.* Berkeley: University of California Press.

Walder, Andrew G. 1986. *Communist Neo-Traditionalism: Work and Authority in Chinese Industry.* Berkeley: University of California Press.

———. 1989. "Factory and Manager in an Era of Reform." *China Quarterly* 118: 242–64.

———. 1991. "A Reply to Womack." *China Quarterly* 126: 333–39.

Waldron, Arthur. 1990. *The Great Wall of China: From History to Myth.* Cambridge: Cambridge University Press.

Wang Guiling, Dou Kun, and Lü Kenong, eds. 1988. (王桂玲) (窦坤) (吕克农) 《北京的黎明》 (*Beijing's Dawn*). Beijing: 北京出版社 (Beijing Press).

Wang Haibo. 1994. (王海波) 《新中国工业经济史（1949.10–1957）》 (*A History of New China's Industrial Economy: October 1949–1957*). Beijing: 经济管理出版社 (Economics and Management Press).

———. 1995. 《新中国工业经济史（1958–1965）》 (*A History of New China's Industrial Economy: October 1958–1965*). Beijing: 经济管理出版社 (Economics and Management Press).

Wang Heling. 1988. (王鹤龄) "接管内三区，建立街政府" ("Taking Over the Third Inner District, Establishing Street Government"). In 《北京的黎明》 (*Beijing's Dawn*), ed. Wang Guiling (王桂玲), Dou Kun (窦坤), and Lü Kenong (吕克农), 252–58. Beijing: 北京出版社 (Beijing Press).

Wang Huajun and Gu Mengchao, eds. 1991. (王化君) (顾孟潮) 《建筑，社会，文化》 (*Architecture, Society, Culture*). Beijing: 中国人民大学出版社 (People's University of China Press).

Wang Hui. 2001. "On Scientism and Social Theory in Modern Chinese Thought." Trans. Gloria Davies. In *Voicing Concerns: Contemporary Chinese Critical Inquiry,* ed. Gloria Davies, 135–56. Lanham: Rowman and Littlefield.

Wang Hui and Leo Ou-fan Lee, with Michael M. J. Fischer. 1994. "Is the Public Sphere Unspeakable in Chinese? Can Public Spaces (*gonggong kongjian*) Lead to Public Spheres?" *Public Culture* 6 (3): 598–605.

Wang Min and Liu Yipeng, eds. 1994. (王敏) (刘义鹏) 《最新劳动人事管理政策法

律实务》 (*Practical Guide to the Latest Policies and Laws for Labor and Personnel Management*). Beijing: 国际文化出版公司 (International Culture Press).

Wang, Ya Ping, and Alan Murie. 1996. "The Process of Commercialization of Urban Housing in China." *Urban Studies* 33 (6): 971–89.

———. 1999. "Commercial Housing Development in Urban China." *Urban Studies* 36 (9): 1475–94.

Wang Yongxi, Xie Anbang, Gao Aidi, and Cao Jianzhang. 1992. (王永玺) (谢安邦) (高爱娣) (曹建章) 《中国工会史》 (*A History of China's Trade Unions*). Beijing: 中共党史出版社 (Chinese Communist Party History Press).

Warner, Malcolm. 1992. *How Chinese Managers Learn: Management and Industrial Training in China*. Hampshire, UK: Macmillan.

Watson, Andrew, ed. and trans. 1980. *Mao Zedong and the Political Economy of the Border Region*. Cambridge: Cambridge University Press.

Weston, Timothy B. 2000. "China's Labor Woes: Will the Workers Crash the Party?" In *China Beyond the Headlines*, ed. Timothy B. Weston and Lionel M. Jensen, 245–72. Lanham, MA: Rowman and Littlefield.

Wheatley, Paul. 1971. *The Pivot of the Four Quarters: A Preliminary Enquiry into the Origins and Character of the Ancient Chinese City*. Edinburgh: Edinburgh University Press.

White, Gordon. 1987. "The Politics of Economic Reform in Chinese Industry: The Introduction of the Labor Contract System." *China Quarterly* 111: 365–89.

———. 1998. "Social Security Reforms in China: Towards an East Asian Model?" In *The East Asian Welfare Model: Welfare Orientalism and the State,* ed. Roger Goodman, Gordon White, and Huck-ju Kwon, 175–97. London: Routledge.

Whyte, Martin, and William Parish. 1984. *Urban Life in Contemporary China*. Chicago: University of Chicago Press.

Wolf, Arthur, and Huang Chieh-shan. 1980. *Marriage and Adoption in China, 1845–1945*. Stanford, CA: Stanford University Press.

Womack, Brantly. 1991. "Transfigured Community: Neo-Traditionalism and Work Unit Socialism in China." *China Quarterly* 126: 313–32.

World Bank. 1992. *China: Implementation Options for Urban Housing Reform*. Washington, DC: World Bank.

Wright, Arthur F. 1977. "The Cosmology of the Chinese City." In *The City in Late Imperial China,* ed. G. William Skinner, 33–73. Stanford, CA: Stanford University Press.

Wu, Fulong. 1996. "Changes in the Structure of Public Housing Provision in Urban China." *Urban Studies* 33 (9): 1601–27.

———. 2002. "Real Estate Development and the Transformation of Urban Space in China's Transitional Economy, with Special Reference to Shanghai." In *The New Chinese City: Globalization and Market Reform,* ed. John R. Logan, 153–56. Oxford: Blackwell.

Wu Liangyong. 1994. (吴良镛) 《北京旧城与菊儿胡同》 (*The Old City of Beijing and its Ju'er Hutong Neighborhood*). Beijing: 中国建筑工业出版社 (China

Architecture Industry Press).

Wu Luoshan. 1959. (吴洛山) "关于人民公社规划中几个问题的探讨" ("Several Questions and Explorations on the Design of People's Communes"). 《建筑学报》 (*Journal of Architecture*) 1: 1–3.

Wu Qiang and Zhou Qingsu. 1956. (武强) (周庆素) "北京钢铁工业学院设计介绍" ("A Summary of the Design of Beijing Iron and Steel Institute of Technology"). 《建筑学报》 (*Journal of Architecture*) 1: 84–94.

Xiao Xunhua and Chen Deng'ao. 1958. (萧巽华) (陈登鳌) "积极吸取工业建筑设计中贯彻 '勤俭建国'方针的经验" ("Enthusiastically Absorb the Experience of Industrial Construction Design in Putting into Practice the Policy for 'Thrift in National Construction'"). 《建筑学报》 (*Journal of Architecture*) 2: 1–5.

Xie, Yichun, and Frank J. Costa. 1993. "Urban Planning in Socialist China." *Cities: The International Journal of Urban Policy and Planning* 10 (2): 103–14.

Yan Yizhi. 1955. (燕翊治) "国营友谊农场的场部规划介绍" ("A Summary of the Planning and Design of a State Run Friendship Farm"). 《建筑学报》 (*Journal of Architecture*) 3: 86–89.

Yang Dongping. 1994. (杨东平) 《城市季风：北京和上海的文化精神》 (*City Monsoon: The Cultural Spirit of Beijing and Shanghai*). Beijing: 东方出版社 (Oriental Press).

Yang Kuan. 1993. (杨宽) 《中国古代都城制度史研究》 (*Historical Research on China's Ancient Capital Cities*). Shanghai: 上海古籍出版社 (Shanghai Classics Press).

Yang Lu and Wang Yukun. 1992. (杨鲁) (王育琨) 《住房改革：理论的反思与现实的选择》 (*Housing Reform: Rethinking Theory and Making a Practical Choice*). Tianjin: 天津人民出版社 (Tianjin People's Press).

Yang, Mayfair Mei-hui. 1994. *Gifts, Favors, and Banquets: The Art of Social Relationships in China*. Ithaca, NY: Cornell University Press.

Ye Jundong and Zhou Jialu. 1994. (叶俊东) (周甲禄) "国办文化团体的新选择" ("New Choices for State-Run Cultural Troops"). 《了望》 (*Liaowang*) 50: 36–37.

Ye Zugui and Ye Zhoudu. 1958. (叶祖贵) (叶洲独) "关于小面积住宅设计的进一步探讨" ("On Further Explorations into the Design of Small-Scale Residences".) 《建筑学报》 (*Journal of Architecture*) 2: 30–36.

Yeh, Wen-Hsin. 1995. "Corporate Space, Communal Time: The Structure of Everyday Life in Shanghai's Bank of China." *American Historical Review* 99: 97–122.

Yi Zhongtian. 1996. (易中天) 《闲话中国人》 (*Casually Talking Chinese*). Beijing: 华龄出版社 (Hualing Publishing House).

You Zhenglin. 2000. (游正林) 《内部分化与流动：一家国有企业的二十年》 (*Internal Differentiation and Mobility: 20 Years in the Life of a State-Owned Enterprise*). Beijing: 社会科学文献出版社 (Social Science Document Press).

Young, Susan. 1994. "Private Entrepreneurs and Evolutionary Change in China." In *China's Quiet Revolution: New Interactions Between State and Society*, ed. David S. G. Goodman and Beverley Hooper, 105–25. Melbourne: Longman Cheshire.

——. 1995. *Private Business and Economic Reform in China*. Armonk, NY: M. E. Sharpe.

Yu Xianyang. 1991. (于显洋) "单位意识的社会学分析" ("A Sociological Analysis of *Danwei* Consciousness"). 《社会学研究》 (*Sociological Research*) 5: 76–82.

Yuan Jingshen. 1958. (袁镜身) "从反浪费到设计大跃进" ("From the Anti-Waste Movement to Designing the Great Leap Forward"). 《建筑学报》 (*Journal of Architecture*) 3: 38–40.

Yuan Lunqu. 1987. (袁伦渠) 《新中国劳动经济史》 (*A History of the Labor Economy of New China*). Beijing: 劳动人事出版社 (Labor and Personnel Press).

Yuan Zujun. 2001. (袁祖君) "北大缘何重砌南墙" ("Why Is Beijing University Rebuilding Its South Wall?") 《北京青年报》 (*Beijing Youth Daily*), 30 July: 2.

Zha, Jianying. 1995. *China Pop: How Soap Operas, Tabloids, and Bestsellers Are Transforming a Culture*. New York: The New Press.

Zhang, Li. 2001. *Strangers in the City: Reconfiguration of Space, Power, and Social Networks Within China's Floating Population*. Stanford, CA: Stanford University Press.

Zhang Zuoji. 1994. (张左己) 《中国劳动体制改革研究》 (*Research on the Reform of China's Labor System*). Beijing: 中国劳动出版社 (China Labor Press).

Zhao Dongri, Shou Zhenhua, and Feng Ying. 1958. (寿振华) (赵冬日) (冯颖) "北京市白纸坊居住小区改建规划方案" ("Design for the Rebuilding of Beijing's Baizhifang Residential District"). 《建筑学报》 (*Journal of Architecture*) 1: 17–22.

Zhao Guanqian. 1988. (赵冠谦) "建筑标准设计" ("Standard Architectural Design"). In 《建筑、园林、城市规划》 (*Architecture, Gardens and Urban Planning*), ed. Zhongguo Dabaike Quanshu (中国大百科全书), 222–23. Beijing: 中国大百科全书出版社 (Chinese Encyclopedia Press).

Zhao, Minghua, and Theo Nichols. 1996. "Management Control of Labor in State-Owned Enterprises: Cases from the Textile Industry." *China Journal* 36: 1–21.

Zheng Gongcheng. 1996. (郑功成) 《从企业保障到社会保障》 (*From Enterprise Guarantee to Social Guarantee*). Shenyang: 辽宁人民出版社 (Liaoning People's Press).

Zhonggong zhongyang dangxiao dangshi jiaoyanshi, ed. 1979. (中共中央党校党史教研室) 《中共党史参考资料》 (*CCP Party History Reference Materials*). 8 vols. Beijing: 人民出版社 (People's Press).

Zhongguo Dabaike Quanshu. 1988. (中国大百科全书) 《建筑、园林、城市规划》 (*Architecture, Gardens, and Urban Planning*). Beijing: 中国大百科全书出版社 (Chinese Encyclopedia Press).

Zhou, Min, and John R. Logan. 2002. "Market Transition and the Commodification of Housing in Urban China." In *The New Chinese City: Globalization and Market Reform*, ed. John R. Logan, 137–52. Oxford: Blackwell.

Zhu Guanglei. 1994. (朱光磊) "单位的政府职能及其分解" ("The Governmental Functions of the *Danwei* and Its Decomposition"). 《江海学刊》 (*Jianghai Research Journal*) 2: 48–52.

Zhu Huaxin. 1993. (祝华新) "From a 'Person of the Work Unit' to a 'Social Person': Psychological Evolution Under the Impact of Reform." 《人民日报》 (*People's Daily*), 14 December: 11. (Translation in Michael Dutton, *Streetlife China*, 215–20. Cambridge: Cambridge University Press.)

Zhu Wenyi. 1993. (朱文一) 《空间、符号、城市：一种城市设计理论》 (*Space, Symbol, City: A Theory of Urban Design*). Beijing: 中国建筑工业出版社 (China Architecture Industry Press).

Zhu Rongji. 1999. (朱熔基) "政府工作报告" ("Government Work Report"). 《人民日报》 (*People's Daily*), 18 March.

Zito, Angela, and Tani Barlow, eds. 1994. *Body, Subject, and Power in China*. Chicago: Chicago University Press.

Zou Denong. 2001. (邹德侬) 《中国现代建筑史》 (*A History of Modern Architecture in China*). Tianjin: 天津科学技术出版社 (Tianjin Science and Technology Press).

Printed and bound by CPI Group (UK) Ltd, Croydon, CR0 4YY

23/04/2025

14660938-0002